Grammar and Grace

Grammar and Grace

Reformulations of
Aquinas and Wittgenstein

edited by

Jeffrey Stout
and
Robert MacSwain

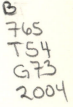

scm press

British Library Cataloguing in Publication data

A catalogue record for this book is available
from the British Library

0 334 02923 6

First published in 2004 by SCM Press
9–17 St Albans Place, London N1 0NX

www.scm-canterburypress.co.uk

SCM Press is a division of
SCM-Canterbury Press Ltd

Printed and bound in Great Britain by
Biddles Ltd, www.biddles.co.uk

This volume is dedicated to

VICTOR STEPHEN PRELLER

25 September 1931–19 January 2001

Professor of Religion at Princeton University
Priest of the Oratory of the Good Shepherd

He did not carry his gift within him
Or wear it draped over his shoulders like a cardigan.
It was not evident to the unaided eye
Or obvious to the casual observer.

Unless, perhaps, it hovered in the constant haze of cigarette smoke
Or sat amid the shamble of books and cat hair, compact discs and
tea cups:
'Ah,' he would say – and there it was!
Hidden in the half-raised arch of an eyebrow.

RCM

Contents

Contents

Notes on the Contributors

John R. Bowlin is Associate Professor of Religion at the University of Tulsa. The author of *Contingency and Fortune in Aquinas's Ethics*, he has also written several articles on Christian moral theology and the history of ethics, including 'Psychology and Theodicy in Aquinas' (*Medieval Philosophy and Theology*, 1998) and 'Sieges, Shipwrecks, and Sensible Knaves: Justice and Utility in Butler and Hume' (*Journal of Religious Ethics*, 2000).

David B. Burrell, CSC, is the Theodore M. Hesburgh Professor in Philosophy and Theology at the University of Notre Dame. He is the author of numerous books on philosophy, theology, and medieval studies, and for the past twenty years has been exploring comparative issues in Jewish, Christian, and Islamic thought. His works include *Analogy and Philosophical Language*; *Exercises in Religious Understanding*; *Aquinas: God and Action*; *Knowing the Unknowable God: Ibn-Sina, Maimonides, Aquinas*; *Freedom and Creation in Three Traditions*; and *Friendship and the Ways to Truth*.

G. Scott Davis holds the Lewis T. Booker Chair in Religion and Ethics at the University of Richmond. He is the author of *Warcraft and the Fragility of Virtue: An Essay in Aristotelian Ethics* and the editor of *Religion and Justice in the War over Bosnia*. He has also written several articles on just war theory, the history of ethics, and the philosophy of religion, including 'Doing What Comes Naturally: Recent Work on Thomas Aquinas and the New Natural Law Theory' (*Religion*, 2001) and 'Humanitarian Intervention and Just War Criteria' (*Journal for Peace and Justice Studies*, 2002).

M. Jamie Ferreira is the Carolyn M. Barbour Professor of Religious Studies at the University of Virginia. She is the author of numerous books and articles on the philosophy of religion, Victorian studies, and twentieth-century philosophy, including *Scepticism and Reasonable Doubt: The British Naturalist Tradition in Wilkins, Hume, Reid and Newman*; *Doubt and Religious Commitment: The Role of the Will in Newman's Thought*; *Transforming Vision: Imagination and Will in Kierkegaardian Faith*; and *Love's Grateful Striving: A Commentary on Kierkegaard's 'Works of Love'*.

Stanley Hauerwas is the Gilbert T. Rowe Professor of Theological Ethics at the Divinity School of Duke University. He is the author of numerous studies in ethics, Christian theology, and cultural criticism, and also a volume of prayers. His many influential works include *A Community of Character: Toward a Constructive Christian Social Ethic*; *The Peaceable Kingdom: A Primer in Christian Ethics*; *Against the Nations: War and Survival in a Liberal Society*; *Suffering Presence: Theological Reflections on Medicine, the Mentally Handicapped, and the Church*; *Wilderness Wanderings: Probing Twentieth-Century Theology and Philosophy*; *Sanctify Them in the Truth: Holiness Exemplified*; and the 2001 Gifford Lectures, *With the Grain of the Universe: The Church's Witness and Natural Theology*.

Jennifer A. Herdt is Associate Professor of Theology at the University of Notre Dame. The author of *Religion and Faction in Hume's Moral Philosophy*, she has also written several articles on modern moral thought and Christian theology, including 'Free Choice, Self-Referential Arguments, and the New Natural Law' (*American Catholic Philosophical Quarterly*, 1998) and 'The Rise of Sympathy and the Question of Divine Suffering' (*Journal of Religious Ethics*, 2001).

Joseph Incandela is Professor of Religious Studies at Saint Mary's College, Notre Dame, Indiana. He is the author of 'The Appropriation of Wittgenstein's Writings by Philosophers of Religion: Towards a Reevaluation and an End' (*Religious Studies*, 1985), 'Duns Scotus and the Experience of Human Freedom' (*The Thomist*, 1992), and other articles on philosophy of religion, medieval theology, and Christian ethics.

Fergus Kerr, OP, is Regent of Blackfriars Hall, University of Oxford, and Honorary Senior Lecturer in Theology and Religious Studies at the University of Edinburgh. He is the editor of the journal *New Blackfriars* and the author of *Theology After Wittgenstein*; *Immortal Longings: Versions of Transcending Humanity*; and *After Aquinas: Versions of Thomism*. He also edited Cornelius Ernst's *Multiple Echo: Explorations in Theology* with Timothy Radcliffe, OP; *John Henry Newman: Reason, Rhetoric and Romanticism* with David Nicholls; and *Contemplating Aquinas: On the Varieties of Interpretation*.

Douglas Langston is Professor of Philosophy and Religion at New College of Florida. He is the author of *God's Willing Knowledge: The Influence of Scotus' Analysis of Omniscience* and *Conscience and Other Virtues: From Bonaventure to MacIntyre*. He has also written many articles on medieval theology and philosophy of religion, including 'Medieval Theories of Conscience' in the online *Stanford Encyclopedia of Philosophy* (http://plato.stanford.edu).

Mark Larrimore is Assistant Professor of Religious Studies and Philosophy at Eugene Lang College and the Graduate Faculty of Social and Political Science, New School University. He edited *The Problem of Evil: A Reader* and has written several articles on ethics and religious studies, including 'Orientalism and Antivoluntarism in the History of Ethics: On Christian Wolff's Oratio de Sinarum philosophia practica' (*Journal of Religious Ethics*, 2000), and 'Substitutes for Wisdom: Kant's Practical Thought and the Tradition of the Temperaments' (*Journal of the History of Philosophy*, 2001).

Bruce D. Marshall is Professor of Historical Theology at the Perkins School of Theology, Southern Methodist University. He is the author of *Christology in Conflict: The Identity of a Saviour in Rahner and Barth*; *Trinity and Truth*; and numerous articles in historical, systematic, and ecumenical theology. He also edited *Theology and Dialogue: Essays in Conversation with George Lindbeck* and the forthcoming *Readings in Modern Christology*.

Victor Preller, OGS (d. 2001) was Professor of Religion at Princeton University and sometime Master of the Graduate College. An Episcopal priest of the Oratory of the Good Shepherd, he was the author of *Divine Science and the Science of God: A Reformulation of Thomas Aquinas*. He also wrote 'Catholic Studies', in *The Study of Religion in Colleges and Universities*, edited by Paul Ramsey and John F. Wilson, and 'Sexual Ethics and the Single Life', in *Men and Women: Sexual Ethics in Turbulent Times*, edited by Philip Turner.

Eugene F. Rogers, Jr, is Associate Professor of Philosophical Theology at the University of Virginia. He is the author of *Thomas Aquinas and Karl Barth: Sacred Doctrine and the Natural Knowledge of God* and *Sexuality and the Christian Body: Their Way into the Triune God*. He also edited *Theology and Sexuality: Classic and Contemporary Readings*, and he is completing a book on the Holy Spirit.

The Editors

Jeffrey Stout is Professor of Religion at Princeton University. He is the author of numerous books and articles in ethics and philosophy of religion, including *The Flight from Authority: Religion, Morality, and the Quest for Autonomy*; *Ethics After Babel: The Languages of Morals and Their Discontents*; and *Democracy and Tradition*. He is a contributing editor to the *Journal of Religious Ethics* and also a co-editor, with Wayne Proudfoot and Nicholas Wolterstorff, of the Cambridge University Press Series on Religion and Critical Thought.

Robert MacSwain is a priest in the Episcopal Diocese of East Carolina. He has published poetry and book reviews in several journals, including *Christianity and Literature, Anglican Theological Review*, and the online *Journal of Religion and Society* (http://www.creighton.edu/JRS).

Preface

I met Victor Preller in the spring of 1993 when I was a first-year student at Princeton Theological Seminary. A fellow seminarian encouraged me to take one of Victor's classes in the Religion Department of Princeton University, and so I did. This particular course was listed as an undergraduate seminar in hermeneutics, but (in addition to a handful of undergraduates) about half the students were from the Seminary, I remember at least one doctoral candidate from the University's philosophy department, and a local Jungian analyst dropped in from time to time. During this term I also began attending All Saints' Church in Princeton, where Victor served as a priest associate. So I came to know him almost simultaneously in his dual role of philosopher of religion and Episcopal priest.

It was a role he found difficult to sustain. Despite a lifetime of exploration at the frontier of faith and reason, Victor never found an easy or complacent harmony between the two – and he abhorred the politics and careerism of both the academic and ecclesiastical establishments. His intellectual integrity prevented many convenient short-cuts, and the 'thickness' of his theology resisted any watering-down. Consequently, labels such as 'liberal' or 'conservative' were wasted on him: he combined traditional (Anglo) Catholic doctrine and devotion with unconventional, even radical, philosophical underpinnings. If he arrived at any standard conclusions, he reached them by following his own path. That's not, of course, how Victor himself saw things: he was just reading the tradition rightly, whereas most of his contemporaries had got it wrong!

So it was with great relief that he retired from Princeton University in 1995 (after over thirty years of teaching) and gave himself entirely to his ministry as a priest and much-sought-after spiritual director. The centre of Victor's life, especially in these later years, was his membership in the Oratory of the Good Shepherd – an Anglican religious society founded in Cambridge, England, in 1913. The Oratory's rule of life and the fellowship of its international family were sources of great joy and solace to him. And while his friends and students hoped that retirement would provide the opportunity to finish some long-delayed research projects, Victor entertained no such ambitions. He was content to celebrate Mass, keep the Daily Office, listen to his vast music collection, and welcome visitors.

Fond of such phrases as 'the hubris of publication', the last thing Victor desired after retirement was any further academic activity. The only event which drew him back to his professorial past was an invitation to deliver a lecture on 31 October 1998 at St Mary's Bourne Street in London in honour of the late Eric Mascall (1905–93), a fellow Aquinas scholar and Priest of the Oratory of the Good Shepherd. That lecture, the last of Victor's career, is included as the penultimate chapter of this book.

For when he came down with pneumonia in December of 2000, several of his friends and students (fearing the worst) began planning a long overdue Festschrift focused on Victor's most enduring and profound research and teaching interests: Thomas Aquinas and Ludwig Wittgenstein. But before the project had barely begun, Victor died in Princeton on 19 January 2001 at the age of 69. His death only intensified our resolve, and so what was conceived as a tribute to a living mentor has now become a posthumous celebration of his life and work. As Mark Larrimore notes in his memoir, Victor often said that he wanted to write *through* his students. While not every contributor to this volume was a student of Victor's in the formal sense, each one has been touched in some way, if only indirectly, by who he was and what he did.

When we began editing this book, Jeffrey Stout told me that Victor Preller taught him what it meant to be a philosopher. I could reply, in turn, that he showed me what it means to be a priest. That jagged juxtaposition between philosopher and priest sums up everything Victor sought to accomplish in his life of study, teaching, listening, conversation, prayer, delight, and friendship. And for that we owe him more than we can say.

Robert MacSwain

xiv

Introduction

JEFFREY STOUT

This book is a collection of new essays on St Thomas Aquinas and Ludwig Wittgenstein written by some of the best theologians and philosophers of religion in the English-speaking world. Why Aquinas? Why Wittgenstein? Because they are profound thinkers and hard to understand. Indeed, each of them inspires controversy not only over the truth of his claims and the validity of his arguments, but also over what his writings mean and what he hoped to accomplish. Both thinkers have acquired fierce loyalists and determined critics. But their intellectual legacies are deeply ambiguous, and have generated much controversy. Even their most ardent defenders do not see eye to eye on how they should be read. In both cases, we have interesting, complicated histories of reception and disputation to grapple with, as well as deep, and deeply puzzling, primary texts.

There are good reasons, then, to invite major scholars to hold forth in public on either of these figures. The possibility that we will understand him – and ourselves – a little better at the end of the day is reason enough. But why consider both of them in the same volume? Why Aquinas *and* Wittgenstein? It so happens that the evolving debates over these two figures in theology and the philosophy of religion became inextricably intertwined in the second half of the twentieth century. Some of the scholars who sought to liberate Aquinas from his most influential defenders did so with Wittgenstein's help. When some of these same scholars sought to liberate Wittgenstein from the views some of his disciples attributed to him, they had a fresh image of Aquinas on their minds. Revisionist interpretations of both figures had a mutually reinforcing effect, while also contributing to new approaches to meaning, justification, philosophy of mind, and ethics.

I

It thus became increasingly difficult, in ways that no-one would have been able to predict when Wittgenstein's *Philosophical Investigations* appeared in 1953, to follow disputes over Aquinas without knowing something about Wittgenstein or disputes over Wittgenstein without knowing something about Aquinas. By the same token, it became increasingly difficult to understand the most sophisticated developments in theology and philosophy of religion without grasping the implications of the mutually reinforcing revisionist interpretations of these two figures. For better or worse, our own intellectual setting remains one in which Aquinas and Wittgenstein are linked. Perhaps it did not have to work out in this way, but it did. This volume attempts to make sense of the linkage, its history, and its implications for theology and philosophy.

As Joseph Incandela points out in his essay, 'Similarities and Synergy', the linkage is initially somewhat puzzling. The two figures are separated by more than half a millennium. While Wittgenstein's *Investigations* begins by referring to St Augustine, a clear indication of respect, there are no references to Aquinas. The only indication we have that Aquinas may have influenced Wittgenstein directly is a single volume of the *Summa Theologiae* that was found sitting on a shelf in Wittgenstein's room. According to Ray Monk's biography, Wittgenstein was baptized Roman Catholic, and before his death arrangements were made for him to live at a Dominican priory in the Midlands.[1] But he seems not to have been a practising Christian, and his writings show respect for faith without explicitly committing himself to it. The Christian thinkers who mattered to him most, like Søren Kierkegaard and Leo Tolstoy, seem to represent a strand of theology quite distinct from Aquinas's. His fragmentary style may owe something to Blaise Pascal, but nothing to the systematic architectonic of a medieval *summa*.

Incandela thinks, however, that something significant can be made of their shared connections to Augustine. For Aquinas, in his attempt to summarize (and thus render coherent) the main elements of theological truth, Augustine is a father of the Church, a theologian whose pronouncements must be accorded weight on any question of faith and morals. For Wittgenstein, in his attempt to understand what it is to live well, Augustine is an edifying spiritual guide, a thinker who confesses what it is like to live while coping with the temptations of a disordered will. What do these two images of Augustine have in common? Incandela argues that the answer lies in a tradition of moral enquiry that bears Augustine's stamp.

According to this tradition, moral or spiritual enquiry is at once theoretical and practical, a matter of intellect and will, mind and heart. Its goals include both understanding and moral virtue. It begins in the imitation and trust of others who, although not perfect, have already acquired wisdom, skills, and habits that novices lack. Each of us has a vocation to ascend into such forms of excellence, and in doing so each of us must rely on the advice and example of those who have ascended higher than we have. Our pride, as Wittgenstein sees no less clearly than Aquinas, must be dismantled; it gets in the way, prevents us from seeing our own faults – not to mention others' suffering and worth – for what they are. The teacher makes an effective spiritual guide in part because he, too, copes constantly with temptations. It is instructive to hear those temptations confessed, to hear them made explicit in speech. In this and many other ways, the student's life comes under criticism and correction, and is thereby, one hopes, transformed. If Aquinas and Wittgenstein both owe much to a conception of moral enquiry like the one Incandela describes, the need to free them from their most influential defenders quickly becomes evident. Incandela makes the case for revisionist readings of both figures in a way that nicely sets up the chapters that follow.

Suppose reasoning about the highest things, the things that matter most, has a process of spiritual transformation as its context. It makes sense to conclude that rational justification of the relevant kind must find its footing within that process, taking for granted the ethical formation that the process has brought about so far. If Aquinas understood this, Incandela explains, then his 'Five Ways' are not free-standing proofs of God's existence, available for all-purpose apologetics, as many modern Thomists have taken them to be. He was not, after all, writing for the conversion of non-believers, but self-consciously exercising his authority as a teacher of theology within the Church. His readers were either teachers or novices who had come to accept the basic framework of scriptural and ecclesial authority he accepted. His proofs, then, must have been meant to provide rational justification within that framework, as Victor Preller argued in *Divine Science and the Science of God*.[2]

It also becomes clear why Aquinas devoted more than half of the *Summa Theologiae* to an explication of the virtues. He was explaining to spiritual novices and their instructors what they were going through morally and spiritually, while spelling out what this process of transformation takes for granted. His summary was intended to help this process along by summing up its main features, not to displace the role of the spiritual advisor or the novice's need to meditate and confess.

By the same token, if Wittgenstein had a similarly structured process of transformation in view, casting himself by turns as teacher and student, his writings suddenly seem at odds with the comforting relativist thought that anything is justified provided only that a home can be found for it within some language-game that is actually played. To defend belief in God by appealing to such a thought is not only to use the notion of a language-game as Wittgenstein himself never did.[3] It is also to lose track of the process of transformation within which aspiring to be appropriately responsive to reasons makes sense as a spiritual quest. The point of the process, let us not forget, is to subject prideful, self-defeating, hateful, obsessive, and otherwise defective individuals and their forms of life to critical scrutiny. That these individuals and forms of life are often self-consciously religious neither protects them from fault nor insulates them from critical scrutiny. Whether any given life, form of life, belief, desire, or intention is rationally justified is to be determined by participating honestly in the social practice of moral enquiry, not by offering a generalized theory of language-games.

Participating in that practice does, of course, sometimes involve paying close attention to how we use words, to the details of usage within some language game we find confusing on reflection. Wittgenstein's philosophical practice owed much to a strategy that Bruce Marshall, following Willard Van Orman Quine, calls 'semantic ascent'. Philosophical problems can sometimes be solved or dissolved by looking closely at how expressions are used, by talking about those expressions and their uses instead of using them to talk about their referents. In Wittgenstein's early work, ascending to the level of semantic discourse is meant to serve the purposes of an overarching theory of sensible speech and its limits. In his later work, semantic ascent is less a theoretical than a therapeutic tool, employed in the hope of curing obsession with philosophical theorizing of the kind that he had formerly prized.

Medieval theologians were also skilled practitioners of semantic ascent. Marshall's 'In Search of an Analytic Aquinas' examines Aquinas in this light, showing in detail how he uses a kind of semantic analysis to make sense of doctrines central to trinitarian orthodoxy. How can it be that God is both three persons and one God? Much hangs, for Aquinas, on how God's essence is conceived – and, in particular, on how one responds to the technical metaphysical question of whether essence generates. Aquinas responds, characteristically, by distinguishing different ways in which the term 'essence' can be used. Here, as in many other aspects of his theology, Aquinas's genius resides in the skill with which he draws distinctions, so that the dogmatic formulations of recognized authorities can be brought in line with one another, with Scripture, and with the practical life of the Church. Parallels between medieval and modern practices of semantic ascent help explain why Aquinas's theology would lend itself so readily to Preller's revisionist interpretation in *Divine Science*. Preller cast his book largely in the idiom of Wilfrid Sellars, one of the first analytic philosophers to adopt the phrase 'language-game' from the later Wittgenstein and to pursue the implications of a conception of meaning as use.

Stanley Hauerwas, the most prolific and influential theologian in the English-speaking world, trades heavily on revisionist readings of both Aquinas and Wittgenstein in his constructive work. His Gifford Lectures, *With the Grain of the Universe*, which may prove to be his most enduring contribution to theology, defend Karl Barth's aversion to any form of natural theology divorced from divine revelation in Jesus Christ.[4] But this tenet is not a modern, Barthian novelty, according to Hauerwas, because Aquinas implicitly accepts it, too. What most modern thinkers have come to mean by 'natural theology' is not what Aquinas means by it. Hauerwas's essay for this volume, 'Connections Created and Contingent', credits Preller's *Divine Science* with discovery of the Barthian Aquinas. Indeed, 'Preller thought and said better in 1967 what I was trying to say in 2001.'

Of course, it is anachronistic to read Aquinas as a Barthian. What the discovery of the Barthian Aquinas actually involves is the rediscovery of the broader Augustinian tradition from which both Aquinas and Barth take their theological bearings. In much of his earlier work, Hauerwas helped his readers see Aquinas's ethics as more deeply Aristotelian than natural law scholasticism had long led them to suspect. After Luther, it might have seemed that an Aquinas who conceived of ethics largely in terms of an Aristotelian ethics of the virtues could not also be an Augustinian theologian at heart. But Hauerwas and a number of other contributors to this volume have another possibility in view. It is crucial, they think, to see Aquinas as *both* more deeply Augustinian (in his recognition of the theological primacy of faith) *and* more deeply Aristotelian (in his recognition of the ethical primacy of the virtues) than modern Thomistic scholarship has granted.

After paying his respects to Preller as an interpreter of Aquinas, Hauerwas considers two themes from the later Wittgenstein – his emphasis on social practices and what Fergus Kerr calls his 'attitude of wonder towards particular things'. Hauerwas's variations on the latter theme merge with a discussion of the poetry of Gerard Manley Hopkins. The essay as a whole is vintage Hauerwas, a complicated, subtle, instructive, and somewhat mercurial meditation on analogies between conceptions of contingency in Aquinas and Wittgenstein. The point is not to portray Wittgenstein as a Christian, but rather to learn from him in the same way Aquinas learned from Aristotle, as a fellow traveller on life's way. To remain faithful all the while to the theological vocation of disciplined reflection on faith, one must remain mindful throughout that the sort of faith that is relevant here is no human achievement, but a gift of grace.

No-one has written with more authority on both Aquinas's theology and the theological uses of Wittgenstein's philosophy than Fergus Kerr. His books *Theology after Wittgenstein* and *After Aquinas: Versions of Thomism* are paradigmatic contributions to the conversation the present volume aims to elucidate and continue.[5] Here, in '"Real Knowledge" or "Enlightened Ignorance"', he takes up the relationship between Preller's *Divine Science* and two other thinkers in the same theological neighbourhood, Eric Mascall and Victor

White. He begins with the scepticism Mascall expressed, in a review of Preller's book, about its minimalist view of human knowledge of God.

According to Preller's reformulation of Aquinas, we are ordered to God as to one whose nature remains unknown to us. The positive assertions of faith, though surely intelligible from God's point of view, are understood by us only as if through a glass darkly. We are bound, on this side of the beatific vision, to construe those assertions analogically, but without being in a position to grasp the relevant analogies from the top down, in terms of that which gives them their intelligibility – namely, God. Interpreted in this way, Aquinas becomes a negative theologian, thus taking his place in an 'apophatic' tradition that goes back to Dionysius the Pseudo-Areopagite, Gregory of Nyssa, and Gregory Palamas, while making him a fitting conversation partner for Barth, who depicted God as 'wholly other'. Mascall's exegetical question was whether Preller had done justice to Aquinas in attributing such a minimalist view of theological language and knowledge to him. His theological question was whether such a view was too close to agnosticism to be squared with the practice and creeds of the Church.

After summarizing Mascall's review, Kerr examines Preller's sympathetic remarks about Victor White, another scholar who worried that mainstream Thomists had 'watered down' Aquinas's apophatic commitments. Kerr then doubles back to consider Mascall's attempt to strike the right balance between negative and positive theological traditions in the Church. Kerr's essay does much to clarify what is at stake in what may appear to be slight differences in emphasis in Preller, White, and Mascall.

David Burrell, no less than Hauerwas and Kerr, has brought to light the connections between Aquinas and Wittgenstein that occupy our attention in this volume. His books *Analogy and Philosophical Language* and *Aquinas: God and Action* integrated Preller's arguments with other recent developments in the scholarly literature, and made something like Preller's interpretation accessible to an audience Preller himself never reached.[6] In 'Religious Life and Understanding', Burrell recalls his appropriation of Preller's work in a 1969 essay (also called 'Religious Life and Understanding'), and then reflects on theological developments over the ensuing three decades.

After touching on Pierre Hadot's recently influential notion of a spiritual 'practice' (echoing a central theme from Incandela's essay), Burrell complements Kerr's account of Thomism in the 1960s with a perspective on what has been happening since. He commends Catherine Pickstock's contrast between Aquinas and Duns Scotus on the nature of religious language as one way of following up on Victor Preller's work, but wisely stops short of concluding that Preller would have approved of her 'radical orthodoxy'. Burrell then comments perceptively on the fresh ways in which two of Preller's former students, Eugene Rogers and John Bowlin, have extended their teacher's influence more directly. Rogers's first book, *Thomas Aquinas and Karl Barth: Sacred Doctrine and the Natural Knowledge of God*, pursues the Aquinas–Barth parallel much more explicitly than Preller's book does, and with much more attention to disputed questions in the secondary literature.[7] John Bowlin's book *Contingency and Fortune in Aquinas's Ethics* gives us an account of Aquinas as a theorist of the virtues that owes much to the seminars Preller taught on this subject in the 1980s.[8] Taken together, these books flesh out the intuition, already mentioned above in reference to Hauerwas, that Aquinas is both more Augustinian and more Aristotelian than most readers have thought.

It is fortunate, then, to have essays from both of these scholars here. Rogers's piece, 'The Eclipse of the Spirit in Thomas Aquinas', focuses on the interrelation between Aquinas's suspicion of mystical experience and his doctrine of the Holy Spirit. The work of the Spirit, for Aquinas, *inhabits* the practices of the community known as the Church. That, by Wittgensteinian lights, is where anything spiritual must be found, if it is to be something with which human beings actively concern themselves while communicating with one another and appealing to shared norms. A perfectly private experience of rapture would be incommunicable in a way that rendered its normative significance obscure. The Spirit, rightly construed, resides in the habits the community exhibits and the norms its members use to hold each other accountable. It is in terms of their common life that such raptures as they experience are to be interpreted, and thus given a normative significance. Realizing this helps us understand how Aquinas negotiates his way through Augustinian controversies about grace when working out the details of his doctrine of the Spirit.

Introduction

John Bowlin's essay, 'Nature's Grace', argues that Aquinas and Wittgenstein both need to be read as members of the natural law tradition – indeed, a single strand of that tradition. What makes this hard to see is a misleading story about what the tradition of natural law is and how it has developed. Aquinas plays a major role in this story, while Wittgenstein plays none. Aquinas is seen as the great medieval synthesizer of natural law ideas drawn from Aristotle, the Stoics, and Ulpian. His major contribution, according to this story, is not his lengthy reflections on the virtues, but rather his deduction of a normative ethical system from the first principles of the natural law. This contribution supposedly went into eclipse for a time, and was then recovered, in somewhat different forms, by Catholics like Suarez and Protestants like Grotius. What these natural lawyers bequeathed to their most important heirs – Pufendorf, Hobbes, and Locke – was a way of spelling out the normative guidance that nature itself has to offer, a kind of guidance thought to be both clear to and binding on anyone equipped with the natural light of human reason.

Bowlin has a different story to tell. Without denying that a major strand of natural law thinking, especially in the modern period, aims to construct a system of ethical guidance of this type, Bowlin sees Aquinas as engaged in a different sort of project, centred mainly on an explication of the virtues. The role that natural law thinking plays in this project is theological and explanatory rather than normative; what natural law helps Aquinas explain is 'how human action and its proximate causes, reason and will, are created by God and governed by providence'. Wittgenstein, being no theologian, is not trying to answer this question, but neither is he constructing an ethical system that tells us what to do. His task, Bowlin says, is 'to mark the boundary between sense and nonsense, between intelligible human action and madness'. This is the same task Aquinas takes up for his own theological reasons in what tradition came to call his treatise on law.

Once we rightly describe what Aquinas and Wittgenstein were up to – the former in his theological discussion of 'natural law', the latter in his philosophical reflections on our 'natural history' – we can begin to perceive the outline of a tradition that turns to nature not for a system of ethical norms that can stand up to a modern sceptic's doubts, but simply for sound reflective understanding of the constraints we experience as social animals (or 'creatures') of a certain kind. And once we see this much, we can see more clearly why Preller, Hauerwas, Kerr, and Burrell have had success in making Aquinas and Wittgenstein into partners in a conversation that would be edifying for anyone who takes either of these figures seriously on his own terms.

They make good conversation partners with one another and with such other thinkers as Aristotle and Hume because they belong to a relatively continuous tradition of philosophical and theological reflection on human nature. The irony is that seeing Aquinas's interest in natural law as motivated by a theological interest in providence, rather than in a kind of ethical rationalism easily detached from theology, makes him seem all the more interesting from a point of view like Wittgenstein's (or mine) – that is, from a perspective that takes a secular, philosophical interest in what the natural history of human beings implies for our self-understanding.

Bowlin remarks in passing that he arrived in graduate school intending to write a dissertation that would use Wittgenstein and the neo-pragmatists to 'rescue philosophy of religion from its analytic captivity', but soon discovered that Scott Davis had already done what he had hoped to do, and 'brilliantly'. Davis's paper, 'Wittgenstein and the Recovery of Virtue', reworks some of the arguments he first hammered out in the still-unpublished dissertation he completed under Victor Preller's direction in 1984.[9] Readers familiar with Davis's book on just war thinking, *Warcraft and the Fragility of Virtue*, may know him primarily as an Aristotelian philosopher of virtue.[10] His essay for this volume artfully connects Wittgenstein to the recovery of virtue thinking that has been under way in theology and philosophy for almost half a century.

As becomes clear at the beginning of his essay, Davis's concerns as a secular Aristotelian have much more in common with Bowlin's theological retrieval of Aquinas's ethics of the virtues than with the updated philosophical Thomism of thinkers such as John Finnis and Robert P. George. The 'new natural law theory' of the latter thinkers, while it differs significantly from the scholastic Thomism of their Catholic predecessors, is nonetheless what Bowlin would classify as a species of systematic normative ethical theory (and thus something quite distinct from what Aquinas was doing, before ethical theorists took on the task of responding to modern scepticism). Finnis and George, being both morally conservative Roman Catholics and politically conservative philosophers of law, define their position over against the liberalism of thinkers like John Rawls and Ronald Dworkin. Davis rejects the new natural law theory largely on Wittgensteinian grounds, but he does not do so in the name of liberalism. To the contrary, he thinks of liberalism, qua ethical and political theory, as another species of the same style of thinking.

The project of recovering virtue-oriented ethical reflection, for Davis, is an alternative to natural law in the traditions of Suarez and Grotius, the new natural law theory, *and* procedural and rights-centred forms of liberalism. But what kind of alternative can it be, if it eschews the style of normative system-building that new and old natural lawyers and liberal social-contract theorists have in common? What can it tell us about justice, for example? Davis remarks that there is something right about the idea, expressed by Gilbert Harman, that our current conception of justice is a product of 'ongoing implicit bargaining and adjustment' within our own community. In Harman's hands, this idea becomes the key premise in an argument for moral relativism, a position intended to debunk the 'naïve' view of morality as an endeavour in which we are bound by objective constraints.

Many readers have taken Wittgenstein's way of reflecting on our natural history, in particular his notion of language-games, to lead in the same direction. But Davis draws subtle distinctions between Wittgenstein and the relativists. It is true that our conception of justice, like our conception of number or colour, is embedded in social practices that could, in theory, have developed differently. That it is the product of a long history of give and take, however, does not make it a merely 'subjective' affair. We cannot manipulate it at will simply by agreeing to adopt different conventions.

To participate competently in a social practice – for example, by correcting a child's misbehaviour in the hope of producing a 'just' and 'temperate' adult in the long run – is to find oneself constrained by more than the mere fact of membership in a group that happens to accept certain conventional notions. Davis illustrates the force of the constraints that belong to our natural history in a subtle discussion of the example of the wood-sellers in Wittgenstein's *Remarks on the*

Foundation of Mathematics, and then relates his analysis explicitly to Aristotelian virtue ethics of the same sort that Aquinas baptized for his own theological purposes. 'The possibility for variation in local practice is great,' Davis concludes, 'but to the extent that the ramifications involve more and more departures from the cardinal virtues, the more that form of life is unintelligible.'

Hauerwas, Bowlin, and Davis all emphasize Aquinas's appropriation of themes from Aristotle's ethics. But Aquinas was nothing if not eclectic in his borrowing habits, so it should not be surprising to find Douglas Langston, in 'The Stoical Aquinas', emphasizing the impact of another philosophical tradition on Aquinas's thought. If one looks, for example, at Aquinas's treatment of weakness of will, Aristotle's influence is much in evidence, but so is that of Cicero and Chrysippus. This raises the possibility that similar Stoic influences can be found elsewhere in Aquinas's writings. Langston argues with admirable concision that such influences are probably at work in Aquinas's conception of charity, a key theological virtue.

Langston prepares the way for this conclusion by offering an overview of Stoic philosophy and its influence on Augustine. Chapter XV of *On the Morals of the Catholic Church*, according to Langston, does not set out to show 'that Christians must add a level of orientation towards God to a basic Aristotelian account of the virtues'. The underlying account of virtue is more Stoic than Aristotelian. For the Stoics, the right intention – of living in accordance with Nature – is crucial. Acts expressive of this intention are virtuous; acts not expressive of this intention are vicious. The parallel notion in Augustine is love of the true God. 'If a person comprehends that God is the final good and acts with the intention of loving God, the person performs a virtuous action. If a person lacks the comprehension or the intention, the actions performed are vices.'

Augustine exerts a strong influence on Aquinas's account of virtue, but one must know where to look for it. Aquinas does not endorse Augustine's severely negative view of so-called 'natural virtues' as they are exhibited in the lives of non-Christians. That is, he does not declare them mere vices; they are rightly called virtues, he thinks. But when it comes to the theological virtue of charity, Langston argues, the Stoical Augustine matters greatly. Charity or love of God, Aquinas says, is the form of all the virtues. It impresses its form on the other virtues by directing them towards God, and does so in a way that has weighty implications for the proper theological appraisal of virtues not so directed. Such virtues are not virtues in an unqualified sense.

When a person's other virtues are transformed by charity, then, may we conclude that they are virtues without qualification? We must keep in mind, Aquinas adds, that charity comes in degrees of perfection. The highest of these is attainable only in heaven, the second only by the especially virtuous in this life, the third by those who succeed only in refraining from acting against what love of God entails. Only the highest degree of charity, by impressing itself on the other virtues of the blessed, transforms them perfectly. The second and third grades of charity are therefore bound to leave a person's other virtues less than perfectly transformed. So here, too, there is some qualification of their excellence.

Langston proceeds to make an interesting connection with Preller's *Divine Science* – a somewhat surprising one, given that Preller did not himself draw attention to Stoic influences on Aquinas and was often concerned in the classroom to drive a wedge between Aquinas and Augustine as theological authorities. *Divine Science* argues that for Aquinas we are powerless, on our own, to make God and his properties objects of our thought and speech. We are equipped to think and talk intelligibly about ordinary things like tables, trees, and tones, but God thoroughly transcends our unaided powers of thought. Nothing we do can render God intelligible. According to Preller's Aquinas, however, by infusing in us the theological virtue of charity, God brings it about that our religious thought and language are directed towards the unknown God. And at this crucial point, says Langston, Preller was explicating an idea in Aquinas that bears a Stoic-Augustinian stamp.

Langston's essay aims to clarify the relationship between love and character in Aquinas's theological ethics. It does so in a way that reinforces Aquinas's links to the Augustinian tradition of moral enquiry in which Incandela places both Aquinas and Wittgenstein. In 'Vision and Love', M. Jamie Ferreira pursues the relationship between love, character, and vision in Wittgenstein's later work. Her exegetical task appears much more daunting than Langston's given the scant, aphoristic references Wittgenstein makes to these topics after his lectures in the early 1930s. But Ferreira manages in the end to extract a great deal from her limited textual resources, focusing mainly on the remarks gathered together posthumously by G. H. Von Wright in *Culture and Value*.

It goes without saying that Wittgenstein has no normative ethical theory to offer. He makes no attempt to construct a system of principles that explain the force of our ethical intuitions and stand ready to resolve our future dilemmas. One can have a normative ethical stance, however, without wishing to construct a theory of this kind. For Ferreira, Wittgenstein may be a quietist with respect to theory, but he is not a quietist with respect to his own ethical condition as a human being. The drive for clarity that animates his philosophical writings early and late is not confined to the resolution of philosophical problems by means of semantic ascent. Wittgenstein demonstrates in scattered remarks from various phases of his life that he is motivated throughout by a desire to see himself clearly in an ethical sense. He is always conscious of the temptation to deceive himself, not merely about the world he is living in but about what he himself is like. To do philosophy is to love the wisdom of clear vision, which includes accurate knowledge of oneself. Making progress in this pursuit necessarily involves self-consciously undertaking a process of self-transformation.

In its description of Wittgenstein's concern with a spiritual practice of self-transformation, this essay echoes themes from Incandela's account of the Augustinian tradition of moral enquiry as well as Burrell's references to Hadot. But Ferreira, whose most important book is a learned commentary on *Works of Love*,[11] stresses Wittgenstein's admiration for Søren Kierkegaard as a key to understanding the ethical stance expressed in his philosophy. If we take Ferreira's essay as an extension of Incandela's argument, Kierkegaard emerges as Wittgenstein's most concrete point of connection with the tradition Incandela sketches.

While Ferreira's essay brings into focus a major Christian thinker's influence on Wittgenstein, Jennifer Herdt's essay, 'Justification's End', begins by examining Wittgenstein's influence on recent Christian ethics – in particular, on Hauerwas. Many of Wittgenstein's examples and thought experiments undermine the sort of philosophy that implicitly seeks to escape the human condition, one mark of which is the embeddedness of meaning in social practices, in what we do. Hauerwas and others have treated this Wittgensteinian motif as a reason for insisting that ethical thinkers own up to their dependence on the practices of their own communities. If ethical concepts reside in the practices of particular communities, then anyone engaged in the analysis of such concepts had better make clear what community he or she is speaking for and whose practices he or she is bringing to reflective expression.

Ethics, as Hauerwas once put it, always needs a qualifier. *Christian* ethics is reflection on the ethical practices of the Christian community, undertaken by individuals committed to those practices, and addressed primarily to others similarly committed, in the hope of helping them discern the nature and implications of their own commitments. But if the reason for adopting this particularist conception of Christian ethics is a collection of reminders and arguments from Wittgenstein, rather than something internal to the Christian tradition, it becomes hard to maintain the sharp contrast between particularism and universalism that Hauerwas appears to have in mind. More important, says Herdt, Hauerwas's particularism seems to have trouble living up to its theological ambitions. On Christian theological grounds, it aspires to speak mainly about God, but in the end it has much more to say about church – because it is the Church, rather than God, that satisfies its original methodological interest in the social practices of a particular community.

Herdt is not setting out to refute Hauerwas; she is simply taking note of two issues that require the attention of anyone who shares his goal of doing Christian ethics in a Wittgensteinian spirit. She approaches these issues, as she puts it, in a somewhat 'roundabout way' – by explicating Aquinas's account of the virtues while drawing parallels to Wittgenstein's reflections on learning a language game. In the course of her discussion, an apparent difference between Aquinas and Wittgenstein emerges with respect to justifying our actions and practices. Aquinas's account is vertical in the sense that it locates the justification of our actions and practices in their last end, which, rightly understood, is God. Wittgenstein's account, in contrast, is horizontal. For him, according to Herdt, 'justification comes to an end in a form of life as a whole, which we can only describe'.

Herdt thinks that the apparent stand-off represented by these contrasting conceptions of how practical justification comes to an end is somewhat misleading, however, because it leaves out an important dimension of Wittgenstein's thinking. This is his attitude towards wonder. The attempt to justify our actions or practices at some point comes to an end. When it does, we have no reply to our why-questions beside such remarks as, 'This is how we do things.' This means that our capacity to give reasons has limits, limits that should inspire neither despair nor philosophical bootstrapping. Acceptance of these limits is part of the wisdom Wittgenstein hopes to achieve and instil. Yet it is also an occasion for wonder at the existence of such contingent things as human beings, our forms of life, and the world we find ourselves in. This wonder can be interpreted in any number of ways, not least of all in Christian theological ways. It therefore becomes possible for someone like Hauerwas to combine Wittgenstein's horizontal account of justification with Christian theological talk about that which transcends mere contingency.

Herdt is as anxious to avoid what she calls the 'reductionism' of some religious followers of Wittgenstein as Davis is anxious to avoid Wittgensteinian relativism. The two sets of anxieties are closely related; they converge on the so-called Wittgensteinian fideists. (Hauerwas, who is much less worried about these tendencies than either Herdt or Davis, speculates in his essay that no-one, including D. Z. Phillips, has actually accepted Wittgensteinian fideism; Herdt quotes a passage from Phillips that makes him seem a plausible candidate.) What do the reductionists reduce, according to Herdt? Among other things, the content of Christian talk about God as our last end. To what do they reduce it? The practices of the Christian community. Those practices are the right place to look for what Christian talk about God means, because meaning has much to do with how expressions are used. But it does not follow from this Wittgensteinian insight that the linguistic practices of the Christian community make reference to or make assertions about nothing but those very practices.

Herdt grants that Wittgenstein's philosophy can be translated into Christian terms in various ways. But there are Christian reasons, she thinks, for preferring her wonder-centred translation to the reductionist translation she attributes to Phillips. Her translation, she thinks, is the most revealing way in which Wittgenstein's 'grammar' and Aquinas's 'grace' can be brought into contact with one another. Bringing them together in this way involves treating Wittgenstein not as the source of a general methodology applicable to all language games, but rather as someone who sees the world in quite particular, quasi-religious terms. By speaking of wonder as he does, Wittgenstein 'opens the door' to an affirmation of creation, and does so in a way that allows Christians in dialogue with him to develop a better understanding of what they are trying to say about God as creator.

The mode of speech in which Christians say these things is analogical in the sense Aquinas defines in the *Summa Theologiae*. Herdt joins other contributors to this volume in acknowledging Victor Preller's authority as an interpreter of this aspect of Aquinas's theology. 'God', she says in a Prellerian turn of phrase, functions in Christian discourse as the name of 'that which would, if we could know it, render intelligible the finite, contingent existence of everything that is'. Herdt cites not only Burrell's *Analogy and Philosophical Language* and Preller's *Divine Science*, but also Preller's 1998 Mascall Lecture, which appears here, posthumously, as the chapter following hers.

Being the transcript of a lecture, Preller's contribution differs in style from the preceding papers. I shall not attempt to summarize it. The many references I have already made to Preller's influence should suffice to make it intelligible. It is a delight to include the piece here, because it represents an eloquent, condensed statement of Preller's account of Aquinas's appropriation of Aristotle – indeed, his first public remarks on Aquinas in many years, as well as his last. Preller was an exceedingly reticent author, whose published writings consist in one book and a few articles. All the more important, then, to give his provocative Mascall Lecture wider distribution than it has heretofore received.

Mark Larrimore's personal reflections on Victor Preller bring our volume to a close. Again, there is no point in summarizing – or even in commenting, except to say that every word in it rings true to my ear. It has been a great blessing to have Victor as my teacher, colleague, and friend. He changed my life by bringing his favourite authors alive for me – Sellars and Aquinas early on, Wittgenstein and Gadamer a bit later. My first course with him was a graduate seminar putatively on religious language and knowledge. We read Sellars for ten weeks, the Upanishads for two, and then pondered the connections. At the time, I felt I understood neither the Sellars nor the Hinduism, let alone the relation Victor saw between them. It wasn't until a semester later, when I audited an undergraduate course on the same topic, that the penny dropped. One day I found myself sitting in the departmental lounge, explaining the Sellarsian mysteries to the novices, and realized that I grasped what I was saying. That might have been the first moment in which I understood what it means to think philosophically. There is no repaying such debts.

Victor and I advised many students together, and conspired to make our little precinct of the university safe for serious normative enquiry, for the love of wisdom. The high point, for me, was a graduate seminar we once taught together on interpretation, in which we spent weeks explicating Wittgenstein and Gadamer in two-part harmony. (If I am not mistaken, Joe Incandela took that course.) We occasionally joked that we agreed on everything – except the existence of God. Vic and I even tried for a couple of years to write a book together, but it was not to be. My hope is that the present collection of essays will take that book's place, and give readers a vivid sense of the difference he made for those of us who knew him well. I can think of no better discursive way to honour his memory than by pressing forward, in the way this volume does, with the project of trying to say why Aquinas and Wittgenstein continue to matter.[12]

Notes

1. Ray Monk, *Ludwig Wittenstein: The Duty of Genius* (London: Jonathan Cape, 1990), pp. 575–80.

2. Victor Preller, *Divine Science and the Science of God: A Reformulation of Thomas Aquinas* (Princeton: Princeton University Press, 1967).

3. On this point, see Incandela's early article, 'The Appropriation of Wittgenstein's Writings by Philosophers of Religion: Towards a Reevaluation and an End', *Religious Studies* 21 (1985): 457–74.

4. Stanley Hauerwas, *With the Grain of the Universe: The Church's Witness and Natural Theology* (Grand Rapids: Brazos Press, 2001; London: SCM, 2002).

5. Fergus Kerr, *Theology After Wittgenstein*, 1st edn (Oxford: Blackwell, 1986), 2nd edn (London: SPCK, 1997) and *After Aquinas: Versions of Thomism* (Oxford: Blackwell, 2002). A figure of comparable stature is the late Herbert McCabe, an influential British Dominican.

6. David Burrell, *Analogy and Philosophical Language* (New Haven: Yale University Press, 1973) and *Aquinas: God and Action* (Notre Dame, Ind.: University of Notre Dame Press, 1979).

7. Eugene F. Rogers, *Thomas Aquinas and Karl Barth: Sacred Doctrine and the Natural Knowledge of God* (Notre Dame, Ind.: University of Notre Dame Press, 1995).

8. John Bowlin, *Contingency and Fortune in Aquinas's Ethics* (Cambridge: Cambridge University Press, 1999).

9. Grady Scott Davis, 'The Base of Design: Relativism and Rationality in Philosophy of Religion' (Ph.D. thesis, Princeton University, 1984).

10. Grady Scott Davis, *Warcraft and the Fragility of Virtue: An Essay in Aristotelian Ethics* (Moscow, Id.: University of Idaho Press, 1992).

11. M. Jamie Ferreira, *Love's Grateful Striving: A Commentary on Kierkegaard's 'Works of Love'* (Oxford: Oxford University Press, 2001).

12. I wish to thank Scott Davis and Rob MacSwain for their comments on the first draft of this introduction. Rob MacSwain deserves credit for involving the rest of us in the creation of this volume and for doing much of the organizational work required to bring it to publication. It has been a pleasure editing this volume with Rob, and getting to know him, over the course of the last two years. Stan Hauerwas also deserves thanks for his strong encouragement of the project early on.

1. Similarities and Synergy

An Augustinian Reading of Aquinas and Wittgenstein

JOSEPH INCANDELA

Well, neither was married (though, it seems, for different reasons). And both came from prominent, well-to-do families. Each had notable siblings who distinguished themselves in the military. Both renounced lives of material privilege for more ascetic pursuits. Thomas was a composer of hymns, and Wittgenstein demonstrated his own rather substantial musical talents.[1]

Beyond these relatively minor biographical similarities, little seems at first glance to join these men whose respective births and deaths history has separated by almost seven hundred years. The tightly enforced organization of the *Summa* seems much at odds with the numbered meanderings of Wittgenstein's literary Nachlaß. The grand system-builder and apostle of synthesis that so many see in St Thomas seems deliciously antithetical to the determined iconoclast that others see in Wittgenstein. Indeed, the latter once commented to M. O'C. Drury, 'The symbolism of Christianity is wonderful beyond words, but when people try to make a philosophical system out of it I find it disgusting.'[2] Such determined attacks by Wittgenstein upon philosophy of a certain sort make intelligible his self-assessment: 'It came into my head today as I was thinking about my philosophical work and saying to myself: "I destroy, I destroy, I destroy –"'.[3] In light of these differences, why then are so many contemporary theologians and philosophers (including many of the contributors to this volume as well as the person to whom it is dedicated) drawn to, vitally concerned with, and intellectually animated by *both* of them? Indeed, it is hard to think of

Victor Preller without thinking of him in equally pleasant company with both Aquinas and Wittgenstein. For this reason, it is somewhat surprising that *Divine Science and the Science of God* has but one reference to Wittgenstein – and a very general one at that,[4] but it was not long before Wittgenstein's name was tied to Preller's project in reviews of his book.[5]

What I propose to do in this essay is examine the ties that bind both Aquinas and Wittgenstein in a way that may make clearer Vic's – and others' – choice of friends. In particular, I want to suggest that a type of Augustinianism recently described by Alasdair MacIntyre helps us understand the relationship between St Thomas and Wittgenstein, and I follow that through with four points on which this Augustinianism depends. In the second part, I assess the implications of this for con-temporary readings of Aquinas by offering some suggestions for why a certain understanding of Aquinas as theologian is only possible in a post-Wittgensteinian age. That is, not only are there important simi-larities between Aquinas and Wittgenstein that justify why many are drawn to both, but Wittgenstein makes possible a corrective interpre-tation of Aquinas that started in Vic's book and which has continued in the work of many indebted to him. Thus I defend the synergy mentioned in my title.

I

The ambiguity of influence

There are clearly more references to Wittgenstein in books about Aquinas than there are to Aquinas in books about Wittgenstein. Wittgenstein himself claimed very few intellectual forebears, and St Thomas apparently wasn't one of them. He once laughingly stated 'that no assistant lecturer in philosophy in the country had read fewer books on philosophy than he had'.[6] There are to my knowledge no direct references to Aquinas in Wittgenstein's published writings; though Rush Rhees tells us that one of the few philosophical volumes Wittgenstein kept on his bookshelf was a copy of the Prima Pars of the *Summa Theologiae*.[7] Nor will one find many references to Aquinas in books or articles *about* Wittgenstein, even ones directly on

Wittgenstein and religion.[8] The same goes for intellectual biographies and ancestries of Wittgenstein.[9]

Some have recently tried to forge these links in the opposite direction. That is, if Wittgenstein doesn't point back to Aquinas's work, perhaps Aquinas's work points forward to Wittgenstein. Bruce Marshall, for example, has picked up on Wittgenstein-inspired categories from George Lindbeck's *The Nature of Doctrine* and produced an essay entitled 'Aquinas as Postliberal Theologian'.[10] Such attempts have not been without controversy,[11] and David Kolb was most likely right when he said twenty years ago, 'Any Aquinas who looks more like Wittgenstein than Avicenna should probably give us pause.'[12] This is not to say, of course, that Wittgensteinian categories cannot and should not be useful to contemporary theologians writing about Aquinas. Indeed, many have skilfully and explicitly incorporated Wittgenstein into their own expositions of St Thomas while allowing the latter to remain very much a child of his own times, thereby successfully resisting the urge to reduce him to a proto-Wittgensteinian.[13] But what, despite the evident divergences in style and substance between these two thinkers, allows both men sympathetic treatment by the same authors? Or to put the matter more bluntly – if they seem so different, why do they tend to get invited to the same parties?

Language

There is room here to speak first in very general terms. The most obvious place to begin is in the concern each man had for language. St Thomas is frequently associated with analogy (largely due to *Summa Theologiae* I.13.5), and Wittgenstein is linked to the notion of a language-game. Certainly, the comparison of language to a game is itself an analogy[14] which helps Wittgenstein get out the point that meaning is related to use. As he explained, the meaning of a particular piece in chess refers to nothing outside the game, nor to anything 'essential' to the piece. The meaning lies in what the piece can do, what its *use* is. Moreover, language as such is a motley. It has no general form or essential element.[15] Different forms of discourse are related to each other as different games are. Across the universe of games, 'similarities crop up and disappear'.[16] Some use balls, some use cards; in some a score is kept and a winner identified, in others (ring-around-the-rosy, for example) amusement is its own end. This led Wittgenstein to his notion of 'family resemblances',[17] which is a description of the relationship that both different games and different modes of discourse have to each other.

What Aquinas says about analogy in the *Summa* is not dissimilar to Wittgenstein's notion of family resemblances.[18] In I.13.5, Thomas explains that analogical usage falls somewhere between complete univocity (viz., the view that there is some common property in chess and ring-around-the-rosy that makes them both games) and complete equivocation (viz., the view that 'game' applied to chess has no relationship to 'game' applied to ring-around-the-rosy).

Despite those who may wish to speak of Thomas's 'doctrine' of analogy,[19] the *Summa* admits no tidy theories of linguistic lineage (there are myriad family resemblances); but it does call attention to the dangers attendant upon careless conceptual consanguinity. Wittgenstein stated that the goal of *his* investigation was 'clearing misunderstandings away. Misunderstandings concerning the use of words, caused, among other things, by certain analogies between the forms of expression in different regions of language'.[20] In Thomas's case, his use of analogy sought to oppose eliding the differences between the divine creator of all things and the creature. Nowhere is this clearer than in the opening questions of Part I of the *Summa*, where Aquinas endeavours to show that God and only God is *simple* (Q. 3), God and only God is *perfect* (Q. 4), God and only God is *good by nature* (Q. 6), God and only God is *infinite* (Q. 7), God and only God *exists everywhere* (Q. 8), God and only God is *unchangeable* (Q. 9), God and only God is *eternal* (Q. 10), and God and only God is *absolutely one* (Q. 11). The only way to understand the italicized expressions is via some analogy with their use (or their negation) in language about creatures. Otherwise, we would be forced to identify some 'property' common to God and human beings. But how to do this without collapsing divine transcendence and imperilling God's role as creator? That is, if God's existence is univocal to our own in some important sense, then the deity becomes simply the biggest thing around, and the ability of such a being to create both *freely* and *from nothing* diminishes in exact proportion to its fundamental similarity to what gets created.[21] As Anthony Kenny has said with tongue in cheek, if 'to say that God exists is to say that God possesses that property which is held in common by a potted shrimp and the battle of Thermopylae', then 'it is not surprising that many have preferred agnosticism'.[22]

Lacking such a common property, we cannot in this life understand God as God is in Godself.[23] Wittgenstein fully concurs with Aquinas in understanding the distinctiveness of language about God: 'Our statements about God have a different grammar from our statements about human beings. And if you try to talk about God as you would talk about a human being, you are likely to come to talk nonsense, to ask nonsensical questions and so on.'[24] As Vic Preller said, 'In this life "God" remains a word in *another* language.'[25] For Aquinas, the theological payoff for this lack of epistemic access is to place God beyond the reach of or manipulation by the creature and thereby to affirm that the work of the deity in creation, revelation and redemption is solely due to divine gratuity. Thus, Preller again: 'God is not "at the disposal" of man until, in his freedom, he chooses to place himself at man's disposal under the formality of grace or "gift".'[26] Only then can our words illuminate.

The 1992 summer Olympic Games in Barcelona began with an archer shooting a flaming arrow from the ground inside the stadium in a high arc over one of the stadium walls. When the arrow passed over a cauldron spewing natural gas, it ignited the olympic torch, then landed somewhere outside the stadium. Much like this flaming arrow, our words for God aim at their target (perfection terms have a Godward trajectory says St Thomas in *ST* I.13.3), but they all ultimately miss their mark. The target we aim at exceeds the range of our language, and we know not where our terms land. Yet, if shot with a steady hand and a stalwart spirit, they truly enlighten.

St Augustine

Wittgenstein's concerns about language were also one of the things that led him to St Augustine. It is fair to say that both Aquinas and Wittgenstein revered Augustine.[27] In the *Summa Theologiae*, Aquinas cited Augustine 2,738 times and never once directly disagreed with him.[28] Augustine was also one of the few authors that Wittgenstein referred to by name. He considered the *Confessions* possibly 'the most serious book ever written'[29] and said that he began the *Investigations* with a quotation about language from Augustine's *Confessions* (which seems to be the only work by Augustine which Wittgenstein read[30]) because, as he explained to Norman Malcolm, the idea *had* to be important if so great a mind held it.[31]

Stanley Cavell has even suggested that Wittgenstein looked to the *Confessions* as a model for how he expressed himself in the *Investigations*. In particular, Cavell notes parallels between the confessional tone of Augustine's writing in the *Confessions* and how Wittgenstein typically proceeded to lay out problems and then address them:

> In its defense of truth against sophistry, philosophy has employed the same literary genres as theology in its defense of the faith . . . Wittgenstein chose confession and recast his dialogue. It contains what serious confessions must: the full acknowledgement of temptation ('I want to say . . .'; 'I feel like saying . . .'; 'Here the urge is strong . . .') and a willingness to correct them and give them up. . . . (The voice of temptation and the voice of correctness are the antagonists in Wittgenstein's dialogues.)[32]

Along similar lines, Ray Monk has explained that for Wittgenstein, *all* philosophy begins with confession. Wittgenstein often said that writing good philosophy and thinking well about philosophical problems was more a matter of *will* than of *intellect*, and certainly his many comments about temptation conform to this perspective.[33] Pride, he thought, is more of an obstacle to genuine understanding than lack of intelligence.[34] Wittgenstein wrote, 'The *edifice of your pride* has to be dismantled. And that is terribly hard work'[35] and 'If you are unwilling to know what you are, your writing is a form of deceit.'[36]

Aquinas and Wittgenstein's shared appreciation of Augustine is more than a historical curiosity. In fact, it illuminates important commonalities in each man's thinking and approach. In his book *Three Rival Versions of Moral Enquiry*, Alasdair MacIntyre laid out what he termed an Augustinian conception of moral enquiry which he finds both in Augustine himself and in 'medieval Augustinian culture'[37] running through the time of Aquinas. I want to distil MacIntyre's description into four components: the authority of the teacher, the transformation of the student, the type of rational justification offered by and through this enquiry, and the outcome of the process.

This approach begins with accepting the authority of a teacher who introduces certain texts and 'educates one into becoming the sort of person capable of reading those texts with understanding, texts in which such a person discovers the story of him or herself, including the story of how he or she was transformed into a reader of these texts'.[38]

In this way, theoretical and practical enquiry are closely related (or we might say, the mind and will are joined), since the person can only come to see the world truthfully if she is transformed by acquiring the intellectual and moral virtues required to be redirected from embracing error to apprehending truth. Because the truth is not seen at the start of this process, trust in some authority as leading one there is absolutely central. As Augustine himself said, 'for those who seek to learn great and hidden truths, authority alone opens the door'.[39]

Accordingly, rational justification can never come at the beginning of such an enquiry, for the novice student could never accurately test what it requires transformation even to understand. The cement first needs to set before its strength can be measured. As MacIntyre says, 'Hence faith in authority has to precede rational justification. And hence the acquisition of that virtue which the will requires to be so guided, humility, is the necessary first step in education or in self-education. In learning therefore we move towards and not from first principles. . . . Rational justification is thus essentially retrospective.'[40] And thus it must ever be in this perspective, for (as Wittgenstein said above in remarks completely faithful to Augustine's spirit in the *Confessions*) pride must first be dismantled before the world can be seen aright. Pride is so dangerous on an Augustinian view because it seduces the student away from the authority of the master, which is why Aquinas considered pride 'the most grievous of sins' inasmuch as it 'denotes aversion from God simply through being unwilling to be subject to God and His Rule'.[41] Moreover, because on this Augustinian view moral transformation must always accompany proper intellectual enquiry, no such enquiry can ever – in this life – end. It is, in MacIntyre's words, 'essentially incomplete'.[42] He explains:

> Except for the finality of Scripture and dogmatic tradition, there is and can be no finality. The narrative of enquiry always points beyond itself with directions drawn from the past, which, so that past itself teaches, will themselves be open to change. And the narrative of enquiry is of course itself embedded in that larger narrative of which enquiry speaks in setting out the intelligibility of the movements of creatures from and to God.[43]

Gandhi said that our goal should always be to bring our adversary to his senses, not to his knees.[44] Because rational justification is essentially retrospective on the Augustinian view, the master's aim can never be to *dominate* (for such would for ever close off the possibility of the student coming to the truth), but to *transform* the disciple into the kind of person for whom domination is not necessary because the truth has become so transparent. In short, the outcome of this 'process' must be a kind of peace.

Both Aquinas and Wittgenstein are Augustinians in the sense that each man's work features these four components.[45] Let me take up each of these in the order just presented.

Authority of the teacher: The journey of the rational creature from God and back to God is one undertaken for St Thomas under the authority of Scripture (*ST* I.1.8), which is what ultimately secures theology's place as the highest science since its principles come from the highest science or knowledge there is: 'God's very own'[46] (the 'scientia Dei' to which Preller called our attention[47]). But not only in his allegiance to Scripture did Aquinas urge submission to authority. In *ST* I-II.95.1, he explained that 'the perfection of virtue must be acquired by man by means of some kind of teaching'. And in II-II.49.3: 'Thus it is written (Prov. 3.5): "Lean not on thy own prudence", and (Ecclus. 6.35): "Stand in the multitude of the ancients (i.e. the old men), that are wise, and join thyself from thy heart to their wisdom." Now it is a mark of docility to be ready to be taught: and consequently docility is fittingly reckoned a part of prudence.' The movement towards God is the movement towards perfect happiness; but the condition of the wayfarer may be marked by frustration and disappointment, for as he says in *ST* I-II.3.8, 'man is not perfectly happy, so long as something remains for him to desire and seek'.[48]

Wittgenstein keenly felt a similar frustration. About a year before his death, he wrote, 'Philosophical unclarity is tormenting. It is felt to be shameful. We feel we don't know our way around where we *ought* to.'[49] There is a kind of fallenness here, and there is a way of redemption for Wittgenstein which, as the one Aquinas articulated in the *Summa*, was similarly Augustinian in approach. Just as Aquinas did, Wittgenstein held that one must accept certain things on authority in any enquiry, that one can never divorce the advancement of the intellect from the moral progress of the will, and therefore that the search for greater wisdom and insight is both transformative and never-ending. He wrote in *Culture and Value*, 'Believing means submitting to an authority. Having once submitted, you can't then, without rebelling against it, first call it in question and then once again find it acceptable.'[50] That is to say, one cannot coherently argue both *from* and *to* first principles. True, Wittgenstein had a slightly different rhetorical posture than Aquinas. The latter was always the *magister* who explicitly identified himself as a 'teacher of Catholic truth' (Prologue to the *Summa*). But Wittgenstein was both teacher and student, both philosophical redeemer and philosophically redeemed, both the one who releases the fly from the fly-bottle and the one who was thus set free (cf. *Philosophical Investigations*, §309).

This does muddle the picture a bit, but really no more so than in any other published confession; which, as *confession*, features an author acknowledging personal misdeeds or weakness, but which, as *published*, seeks to instruct others as well – at the very least, as an example; at the most, as one whose own transgressions have provided a unique vantage point from which to observe larger points about the human condition and what constitutes the healthy living of a life finally released from certain burdensome weights in its past. For this reason, Wittgenstein's writings, as Augustine's genre, cannot but make the teacher a student and the student a teacher.

So at some points in his writings, he clearly shares the 'mental cramps' he seeks to cure.[51] And the authority that must be accepted to help relieve those cramps is language itself. I believe that's the sense in which to understand both the famous remark, 'What has to be accepted, the given, is – so one could say – *forms of life*[52] and the Wittgensteinian move to pass from explanation to *description*.[53]

> There is no common sense answer to a philosophical problem. One can defend common sense against the attacks of philosophers only by solving their puzzles, i.e. by curing them of the temptation to attack common sense; not by restating the views of common sense. A philosopher is not a man out of his senses, a man who doesn't see what everybody else sees; nor on the other hand is his disagreement with common sense that of the scientist disagreeing with the coarse views of the man on the street. That is, his disagreement is not founded on a more subtle knowledge of fact. We therefore have to look around for the source of his puzzlement. And we find that there is puzzlement and mental discomfort, not only when our curiosity about certain facts is not satisfied or when we can't find a law of nature fitting in with all our experience, but also when a notation dissatisfies us – perhaps because of various associations which it calls up. Our ordinary language, which of all possible notations is the one that pervades all our life, holds our mind rigidly in one position, as it were, and in this position somehow it feels cramped, having a desire for other positions as well. Thus we sometimes wish for a notation which stresses a difference more strongly, makes it more obvious, than ordinary language does, or one which in a particular case uses more closely similar forms of expression than our natural language. Our mental cramp is loosened when we are shown the notations which fulfil these needs.[54]

Here then we have a very rich paragraph, which identifies the nature of the problem (mental cramps which Wittgenstein evidently shares[55]), diagnoses its symptoms (discomfort at a lack of answers or congruity with other 'associations'[56] – not unlike what we just saw Aquinas say in *ST* I-II.3.8), speaks of its capacity to be spread ('the temptation to attack common sense'), and proffers a cure. Moreover, if Wittgenstein is indeed an Augustinian here, that cure can never be simply intellectual in nature. Thus, in *Remarks on the Foundations of Mathematics*, he states, 'The sickness of a time is cured by an alteration in the mode of life of human beings, and it is possible for the sickness of philosophical problems to get cured only through a changed mode of thought and life.'[57] Rather than hoping that others would continue his work, Wittgenstein voiced his preference for 'a change in the way people live which would make all these questions superfluous'.[58]

At other points in his writings, Wittgenstein adopts the rhetorical space of standing outside the problem to help others who may be afflicted. Where Aquinas speaks in the prologue to the *Summa* of instructing beginners by giving them milk to drink rather than meat (1 Cor. 3.2), Wittgenstein said, 'A present-day teacher of philosophy doesn't select food for his pupil with the aim of flattering his taste, but with the aim of changing it.'[59] Here the authority is not so much language, but Wittgenstein himself: 'I wanted to put this picture before your eyes, and your *acceptance* of this picture consists in your being inclined to regard a given case differently; that is, to compare it with *this* series of pictures. I have changed your *way of seeing*' (italics his).[60]

The transformation of the student: St Thomas writes in *De Veritate*, 'since the perfect operation of the intellect consists in its knowing the true, that is its good. . . . Hence, since every good and every form is from God [creation], one must say, without any qualification, that every truth is from God.'[61] But note the complexity of these points. The true is the good of my mind (that is, what it seeks – its goal); and so when I am pursuing truth, I am pursuing goodness. And if *that's* the case, if we pursue goodness whenever we pursue truth, the pursuit of truth *morally* transforms us. In Wittgenstein's terms, when my way of seeing changes, my way of living does as well. Both are necessary, and neither is sufficient by itself to cure the 'sickness of a time'. Thus it is not surprising that St Thomas explains that 'truth or truthfulness must needs be a virtue, because to say what is true is a good act: and virtue is "that which makes its possessor good, and renders his action good"'.[62] I think we can see this point more clearly if we slightly rephrase it: Those who habitually pursue truth turn into honest people. Honest people care about what's true. Therefore, the pursuit of truth must be a virtuous activity. When we act virtuously, we become like unto what we love. And so the pursuit of truth, whose source and goal is God, is an adventure in holiness and *towards* holiness.

For this reason, it is perfectly appropriate and we ought not to be at all surprised that the *Summa* is *mostly* ethics. Part II on the moral life takes up 55 per cent of the whole work. We ought not to be surprised because of the prevalence in Parts I and III of the quest for truth and the necessity for faith. And to say, as Thomas does, that *truth* is a *virtue* (II-II.109.1), for reasons previously explained, and that *faith* is a *virtue* (II-II.4.5) – in part, Aquinas says, because 'it belongs to the very essence of faith that the intellect should ever tend to the true'[63] – makes the entire *Summa* an invitation to virtue, a summons to moral adventure. Part II's girth merely advertises this invitation. Like Thomas himself, the *Summa* is inflated in the middle.

For Thomas, the ultimate destination and resting-place for human striving is the beatific vision of God which is our full and complete happiness (I-II.3.8). Our proper goal as human beings, then, is to see the Truth pure and entire. And for this, we need faith. And faith for Aquinas is instruction in the truth from a higher power in a kind of spiritual apprenticeship: He writes, 'man's ultimate happiness consists in a supernatural vision of God: to which vision man cannot attain unless he be *taught* by God the teacher (*a Deo doctore*). Hence, in order that a man arrive at the perfect vision of heavenly happiness, he must first of all believe God, as a disciple believes the master who is *teaching* him'.[64] The progress of the *viator* through the divine curriculum requires a refining of one's loves and a changing of one's ends which Thomas understands as the work of grace such that 'the will, which hitherto willed evil, begins to will good'.[65]

Retrospective rational justification: Aquinas's starting-point in the authority of divine revelation puts in context what weight should be given to the Five Ways of question 2 of the Prima Pars. Those who regard those arguments as *Aquinas's* proofs for God and consider them the foundation of the *Summa* seem to pretend that question 1 on the authority of Scripture simply doesn't exist. Aquinas himself needs no proof for God, since the authority of Scripture (Exod. 3.14) completely suffices to answer the question whether God exists (*ST* I.2.3). He does, however, seem to need to affirm something like arguments for God's existence since, again, the authority of Scripture (Rom. 1.20) guarantees such (*ST* I.2.2).

There is an evident difference that shows up clearly in the Latin between the Five Ways ('quinque viae') of I.2.3 and what Aquinas said about Christ in the prologue to the second question of the Prima Pars, where he identified Christ as '*our way* to God' ('*via nobis* tendendi in Deum' – italics mine) or what he said in the prologue to the Third Part of the Summa, where he spoke of how Christ 'showed unto us, in His own person the *way* of truth' ('*viam* veritatis nobis in seipso demonstravit' – italics mine again). Simply put, the Five Ways as arguments for the existence of God are just not all that important. Aquinas was as clear as he could be that faith (which 'is founded on the Divine truth') is more certain than science (which is 'based on human reason').[66] Therefore, requiring reasons *before* one believes in God lessens the merit of faith by impugning the authority of God. But to employ reason and human rationality 'consequent to the will of the believer' as a kind of retrospective justification in MacIntyre's rendering of Augustinianism only increases the merit of faith. 'For when a man's will is ready to believe, he loves the truth he believes, he thinks out and takes to heart whatever reasons he can find in support thereof; and in this way human reason does not exclude the merit of faith but is a sign of greater merit.'[67] Thus, as Jamie Ferreira explained, 'The relation of reason to faith, for Aquinas, is a retrospective one, not a prospective one: reason is used within faith only in terms of elaborating the articles of faith and defending them from philosophical attack.'[68] So to elevate the Five Ways to the foundation of Aquinas's project confers an importance on them that was not Aquinas's. Yet, as I'll show in section II below, that seems to be exactly what happened. Since Thomas holds that it is necessary for salvation to believe things above natural reason (*ST* II-II.2.3) and that one of those things is an explicit belief in the mystery of Christ (*ST* II-II.2.7), Aquinas would be disabling his entire project from the start if he put any great weight on those five ways as foundational for his enterprise.

For any subsequent interpreter to do the same would also successfully occlude Aquinas's Augustinianism by turning him into a philosopher offering arguments for everyone apart from a distinctively Christian *telos*, rather than a theologian who appealed to the authority of God, and hence the gratuity of God in revealing and redeeming, to bring all things under and to Christ.[69]

The outcome of the process: For Aquinas, it is almost axiomatic that those who pursue truth become certain kinds of people and *should appear this way to others*. Aquinas follows St Paul in Galatians 5.22–3 in identifying the fruits of the Spirit. Among them are joy ('because every lover rejoices at being united to the beloved') and peace ('the calm of restless desire – for he does not perfectly rejoice, who is not satisfied with the object of his joy').[70]

For Wittgenstein, as for Aquinas, *as for Augustine*, the way of redemption leads to peace. Here the loop closes, and differences of genre fade in significance. So Wittgenstein wrote, 'The real discovery is the one that makes me capable of stopping doing philosophy when I want to. – The one that gives philosophy peace.'[71] The enemy (who may sometimes even be ourselves) must be brought to its senses, not its knees.

This leads me to the next part of the essay in which I describe how a shared Augustinianism affects contemporary interpretations of Aquinas and Wittgenstein, and how its neglect all but guarantees significant misreadings.

II

In *Three Rival Versions of Moral Enquiry*, MacIntyre identifies the encyclopaedist approach with the desire of post-Enlightenment culture[72] for timeless standards of intelligibility fuelled by unitary and ahistorical conceptions of rationality.[73] In relation to the pacifistic approach of bringing one's enemy to its senses, the encyclopaedist approach is intellectual just war.[74] If Aquinas and Wittgenstein are each Augustinians in MacIntyre's sense, then the interpretation of each has to have been negatively affected by inserting encylopaedist strivings into how they were received. In each man's case, this has involved taking one element of his writings and promoting it to a level of prominence neither intended. For Aquinas, this was the Five Ways, which many to this day continue to view as *his* proofs for God despite Victor Preller's (among others) best efforts to counter that view.[75] For Wittgenstein, it has been in extending the notions of form of life and language-game as tools for epistemological justification of diverse discourses and practices. Let me begin with the latter.

In the mid-twentieth century, those seeking the universal intelligibility of religious discourse seemed to get the next best thing in a kind of non-aggression pact based upon a questionable appropriation of some of Wittgenstein's categories. So Norman Malcolm proclaimed, 'Religion is a form of life; it is language embedded in action – what Wittgenstein calls a "language-game". Science is another. Neither stands in need of justification, the one no more than the other.'[76] Similarly, 'By destroying philosophy', Ernest Gellner wrote in 1958, Wittgenstein 'made room for faith . . . religious believers can find in Wittgensteinianism not merely a device for ruling out philosophic criticism, they can find in it a positive validation of their beliefs.'[77] Never mind that Wittgenstein himself had never referred to religion as a separate language-game or form or life.[78] Nor had he ever used these categories in a broad epistemological validation of religion, for as said above, that was never his goal. One could with some legitimacy survey the field of articles and books on Wittgenstein and religion and conclude that he was indeed prophetic in his comment from 1939 that 'The seed I am most likely to sow is a certain jargon.'[79]

Now, in itself, there is nothing wrong with extending Wittgenstein's work in a new direction, though Wittgenstein himself viewed such efforts negatively.[80] But we must be especially careful here in cloaking a project in Wittgenstein's name that is still very much indebted to a kind of philosophical justification which it *was* the burden of his work to critique. What does this mean? Assume for a moment that the thrust of Wittgenstein's work is against wholesale justification of any type of discourse or practice and that any 'method' for doing such is alien to his later work and its full embrace of human contingency and finitude (more later on this).[81] As Mark Cladis has helpfully put it, 'Theological beliefs, then, like scientific beliefs, are argued about, weighed, and evaluated in a variety of ways, but always in the absence of a sure method or universal foundation. To admit as much is to embrace an aspect of human finitude.'[82] Wittgenstein was quite clear that justification of belief and practice comes to an end – it hits 'bedrock' as he puts it in *Investigations* §217 or 'rock bottom' as he says in *On Certainty* §248. If this is true of the rationale one gives to oneself, it is *a fortiori* true of any justifications that one could give in an external forum, philosophical or otherwise. Here's the problem then: those who use Wittgenstein for some wholesale justification of religious belief have not followed him in abandoning that project. Nor, despite appearances, have the attempts to insulate religious belief from criticism by hermeneutically sealing it into separate language-games or forms of life. The quest for universal intelligibility does not disappear with such attempts. It just gets franchised out, with each franchise sharing the values of the parent company, but now imbued with its own local flavour and insisting on its own autonomy. Put another way: those like Malcolm and Gellner (one could add D. Z. Phillips) on defence are playing the same game as those on offence (viz., positivists of various stripes). Brian Clack has written,

> Far from defending religion from attack, the Wittgensteinian is stripping it of any substantial content. Viewed in this manner, Wittgensteinian philosophy of religion is not a protective strategy but a full capitulation to positivism. Accepting that after Hume and Ayer there can be no way of justifying the metaphysical claims made by religion, Phillips and other writers of his ilk choose, from some kind of nostalgic yearning, to preserve the *language* of religion while rejecting the objects to which that language had formerly been believed to refer.[83]

Aquinas has suffered as Wittgenstein has by well-intentioned followers who, selectively avoiding important emphases in both the spirit and the letter of each man's work, have nonetheless sought to turn them into philosophers concerned primarily with questions of epistemological foundations. But the upshot of both analogy (for Aquinas) and family resemblances (for Wittgenstein) is that all knowledge is contextual, that epistemological bedrock is no more possible in our understanding of divinity, goodness, and truth than it is possible in our understanding of games. As Wittgenstein said, 'To understand a sentence means to understand a language.'[84]

Across the street from where I write this sits the University of Notre Dame, perhaps the intellectual epicentre of American Catholicism. And at the epicentre of the epicentre stands Sacred Heart Basilica, whose cornerstone was laid in 1871 but whose final spire was topped off only in 1892. Inside Sacred Heart above the nave of the basilica is a mural of St Thomas Aquinas by the Italian painter Luigi Gregori which depicts Aquinas holding up five fingers of his left hand and pointing to those fingers with his right hand.[85]

In 1879, Pope Leo XIII issued his encyclical *Aeterni Patris*, which commended Thomas as 'the special bulwark and glory of the Catholic faith' because:

> single-handed, he victoriously combated the errors of former times, and supplied invincible arms to put those to rout which might in after-times spring up. . . . reason, borne on the wings of Thomas to its human height, can scarcely rise higher, while faith could scarcely expect more or stronger aids from reason than those which she has already obtained through Thomas.[86]

The pope continued:

> Philosophy has no part which he did not touch finely at once and thoroughly; on the laws of reasoning, on God and incorporeal substances, on man and other sensible things, on human actions and their principles, he reasoned in such a manner that in him there is wanting neither a full array of questions, nor an apt disposal of the various parts, nor the best method of proceeding, nor soundness of principles or strength of argument, nor clearness and elegance of style, nor a facility for explaining what is abstruse.[87]

Leo was in many ways riding atop currents that he himself did not unleash but which flowed steadily in and from late-nineteenth-century Europe, while Gregori (above the nave but not the tide) painted on. Nine years earlier, in a document issued on 24 April 1870 from the third session of the First Vatican Council, the Council Fathers anathematized all those who denied that the existence of God 'cannot be known with certainty . . . by the natural light of human reason'.[88] Due to the confluence of these events, I view the depiction of Aquinas inside Sacred Heart – five fingers aloft, pointing didactically, patiently reminding the nineteenth century of a 600-year-old lesson – as offering something akin to an obscene gesture directed at the Enlightenment. With the Five Ways held up by the Church's *philosopher*, Catholicism was, as others before me have stated, reaching back to the Middle Ages to combat the Enlightenment. Turning back the clock was judged the best way to go forward. The neo-Gothic style of Sacred Heart Basilica echoing in stone, mortar, and glass the great medieval English and French Gothic cathedrals was self-consciously part of the restoration of intellectual and cultural aspects of the Middle Ages going on in the Catholic Church after 1860.[89]

In *Thomas Aquinas: Theologian*, Thomas O'Meara described three ages of Thomism: one from the 1200s to the 1400s, one from the 1500s to the 1800s, and one from the 1840s to the 1960s.[90] Third-wave Thomism, O'Meara explained, 'identified truth and life with immutability and rationality; it opposed being to history and ignored concreteness in human life and in the economy of salvation'.[91] This brand of Thomism had much in common with, and was the contemporary of, what MacIntyre has characterized as the post-Enlightenment culture of the encyclopaedia: 'So the narrative of the encyclopaedist issues in a denigration of the past and an appeal to principles purportedly timeless. . . . the comprehensive and unitary conception of reason in the name of which this appeal is made has the corresponding function of providing an unwarranted privileged status to those who identify their own assertions and arguments with the deliverances of reason thus conceived.'[92] The finitude of temporality renders one and one's arguments vulnerable, as all (people and traditions) are captive of their past in some sense. What better way to seek release than to appeal to a perspective that the past cannot infect or limit, a timeless view that the past may have anticipated or adumbrated but never quite attained in virtue of its being tradition-bound? And what better way to conceal one's prison record than to agree with one's opponents (also owners of a past) in wiping the record clean and starting over from scratch?

The danger one always faces in life, philosophy, or war is to win the battle but lose oneself. That is, the act of opposing the enemy can make one indistinguishable from the target of one's opposition. Third-wave Thomism and Wittgensteinian fideism both did this by adopting timeless notions of rationality that left both unable to explain themselves to themselves. Such a strategy may have had its short-term appeal or effect, but it lacked the perspective required to explain why either of them arose in the first place; and thus left both ultimately unable to combat masters they were unable to acknowledge: human finitude and history (that is, their grounding in a tradition of thought and problems which exhibits their emergence as anything but timeless and which exhibits their survival as anything but necessary).

In this way, a certain brand of neo-Thomism which uses Thomas defensively as first and foremost a philosopher battling the forces of modern secularity has had deleterious effects. And perhaps ultimately what Wittgenstein does for Aquinas, in part despite, and in part because of, the former's aversion to system-building and a reluctance to use philosophy as a blunt weapon routing the enemy and clearing the field of battle, is the more peaceable *and local* task of 'assembling reminders for a particular purpose'.[93] In *Zettel*, Wittgenstein wrote, 'sometimes the voice of a philosophical thought is so soft that the noise of spoken words is enough to drown it and prevent it from being heard'.[94] As in other things, yelling too loudly loses the wisdom of the whisper, swinging too wildly loses the deft touch of the artist, and arguing too boldly loses the nuance amidst the noise. Wittgenstein's conception of philosophy helped to liberate Aquinas from a neo-Thomism that stifled the riches of the *Summa*. Ironically, authority is liberated when it is disarmed (a point rather compatible with Christian non-violence). After Wittgenstein, Aquinas can speak *to* us, rather than silence others. Recent books like Fr Michael Barron's *Thomas Aquinas: Spiritual Master*[95] simply could not and would not have been written fifty years ago.

As one commentator has written, in the wake of Pope Leo's encyclical commending the study of Aquinas,

> soon a dark side to this renewal began to show itself. As an official doctrine, Thomism began to take on the color of the Church's institutional structures; it became both authoritative and defensive, both traits that were not intrinsic to Thomism, itself, or to St Thomas. These two attitudes, mixed with the need to teach large

numbers of students, led to the Thomism of the manuals, and it must be said that the old medieval forms of disputation and medieval scholasticism's inclinations to indulge in endless distinctions only added to the overlogical structure of so many philosophical and theological manuals used in the Church's seminaries. The result at its worst was a neo-scholastic doctrine shattered into a thousand pieces and welded back together in the form of syllogisms. The correct expression of verbal formulas gained the upper hand in the classroom and stifled insight and creativity. The concrete sense of life and intellectual activity was buried under the dust of a rabid conceptualism which had no use for the modern world and its ideas, which were reduced to straw men and destroyed in a few lines at the end of an article.[96]

David Burrell has pointed out that a unilateral focus on such 'arguments' can inhibit the symbolic dimensions of language,[97] the ones which (in Christianity at least) Wittgenstein found so ennobling and the ones which (if this discourse be about the creator of all things) theology most needs. For the symbolic is the congealing of the analogical, and the analogical is the best tool in the shed for displaying 'the distinction' (a notion Burrell borrows from Robert Sokolowski[98]) between all and the source of all, a distinction which we have seen Aquinas depict as an analogical one and Wittgenstein describe as a grammatical one.

One of the most oft-quoted statements from the *Investigations* is §373: 'Grammar tells what kind of object anything is. (Theology as grammar.)' Attention to grammar takes us to use, to practice, to how (in this case) the life of faith is lived. Philosophy can never be an end unto itself in such a scheme. Truly, it does leave everything as it is (cf. *Philosophical Investigations*, §124) in that sense. At best, its value is instrumental (or therapeutic). Wittgenstein wrote, 'To understand a language means to be master of a technique.'[99] That ethicists, or those writing on ethics, gravitate to Wittgenstein is wholly unsurprising.[100] Stanley Hauerwas, for example, has claimed Wittgenstein in the following way:

[Wittgenstein] slowly cured me of the notion that philosophy was primarily a matter of positions, ideas, and/or theories. From

Wittgenstein, and later David Burrell, I learned to understand and also to do philosophy in a therapeutic mode. . . . Moreover, Wittgenstein ended forever any attempt on my part to try to anchor theology in some general account of 'human experience', for his writings taught me that the object of the theologians' work was best located in terms of the grammar of the language used by believers.[101]

Therefore, Wittgenstein will also be (and has been) understandably quite useful to those who think that philosophy – and to a certain extent, theology – are not ends unto themselves, but point beyond themselves to a relationship (between creator and created for Burrell, between Christian and church for Hauerwas) which may be narrative in form, but which cannot itself take place in the pages of a book. I think that's the best sense in which to understand Wittgenstein's remark that 'If Christianity is the truth then all the philosophy that is written about it is false.'[102] Elsewhere he wrote, '[Christianity] offers us a (historical) narrative and says, now believe! But not, believe this narrative with the belief appropriate to a historical narrative, rather: believe, through thick and thin, which you can do only as the result of a life.'[103] One must, Wittgenstein said, live in the pages of a book.[104] Trust precedes justification.[105]

This is why it must be a misinterpretation of Wittgenstein to put religion forward as a self-enclosed language-game or form of life. For he is elsewhere clear that the trust about which he speaks is a 'passionate commitment'.[106] As Dallas High reminds us, passions tend to be absorbing. They get in the way of other things, and hence are not generally the kinds of things susceptible to tidy enclosure.[107] High also appropriately draws attention to how thoroughly Kierkegaardian this is.[108] This is appropriate because Kierkegaard, an Augustinian through his Lutheranism, was considered by Wittgenstein 'by far the most profound thinker of the last century'.[109] And certainly, submission to authority is at the heart of Kierkegaard's discussion of Abraham.[110] The teleological suspension of the ethical and the paradoxes of Abraham's faith require an exalted notion of authority, or else they are not in the least bit compelling.

Wittgenstein's focus on language quite naturally inclines communitarians of various stripes to him. The rule-making he describes as constitutive of grammar is an inherently social activity.[111] That's the true significance, I would argue, of Wittgenstein's rejection of a private language. Namely the point is less narrowly epistemological than fundamentally moral:[112] Is healthy human life lived with others or for purely private ends? Indeed, for the later Wittgenstein to make 'an argument' designed to 'solve' some fundamental philosophical problem would run counter to so much else he says about the historicity of thought and concepts:

> What I am opposed to is the concept of some ideal exactitude given us *a priori*, as it were. At different times we have different ideals of exactitude; and none of them is supreme.

> One of the more important methods I use is to imagine a historical development for our ideas different from what actually occurred. If we do this we see the problem from a completely new angle.[113]

This is none other than we should expect. A focus on language and its rules naturally leads to concern about the speakers of that language and the followers of those rules. And since, as Wittgenstein said, 'When language-games change, then there is a change in concepts, and with the concepts the meanings of words change',[114] human temporality is a necessary component. In the *Investigations*, the ahistorical nature of logic is compared to 'slippery ice where there is no friction'.[115] Such conditions, Wittgenstein explains, are ideal from one perspective; but precisely as ideal, they are not *real*. His conclusion: 'We want to walk: so we need *friction*. Back to the rough ground!'[116] In so many other places in Wittgenstein's work, there appear notions of movement against something else, whether he was speaking about the engagement of cog-wheels[117] or the movement of water over a river-bed which is itself in flux.[118] As Wittgenstein says, 'the river-bed of thoughts may shift'.[119] Human life is life lived in motion against a backdrop of wider cultural and historical forces themselves in movement. Which in turn affects his ideas about human activity and intentionality, because the givenness of our language, thoughts, and concepts means that we each inherit a horizon beyond which we cannot self-constitute. In *Culture and Value*, Wittgenstein says, 'Tradition is not something that anyone can pick up, it's not a thread, that someone can pick up, if and when he pleases; any more than you can choose your own ancestors.'[120] Philosophy, then, might help in straightening out the messiness of a shared domicile, but it cannot pour the foundations of the structures on which we currently stand. Certain things just belong to what Wittgenstein terms 'the scaffolding of our thoughts'.[121] Thus does he affirm that 'a language-game is only possible if one trusts something'.[122] Authority, not proof, comes first. Justification is inherently retrospective here, as a particular 'world-picture' formed through reliance on authority 'is the substratum of all my enquiring and asserting'.[123]

This essentially Augustinian reliance on authority implies that philosophy will always ask more than it answers. Its task remains incomplete if for no other reason than that its task remains ongoing, just as anyone with children knows that one never *finishes* cleaning the house.

St Thomas, for his part, participated in what Chenu described as a 'new awareness of history' begun in the twelfth century and continuing through Aquinas's own time. The *Summa* itself is organized as a journey with God in time, beginning with the *exitus* of all things from God in creation (literally, the origin of time) through human pilgrimage in salvation history's *reditus* back to God.[124] Indeed, the theme of motion or movement is a crucial one throughout the *Summa*. Each major section of the *Summa* begins with the problem of the movement of the human being towards God,[125] and we've already seen the significance of Aquinas's appellation of Christ as the *via* (road) to God. And just as for Wittgenstein, Aquinas's concern with human historicity and movement in time led to significant limits of his own on the scope of autonomous free choice.[126]

Much has been made of the fact that Aquinas never finished the *Summa*. He stopped writing on 6 December 1273. Different people have drawn different lessons from this, and especially from his purported words at the ending of his labours, 'It's all straw.' Some have seen this remark as tantamount to a repudiation of his previous work, or a severe devaluing of the whole enterprise of writing a *Summa*. I think that there's a much more charitable lesson to be drawn (and I'm certainly not the first to suggest this). And that is that an unfinished *Summa* becomes its own truth, a self-validating artefact, in a very theologically interesting way. Given the subject of the *Summa* – an infinite light which is, in Josef Pieper's words 'lucid and limpid' to its very depths[127] – there will always be more to learn. There will never be a time when all 't's are crossed and all 'i's dotted in anyone's theology. An unfinished *Summa* (almost an oxymoron) makes this point. And so, ironically, only in not finishing the *Summa* did Aquinas really finish it. A finished product would have necessarily been unfinished and necessarily untruthful! The *Summa* is unfinished – necessarily so – because in this life, one never reaches the end of one's search for God. And so, in that way, the unfinished *Summa* is its own truth.

That spirit was very much shared by Wittgenstein. Neither man, despite the significant and obvious differences in the style of their writings, ever really finished his work or dared to answer every question he posed. But this is no accident, since as we've seen, enquiry indebted to Augustine lacks a terminus. There is only one remark that Wittgenstein made *about* Aquinas that has come down through the recollections of his students. 'Asked one day what he thought of St Thomas, he replied that he could not make much of his answers, but he thought his questions were very good. Coming from Wittgenstein, this was high praise. The *Investigations* contain 784 questions. Only 110 of these are answered; and seventy of the answers are *meant* to be wrong.'[128] As he himself said in *Zettel* – again quoting Augustine – 'quia plus loquitur inquisitio quam inventio' ('because the search says more than the discovery').[129]

And because questions always outnumber answers, silence becomes a perfectly acceptable outcome of enquiry. Both St Thomas and Wittgenstein were at important moments of their lives and writings reduced to silence. For Aquinas, of course, the silence descended on 6 December 1273. For Wittgenstein, the last line of the *Tractatus* is the justly famous 'Whereof one cannot speak, one must pass over in silence.' Much has legitimately been made of the discontinuity in the writings of the earlier and later Wittgenstein. But what united the two admittedly disparate phases of his career is the underlying assumption that philosophy has limits, which assumption Aquinas always shared and articulated in the first article of the first question of the first part of the *Summa*.[130] Certainly, the later Wittgenstein would not have subscribed to the *Tractatus*'s earlier notion of *a priori* limits to language. All limits to language in the later Wittgenstein must be in a certain sense 'movable' depending on the kind of discourse in question.[131] Still, the Wittgenstein of the *Investigations* did say, 'So in the end when one is doing philosophy one gets to the point where one would like just to emit an inarticulate sound. – But such a sound is an expression only as it occurs in a particular language-game, which should now be described.'[132]

Wittgenstein once said that his early work has two parts: everything he's written, and everything he hasn't; and it's the second part that's more important.[133] St Thomas could agree, for he knew that the best words could do was point to God, and that the divine reality resisted any attempts to enclose it in human idiom. Yet, our words of God are not useless, for as we have seen they do indeed point in a definite direction down an infinite hallway[134] towards an experience where words fail and silence is the most articulate response. As Wittgenstein said in *Zettel*, 'How words are understood is not told by words alone. Theology.'[135]

It may be that Wittgenstein's work on language and the Augustinian elements of the same finally frees Aquinas from the grasp of the encyclopaedist neo-Thomists. Through Wittgenstein, we are reminded of lessons which we should have grasped long ago from Thomas, that language has a multitude of uses, that an exclusive focus on the 'crystalline purity'[136] of rational argumentation blinds us to deeper truths – chief among which is Wittgenstein's point that this crystalline purity was never 'a *result of investigation*: it was a requirement'.[137] That is, historical factors and not-all-that-dissimilar epistemological crises pushed certain encyclopaedist misinterpretations of Aquinas and Wittgenstein to the fore.

Fortunately, the previous quotation (among many others in this essay) shows how Wittgenstein's own work contains, as Aquinas's certainly does not, a diagnosis of possible misinterpretations of it; and the Augustinianism in Wittgenstein profiled in the previous part of this essay liberates what generations of neo-scholastics had done their best to hide in Aquinas.

When Aquinas and Wittgenstein are used to resolve various epistemological crises, they inevitably get misread. It's like doing a spell check on the text of a play. The point lies not in a scrutiny of a sort that its authors would regard as peculiar. The point lies in the performance. Wittgenstein's philosophical critique of philosophy's ambition to pure, frictionless objectivity allows Aquinas the theologian to re-emerge and thereby suggests a corrective reading of St Thomas and everything in him that resists the Procrustean bed of philosophical 'precision' (so, for example, the second half of the twentieth century witnessed a reemergence of concern with the virtues over the occasionally arcane chicanery of the 'pure' natural law reasoning of the manuals).[138] For these reasons, we can read Aquinas more correctly after Wittgenstein; and the fact that both thinkers tend to show up at the same parties these days is simply testimony to the good taste of their hosts who know enough to invite guests to their gatherings who have much in common and are capable of meaningful interaction.[139]

Notes

1. Norman Malcolm, *Ludwig Wittgenstein: A Memoir* (London: Oxford University Press, 1958), p. 6.

2. M. O'C. Drury, 'Some Notes on Conversations with Wittgenstein', in *Ludwig Wittgenstein: Personal Recollections*, ed. Rush Rhees (Oxford: Basil Blackwell, 1981), p. 101; quoted in Brian R. Clack, *An Introduction to Wittgenstein's Philosophy of Religion* (Edinburgh: Edinburgh University Press, 1999), p. 106.

3. Wittgenstein, *Culture and Value*, ed. Georg Henrik von Wright, trans. Peter Winch (Chicago, Ill.: University of Chicago Press, 1980), p. 21e.

4. Victor Preller, *Divine Science and the Science of God: A Reformulation of Thomas Aquinas* (Princeton, NJ: Princeton University Press, 1967), p. 9. In his comments on an earlier draft of this paper, Jeff Stout observed that the contemporary philosopher Preller admired most at the time he wrote *Divine Science and the Science of God* was Wilfrid Sellars, not Ludwig Wittgenstein. Of course, some parts of Sellarsian philosophy contain Wittgensteinian emphases and examples – especially such essays as 'Some Reflections on Language Games'. This essay originally appeared in *Philosophy of Science* 21 (1954): 204–28; and was reprinted in a revised version in Sellars, *Science, Perception and Reality* (London: International Library of Philosophy and Scientific Method), 1963, pp. 321–58, a work to which Preller claimed to be especially indebted (p. 36, n. 2, in *Divine Science and the Science of God*), and a work containing several references to Wittgenstein – though fewer to his later work than to the *Tractatus*. At some point between the mid-1970s and the mid-1980s, well after *Divine Science and the Science of God*, Wittgenstein displaced Sellars in Preller's teaching.

5. See, for example, David Burrell, 'Religious Life and Understanding', *Review of Metaphysics* 22 (1969): 676–99.

6. Karl Briton, 'Portrait of a Philosopher', in *Ludwig Wittgenstein: The Man and his Philosophy*, ed. K. T. Fann (New York: Dell Publishing, 1967), pp. 60–1. This was quoted on p. 759 of Garth Hallett's *A Companion to Wittgenstein's 'Philosophical Investigations'* (Ithaca, NY: Cornell University Press, 1977).

7. In Hallett, *Companion to Wittgenstein's 'Philosophical Investigations'*, p. 761, and Anthony Kenny, 'Aquinas and Wittgenstein', *Downside Review* 77 (1959): 235. Apparently, Wittgenstein possessed just Questions 1–26 of the Prima Pars. Some do, however, see an oblique reference to St Thomas in a remark from *Culture and Value*, p. 82e, about God's essence vs. God's existence. See Emmanuel Obbo, 'Metaphysical Elements in Wittgenstein's Philosophy' (Dissertatio ad doctoratum in Facultate Philosophiae – Pontificia Universitas Urbaniana, Rome, 1991), p. 123. Fergus Kerr, in *Theology after Wittgenstein* (Oxford: Basil Blackwell, 1986), p. 154, says that the source of this allusion 'must be to the celebrated thesis of Thomas Aquinas'.

8. See, for example, Alan Keightley, *Wittgenstein, Grammar and God* (London: Epworth Press, 1976), and Felicity McCutcheon, *Religion Within the Limits of Language Alone: Wittgenstein on Philosophy and Religion* (Aldershot: Ashgate, 2001). Cyril Barrett's *Wittgenstein on Ethics and Religious Belief* (Oxford: Basil Blackwell, 1991), Fergus Kerr's *Theology after Wittgenstein*, and M. Jamie Ferreira's recent essay, 'Normativity and Reference in a Wittgensteinian Philosophy of Religion', *Faith and Philosophy* 18 (2001): 443–64 are welcome exceptions to the omission of Thomas in books and articles about Wittgenstein. Kenny's article, 'Aquinas and Wittgenstein', is one of the few where both Aquinas and Wittgenstein appear in the title. His essay is less a direct comparison between Aquinas and Wittgenstein than it is a comparison between Aquinas's antagonists (primarily Scotus) and Wittgenstein's (the positivists). Nonetheless, commonalties between Aquinas and Wittgenstein do come out through Kenny's examination of common adversaries, and I have benefited substantially from this piece. Other examples of articles on both Aquinas and Wittgenstein include Patrick Beardsley, 'Aquinas and Wittgenstein on the Grounds of Certainty', *Modern Schoolman* 51 (1974): 301–34, and William Bruening, 'Aquinas and Wittgenstein on God-Talk', *Sophia* 16 (1977): 1–7. Finally, see David Stagaman, SJ (ed.), *Wittgenstein and Religion: A Bibliography of Articles, Books, and Theses in the Twentieth Century that relate the Philosophy of Ludwig Wittgenstein to the Study of Religion and Theology* (Manila: Office of Research and Publications, Ateneo de Manila University, 2001).

9. Ray Monk's *Ludwig Wittgenstein: The Duty of Genius* (New York: Penguin Books, 1990), must be reckoned the standard against which all future intellectual biographies of Wittgenstein should be measured. I find no mention of Aquinas in that book. See also, among many others, C. G. Luckhardt (ed.), *Wittgenstein: Sources and Perspectives* (Ithaca, NY: Cornell University Press, 1979). Hallett's book cited above is a noteworthy exception.

10. Bruce Marshall, 'Aquinas as Postliberal Theologian', *The Thomist* 53

(1989): 353–402. See also his 'Thomas, Thomisms, and Truth', *The Thomist* 56 (1992): 499–554.

11. See Frederick Crosson's 'Reconsidering Aquinas as a Postliberal Theologian', *The Thomist* 56 (1992): 481–98; and John Milbank and Catherine Pickstock's *Truth in Aquinas* (London: Routledge, 2001).

12. David Kolb, 'Language and Metalanguage in Aquinas', *Journal of Religion* 61 (1981): 430.

13. David Burrell's work is probably the best example of this. See particularly his *Aquinas: God and Action* (Notre Dame, Ind.: University of Notre Dame Press, 1979), and his *Knowing the Unknowable God: Ibn-Sina, Maimonides, Aquinas* (Notre Dame, Ind.: University of Notre Dame Press, 1986). More recently, there is the Preller-inspired and -dedicated book (see p. 4) by Eugene F. Rogers, Jr, *Thomas Aquinas and Karl Barth: Sacred Knowledge and the Natural Knowledge of God* (Notre Dame, Ind.: University of Notre Dame Press, 1995).

14. See Clack, *Introduction to Wittgenstein's Philosophy of Religion*, pp. 16–18. I draw much of the following explanation from Clack's helpful exposition. In *Philosophical Investigations*, trans. G. E. M. Anscombe (New York: Macmillan, 1968), §108, the comparison becomes explicit when Wittgenstein writes, 'The question "What is a word really?" is analogous to "What is a piece in chess?"'

15. As Wittgenstein wrote in *Zettel*, ed. G. E. M. Anscombe and G. H. von Wright, trans. G. E. M. Anscombe (Berkeley, Calif.: University of California Press, 1970), §16, 'The mistake is to say that there is anything that meaning something consists in.'

16. See *Philosophical Investigations*, §65.

17. See *Philosophical Investigations*, §67: 'And I shall say: "games" form a family.'

18. Anthony Kenny, 'Aquinas and Wittgenstein', pp. 220–6, first drew my attention to this similarity.

19. See, for example, Bruening, 'Aquinas and Wittgenstein on God-Talk', pp. 1 and 7.

20. Wittgenstein, *Philosophical Investigations*, §90.

21. On this, see David Burrell, *Freedom and Creation in Three Traditions* (Notre Dame, Ind.: University of Notre Dame Press, 1993), pp. 8ff.

22. Kenny, 'Aquinas and Wittgenstein', p. 226.

23. See *Summa Theologiae*, trans. Fathers of the English Dominican Province (New York: Benziger Brothers, 1947), I.12.11 and I.12.13 ad 1.

24. Rush Rhees, 'On Religion: Notes on Four Conversations with Wittgenstein', *Faith and Philosophy* 18 (2001): 413.

25. Preller, *Divine Science and the Science of God*, p. 156.

26. Preller, *Divine Science and the Science of God*, p. 156.

27. I use this verb for Wittgenstein's regard for Augustine quite deliberately and borrow it from Malcolm's *Memoir*, p. 71. For an excellent discussion of the epistemological similarities between Augustine and the later Wittgenstein, see the unpublished Ph.D. dissertation by Alven Neiman entitled 'Augustine: Scepticism

and Philosophy' (University of Notre Dame, 1978). Neiman develops these views in 'The Arguments of Augustine's *Contra Academicos*', *The Modern Schoolman* 59 (1982): 255–79 (especially footnote 44, p. 276).

28. See Julio Burunat, 'Thomas Aquinas' Use of Augustine's Work: A Study in Development' (unpublished Ph.D. dissertation, Fordham University, 1973), p. 21.

29. Monk, *Ludwig Wittgenstein: The Duty of Genius*, p. 282; quoting Rush Rhees (ed.), *Recollections of Wittgenstein* (Oxford: Oxford University Press, 1984), p. 90.

30. Hallett, *Companion to Wittgenstein's 'Philosophical Investigations'*, p. 761. Hallett says there that, at the very least, he has found no evidence of Wittgenstein having read anything other than the *Confessions*. Drury reports that Wittgenstein 'had tried to read *The City of God* but had been unable to get on with it'. See Drury, 'Some Notes on Conversations with Wittgenstein', p. 105.

31. Malcolm, *Memoir*, p. 71.

32. Stanley Cavell, 'The Availability of Wittgenstein's Later Philosophy', in *Wittgenstein: The Philosophical Investigations*, Modern Studies in Philosophy, ed. George Pitcher (Notre Dame, Ind.: University of Notre Dame Press, 1968), p. 183. See also G. H. von Wright's biographical sketch, in Malcolm, *Memoir*, p. 21, and K. T. Fann, *Wittgenstein's Conception of Philosophy* (Berkeley, Calif.: University of California Press, 1971), p. 106.

33. See, for example, *Culture and Value*, p. 3e.

34. Monk, *Ludwig Wittgenstein: The Duty of Genius*, p. 366.

35. Wittgenstein, *Culture and Value*, p. 26e; quoted in Monk, *Ludwig Wittgenstein: The Duty of Genius*, p. 366.

36. Rush Rhees (ed.), *Recollections of Wittgenstein* (Oxford: Oxford University Press, 1984), p. 174; quoted in Monk, *Ludwig Wittgenstein: The Duty of Genius*, p. 367.

37. Alasdair MacIntyre, *Three Rival Versions of Moral Enquiry* (Notre Dame, Ind.: University of Notre Dame Press, 1990), p. 82.

38. MacIntyre, *Three Rival Versions of Moral Enquiry*, p. 92. Wittgenstein voices such retrospective justification well in *Culture and Value*, p. 85e: 'A proof of God's existence ought really to be something by means of which one could convince oneself that God exists. But I think that what *believers* who have furnished such proofs have wanted to do is give their "belief" an intellectual analysis and foundation, although they themselves would never have come to believe as a result of such proofs.' Cyril Barrett said that 'St Thomas' proofs for the existence of God were repulsive to Wittgenstein.' See Barrett, 'The Logic of Mysticism', in *Religion and Philosophy*, ed. Martin Warner (Cambridge: Cambridge University Press, 1992), p. 63. (This of course assumes that Aquinas proposed his own proofs for the existence of God.) Malcolm in his *Memoir*, p. 71, said merely that Wittgenstein 'was impatient' with proofs for God's existence.

39. This remark comes from Augustine, *Divine Providence and the Problem of Evil*, a translation of *De Ordine*, by Robert P. Russell, OSA (New York:

Cosmopolitan Science and Art Service Co., 1942), II.9.26. I owe my discovery of this passage to Alven Neiman's excellent piece, 'Augustine's Philosophizing Person: The View at Cassiciacum', *The New Scholasticism* 57 (1984): 239, in which the author argues against those who would read Augustine as a proto-Cartesian.

40. MacIntyre, *Three Rival Versions of Moral Enquiry*, p. 84.

41. Thomas Aquinas, *Summa Theologiae*, II-II.162.6.

42. MacIntyre, *Three Rival Versions of Moral Enquiry*, p. 124.

43. MacIntyre, *Three Rival Versions of Moral Enquiry*, p. 125.

44. Quoted in 'Talking Peace: An Interview with Colman McCarthy', *Common Sense* (May 2002): 6.

45. Obviously, both Aquinas and Wittgenstein were *more* than Augustinians as well. I don't wish to be taken to reducing them to such. But I would claim that this is a useful (and neglected) lens through which to see both men and the similarities they have to one another. I would, therefore, certainly want to disagree with Norman Malcolm's statement in his *Memoir*, p. 15, that 'The later Wittgenstein, I should say, has no ancestors in the history of thought', which I regard as the pious hyperbole of a devoted student.

46. Aquinas, *Summa Theologiae*, I.1.2.

47. See especially chapter 4 of *Divine Science and the Science of God*.

48. See also *ST* I.12.8 ad 4 for a very similar idea.

49. Manuscript 173; quoted in Hallett, *Companion to Wittgenstein's 'Philosophical Investigations'*, pp. 231–2. The translations from the German are Hallett's.

50. Wittgenstein, *Culture and Value*, p. 45e.

51. See, for example, *The Blue Book* (New York: Harper & Row, 1964), p. 59, where Wittgenstein speaks of '*our* mental cramp' (italics mine).

52. Wittgenstein, *Philosophical Investigations*, §226e.

53. In *On Certainty*, ed. G. E. M. Anscombe and G. H. von Wright, trans. Denis Paul and G. E. M. Anscombe (New York: Harper & Row, 1972), §189, Wittgenstein said, 'At some point one has to pass from explanation to mere description.' Hallett, *Companion to Wittgenstein's 'Philosophical Investigations'*, p. 738, drew my attention to this connection.

54. Wittgenstein, *The Blue Book*, pp. 58–9.

55. The same inability to stop destructive behaviour despite the clear desire to do so that we find in the *Confessions*, we find in Wittgenstein. In a statement to Rush Rhees (quoted in Hallett, *Companion to Wittgenstein's 'Philosophical Investigations'*, p. 230), Wittgenstein lamented, 'In my book I say that I am able to leave off with a problem in philosophy when I want to. But that's a lie. I can't.'

56. In *Philosophical Investigations*, §90, Wittgenstein wrote, 'Our investigation is therefore a grammatical one. Such an investigation sheds light on our problem by clearing misunderstandings away.'

57. Wittgenstein, *Remarks on the Foundations of Mathematics*, ed. G. H. von Wright, Rush Rhees, and G. E. M. Anscombe, trans. G. E. M. Anscombe (New York: Macmillan, 1956), p. 57.

58. Wittgenstein, *Culture and Value*, p. 61e.

59. Wittgenstein, *Culture and Value*, p. 17e.

60. Wittgenstein, *Zettel*, §461.

61. Aquinas, *De Veritate*, trans. Robert W. Mulligan (Chicago, Ill.: Henry Regnery, 1952), q. 1, a. 8.

62. Aquinas, *Summa Theologiae*, II-II.109.1.

63. Aquinas, *Summa Theologiae*, II-II.4.5.

64. Aquinas, *Summa Theologiae*, II-II.2.3.

65. Aquinas, *Summa Theologiae*, I-II.111.2.

66. Aquinas, *Summa Theologiae*, II-II.4.8.

67. Aquinas, *Summa Theologiae*, II-II.2.10. See above n. 38 on Wittgenstein's similar view about retrospective justification and his consequent negative assessment about so-called proofs for God.

68. M. Jamie Ferreira, 'Normativity and Reference in a Wittgensteinian Philosophy of Religion', p. 455.

69. Eugene Rogers's book does an excellent job in showing how thoroughly christocentric Aquinas's project was. In the *Summa Contra Gentiles*, Aquinas cites Augustine only 75 times (vs. the 2,738 of the *Summa Theologiae*). Given the very explicit project of addressing himself to non-believers in the *Contra Gentiles*, this is precisely as we should expect if MacIntyre is right about what an Augustinian approach is.

70. Aquinas, *Summa Theologiae*, I-II.70.3.

71. Wittgenstein, *Philosophical Investigations*, §133.

72. In MacIntyre, *Three Rival Versions of Moral Enquiry*, p. 69, he speaks about 'post-Enlightenment culture, the culture of the encyclopaedia'.

73. See MacIntyre, *Three Rival Versions of Moral Enquiry*, esp. pp. 64ff.

74. I do not mean to suggest by this that Aquinas himself was a pacifist. The evidence to the contrary is overwhelming – we need look no further than *ST* II-II.40 and II-II.64. Nor was he necessarily averse to bringing, quite literally, some to their knees (*ST* II-II.11.3, for example). Rather, I intend to make a point only about Aquinas's method. That method was fundamentally dialectical and deeply charitable in conceding to his intellectual or religious opponents the strength of their own positions, liberally borrowing from them where their pursuit of truth ran parallel to his own, and taking their views seriously enough to engage them without rancour. The goal was not to defeat, but to incorporate; and to incorporate in this way entailed annexing the strengths of other positions even while identifying on their own terms the limitations they bore. And I would argue that this method was displayed even while Aquinas was articulating his own commitment to just war or justified uses of violence. For a wonderfully contextual discussion of Thomas's hermeneutical challenges and achievements, see chapters 10 and 11 of Alasdair MacIntyre, *Whose Justice? Which Rationality?* (Notre Dame, Ind.: University of Notre Dame Press, 1988), pp. 164–208. See also ch. 1 of Paul J. Wadell, *The Primacy of Love: An Introduction to the Ethics of Thomas Aquinas* (New York: Paulist Press, 1992), pp. 7–28.

75. See especially ch. 4 of *Divine Science and the Science of God*.

76. Norman Malcolm, 'The Groundlessness of Belief', in *Reason and Religion*, ed. Stuart C. Brown (Ithaca: Cornell University Press, 1977), p. 156.

77. Ernest Gellner, 'Reply to Mr. MacIntyre', *Universities and Left Review* (Summer 1958); quoted in William Bartley, *Wittgenstein* (Philadelphia, Pa.: Lippincott, 1973), p. 173.

78. See my 'The Appropriation of Wittgenstein's Work by Philosophers of Religion: Towards a Re-evaluation and an End', *Religious Studies* 21 (1985): 457–74. For a similar criticism, see also the chapter 'Neo-Wittgensteinian Philosophy of Religion', in Clack, *Introduction to Wittgenstein's Philosophy of Religion*, pp. 78–105. A helpful supplementary point comes out in J. Kellenberger's 'Wittgenstein's Gift to Contemporary Analytic Philosophy of Religion', *International Journal for Philosophy of Religion* 28 (1990): 153: namely, even if one could rightly associate such concepts as language-game and form of life with religion, it is still undetermined whether religious belief is itself *a* language-game or *a* form of life, or whether it is composed of many language-games or forms of life.

79. This is the concluding remark of Wittgenstein's lectures in the spring of 1939; quoted on p. 111 of Fann, *Wittgenstein's Conception of Philosophy*.

80. He said in *Culture and Value*, p. 61e, 'Am I the only one who cannot found a school or can a philosopher never do this? I cannot found a school because I do not really want to be imitated. Not at any rate by those who publish articles in philosophical journals. I am by no means sure that I should prefer a continuation of my work by others to a change in the way people live which would make all these questions superfluous. (For this reason, I could never found a school.)'

81. See Alven Neiman, 'No More Method! A Polemical Response to Audrey Thompson', in *Philosophy of Education 1995*, ed. Alven Neiman (Urbana, Ill.: The Philosophy of Education Society, 1996), pp. 130–41.

82. Mark Cladis, 'Mild-Mannered Pragmatism and Religious Truth', *Journal of the American Academy of Religion* 50 (1992): 20.

83. Clack, *Introduction to Wittgenstein's Philosophy of Religion*, p. 101.

84. Wittgenstein, *Philosophical Investigations*, §199. Similarly, in *On Certainty*, §141, Wittgenstein says, 'When we first begin to *believe* anything, what we believe is not a single proposition, it is a whole system of propositions. (Light dawns gradually over the whole.)'

85. See the illustration in Fr Thomas O'Meara, *The Basilica of the Sacred Heart at Notre Dame: A Theological Guide to the Paintings and Windows* (Notre Dame, Ind.: Ave Maria Press, 1991). See also online: http://www.saintmarys. edu/~incandel/aquinasSH.jpg. This depiction of Aquinas was certainly not original with Gregori, as other examples do exist. See in particular Plates 3, 4, and 5 of B. H. Molkenboer, *St Thomas van Aquino in de schilderkunst* (Gent: Uitgaven, 1927). Plate 5 is a representation by Pompeo Batoni, an eighteenth-century Italian artist. For another online image of Aquinas holding up five fingers in this manner, see http://www.home.duq.edu/~bonin/thomasbibliography.html.

86. Leo XIII, *Aeterni Patris*, §§17–18. Available online: http://www.vatican.

va/holy_father/leo_xiii/encyclicals/documents/hf_l-xiii_enc_04081879_aeterni-patris_en.html.

87. *Aeterni Patris*, §17.

88. *Dogmatic Constitution on the Catholic Faith*: Session 3, Canon 3 ('On Revelation'). Available online: http://www.piar.hu/councils/ecum20.htm.

89. O'Meara, *The Basilica of the Sacred Heart at Notre Dame*, p. 7.

90. O'Meara, *Thomas Aquinas: Theologian* (Notre Dame, Ind.: University of Notre Dame Press, 1997), p. 156.

91. O'Meara, *Thomas Aquinas: Theologian*, p. 171.

92. MacIntyre, *Three Rival Versions of Moral Enquiry*, pp. 78–9.

93. Wittgenstein, *Philosophical Investigations*, §127.

94. Wittgenstein, *Zettel*, §453.

95. (New York: Crossroad, 1996).

96. James Arraj, 'What is the State of Catholic Philosophy and Theology Today? or Whatever Happened to Thomism?' Available online: http://www.innerexplorations.com/chtheomortext/the.htm. On this period in the history of Thomistic interpretation, see also pp. 167–73 of Fr Thomas O'Meara, *Thomas Aquinas: Theologian*.

97. David Burrell, 'Creation, Metaphysics, and Ethics', *Faith and Philosophy* 18 (2001): 212.

98. Robert Sokolowski, *The God of Faith and Reason: Foundations of Christian Theology* (Notre Dame, Ind.: University of Notre Dame Press, 1982), esp. pp. 31–3.

99. Wittgenstein, *Philosophical Investigations*, §199.

100. See, for example, James C. Edwards, *Ethics Without Philosophy: Wittgenstein and the Moral Life* (Tampa: University Presses of Florida, 1982), which is one of the best treatments of these issues available.

101. Stanley Hauerwas, *The Peaceable Kingdom* (Notre Dame, Ind.: University of Notre Dame Press, 1983), p. xxi.

102. Wittgenstein, *Culture and Value*, p. 83e.

103. Wittgenstein, *Culture and Value*, p. 32e.

104. Wittgenstein, *Zettel*, §233.

105. In *Culture and Value*, p. 72e, Wittgenstein said, 'Religious faith and superstition are quite different. One of them results from *fear* and is a sort of false science. The other is a trusting.'

106. Wittgenstein, *Culture and Value*, p. 64e: 'It strikes me that a religious belief could only be something like a passionate commitment to a system of reference. Hence, though it's *belief*, it's really a way of living, or a way of assessing life. It's passionately seizing hold of *this* interpretation.' For another statement linking passion and belief, see p. 33e.

107. Dallas High, 'Wittgenstein: On Seeing Problems from a Religious Point of View', *International Journal for Philosophy of Religion* 28 (1990): 113. High's essay is an excellent response to those who would argue that Wittgenstein himself either wasn't religious or wasn't vitally concerned with religious issues.

108. See High, 'Wittgenstein', p. 111. Wittgenstein himself draws attention to this connection when he links faith to passion in *Culture and Value*, p. 53e:

'Wisdom is passionless. But faith by contrast is what Kierkegaard calls a *passion*.'

109. Drury, 'Some Notes on Conversations with Wittgenstein', p. 102. See Hallett, *Companion to Wittgenstein's 'Philosophical Investigations'*, p. 769 for a slightly different rendering of this statement. Malcolm (*Memoir*, p. 71) reports that Wittgenstein referred to Kierkegaard 'with something of awe in his expression, as a "really religious" man'.

110. Michael P. Hodges, 'Faith: Themes from Wittgenstein, Kierkegaard and Nietzsche', in *Wittgenstein and Philosophy of Religion*, ed. Robert L. Arrington and Mark Addis (London: Routledge, 2001), p. 71. Hodges on pp. 66–70 also points out the central place that authority has in Wittgenstein's understanding of religious belief.

111. See *Philosophical Investigations*, §199 and pp. 70–2 of Emmanuel Obbo, 'Metaphysical Elements in Wittgenstein's Philosophy'.

112. Or so I have argued in 'The Appropriation of Wittgenstein's Work by Philosophers of Religion: Towards a Re-Evaluation and an End'.

113. Wittgenstein, *Culture and Value*, p. 37e.

114. Wittgenstein, *On Certainty*, §65. See also *Zettel*, §135: 'conversation flows on, . . . and only in its course do words have their meaning'.

115. Wittgenstein, *Philosophical Investigations*, §107.

116. *Philosophical Investigations*, §107.

117. See Wittgenstein, *Philosophical Investigations*, §§136, 271.

118. Wittgenstein, *On Certainty*, §§96–7 and 99.

119. Wittgenstein, *On Certainty*, §97.

120. *Culture and Value*, p. 76. I take this particular translation from Wittgenstein, *Culture and Value*, ed. G. H. von Wright, revised 2nd edn with English translation by Peter Winch (Cambridge, Mass.: Blackwell, 1998), p. 86e. Wittgenstein made Augustine's concerns about time in the *Confessions* his own, and often cited him when discussing time. See *Philosophical Investigations*, §§89–90 and *The Blue Book*, p. 26. On Wittgenstein's use of Augustine when speaking about time, see Hallett, *Companion to Wittgenstein's 'Philosophical Investigations'*, p. 761.

121. Wittgenstein, *On Certainty*, §211.

122. Wittgenstein, *On Certainty*, §509.

123. Augustine, *On Certainty*, §162. Cf. §§140, 160, and 263.

124. See especially Chapter 5 of Chenu's *Nature, Man, and Society in the Twelfth Century*, trans. and ed. Jerome Taylor and Lester K. Little (Chicago, Ill.: University of Chicago Press, 1968).

125. Robert Barron makes these points quite nicely on pp. 66–7 of *Thomas Aquinas: Spiritual Master*. There he explains that if spiritual 'change' or movement is the primary focus of Aquinas's argument, then Thomas's careful denial of self-movement in the first half of the first way in I.2.3 ('omne quod movetur, ab alio movetur') takes on an interesting anthropological significance. In denying that something can change itself, that it can set itself on its own path, Thomas negates the sinful drive toward radical autonomy, toward complete self-direction.

126. See my 'Duns Scotus and the Experience of Human Freedom', *The Thomist* 16 (1992): 229–56.

127. Josef Pieper, *The Silence of St Thomas*, trans. John Murray and Daniel O'Connor (New York: Pantheon Books, 1957), p. 96.

128. Rush Rhees passed this comment along. See Hallett, *Companion to Wittgenstein's 'Philosophical Investigations'*, p. 761. The above quotation comes from Anthony Kenny, 'Aquinas and Wittgenstein', p. 235.

129. Wittgenstein, *Zettel*, §457.

130. Anthony Kenny says in 'Aquinas and Wittgenstein', p. 218: 'One of the first things which might bring one to notice a similarity between Aquinas and Wittgenstein is the fact that there is a measure of agreement between them about which problems a philosopher should *not* raise.'

131. Michael Hodges, 'Faith: Themes from Wittgenstein, Kierkegaard and Nietzsche', p. 80. I'm very indebted here to Hodges's explanation of these issues on pp. 80–1, as well as his calling my attention to the quotation from *Philosophical Investigations*, §261.

132. *Philosophical Investigations*, §261.

133. The quotation comes from a letter to Ludwig von Ficker: 'I wanted to write that my work consists of two parts: of the one which is here, and of everything which I have *not* written. And precisely this second part is the important one.... In brief, I think: All of that which *many* are *babbling* today, I have defined in my book by remaining silent about it.' This is quoted on p. 33 of Clack, *Introduction to Wittgenstein's Philosophy of Religion*, and comes originally from 'Letters to Ludwig von Ficker', ed. Allan Janik, trans. Bruce Gillette, in *Wittgenstein: Sources and Perspectives*, ed. C. G. Luckhardt (Hassocks: Harvester Press, 1979), pp. 34–5.

134. I take this way of putting the matter from Peter Kreeft and Ronald Tacelli, *Handbook of Christian Apologetics* (Downers Grove, Ill.: InterVarsity Press, 1994), p. 79.

135. Wittgenstein, *Zettel*, §144. In *Culture and Value*, p. 85e, Wittgenstein said, 'Actually I should like to say that . . . the *words* you utter or what you think as you utter them are not what matters, so much as the difference they make at various points in your life. . . . *Practice* gives the words their sense.'

136. *Philosophical Investigations*, §107.

137. *Philosophical Investigations*, §107.

138. David Burrell had it exactly correct when he wrote in 1969's 'Religious Life and Understanding', p. 683: 'We are misled only when we fail to recognize that Aquinas's project is explicitly theological, and doubly misled if we expect philosophy to do more than he himself demanded of it.'

139. I wish to thank Gregory C. Higgins and the two editors of this volume for their extremely helpful comments on earlier drafts of this essay.

2. In Search of an Analytic Aquinas

Grammar and the Trinity

BRUCE D. MARSHALL

A Melchizedek among Thomists

One of the signal achievements of Victor Preller's *Divine Science and the Science of God* is to have developed a sustained and penetrating interpretation of Thomas Aquinas by using the resources of analytic philosophy.[1] Wilfrid Sellars, then at the height of his influence, is the analytic philosopher upon whom Preller chiefly draws. But Preller is no mere follower of Sellars. He adapts the ideas of Sellars and other analytic philosophers to his own purpose, which is a critical and highly sympathetic reconstruction of Aquinas's views on the knowledge of God, based on deep engagement with Thomas's own texts. The result is a remarkably creative and thought-provoking interpretation of Aquinas, still fresh nearly forty years after it was written.

Preller offers not only an analytic reading of Aquinas, but a theological one. His interpretation of Aquinas is not theological in the sense that he devotes much time (apart from some tantalizing suggestions) to the central matters of Christian faith, with which Thomas is so preoccupied: the Trinity, grace, the incarnation, Christ's life, passion, and resurrection, the sacraments. But Preller's take on Aquinas is boldly theological in its understanding of the *kind* of thing that Thomas is doing. When Aquinas speaks as a teacher of Catholic truth – which is to say, all of the time – he rejects the very idea of an autonomous philosophy. All philosophical claims, indeed all claims to knowledge, have to be warranted theologically, by establishing some suitable link with the chief convictions of Christian faith.[2] In particular, as Preller reads Aquinas, only faith, and not philosophy, can recognize when human talk of God actually succeeds, despite all its limitations, in referring to God.[3]

In all of this Preller was, and largely remains, ahead of his time. Indeed Preller is a kind of Melchizedek among Thomists, without father or mother or genealogy – at least any genealogy that most other readers of Aquinas could understand. To be sure, interpretations of Aquinas whose interest is chiefly philosophical are now more and more likely to have an overtly analytic character. The possibility of an 'analytical Thomism' is regularly discussed, and various topics in Aquinas now receive philosophical treatment informed in one way or another by the analytic tradition.[4] This development no doubt owes much to the explosive growth of analytic philosophy of religion since the 1970s, though some of the most formative analytically oriented writers on Aquinas got started well before this (like P. T. Geach, Anthony Kenny, and Herbert McCabe).[5] One would like to be able to include Preller on this list of progenitors, but I can't see that later analytic philosophical interest in Aquinas owes anything to him. This may in part be due to his radically theological reading of Aquinas, despite the evident philosophical interest of his topic. It surely also stems from his want of a recognizable Thomistic genealogy. Yet as this volume attests, he is not without heirs, although his descendants are not to be found among those whose interest in Thomas is mainly philosophical.

Despite the rise of analytic Thomism, many Thomistic philosophers remain sceptical of the thought that one could be a Thomist and an analytic philosopher at the same time. They may assume (erroneously) that analytic philosophy commits its practitioners to views that are entirely unacceptable to Thomists, like naturalism or physicalism (though it's one thing to observe that a Thomist can't accept these claims, and quite another to refute naturalism and physicalism as conceived and justified by, say, Quine). Or, conversely, they may assume that Thomism is defined by theses, like the real distinction of existence and essence, that they suppose analytic philosophers are committed to rejecting.[6] Not all philosophical readers of Thomas even get to the point of being suspicious. The world of French- and German-speaking Thomas interpretation remains virtually untouched by analytic philosophy, and *a fortiori* by 'analytical Thomism'.

In any case interpreters of Thomas who share Preller's philosophical bent are unlikely to read him in Preller's radically theological way, or (naturally enough) to have much interest in Thomas's treatment of topics they are inclined to regard as wholly theological.[7] But those who share Preller's interest in a consistently theological interpretation of Aquinas are, in turn, even less likely to use the resources of analytic philosophy as an aid to understanding and assessing Thomas's views, or to see the analytic tradition as a source of critical challenges which Thomas's theological partisans need to address. Indeed the more oriented they are to particular theological topics (the Trinity, the incarnation, and so forth) the less apt they are to have any interest in matters analytic.[8] Of course Thomist theologians are not alone in this. They tend to share a determination to remain innocent of analytic philosophy common to theologians of practically every persuasion – odd though it is for *Thomists* to proceed in this way.[9]

I suspect that the neglect of Preller's approach to Aquinas, at once theological and analytically philosophical, has been unjust. One way to test whether there is in fact good reason to follow Preller on this score is to see whether we can find at the heart of Aquinas's theology any claims or procedures which have an evident kinship, whatever their lineage, with analytic philosophy. Unlike phenomenology, structuralism, or even the amorphous 'postmodernism' – and certainly unlike Thomism – what marks out analytic philosophy is not a set of substantive theses, but a kind of procedural presumption. Careful attention to language and logic, analytic philosophers are inclined to suppose, will probably help us get at the truth of whatever substantive matter we're concerned with. My aim here is not to test whether this or that claim Thomas makes passes analytic muster (a procedure which Thomists may fear, not always needlessly, distorts the teaching of the master). Rather we need to see whether there are already any obvious analytic elements *in* Aquinas – whether he makes theological claims and arguments in ways that analytic philosophers can easily recognize as the sort of thing they think ought to be done, whenever claims are made or arguments advanced.

It's best to avoid generality here, and consider a case in point. I'll first characterize a medieval semantic procedure, much utilized by Thomas, which has obvious analytic resonance. We'll then look in more detail at a particular theological application of this procedure: the question whether, in the eternal coming forth of the Son from the Father, the divine essence itself generates, or is generated.

Semantic ascent

Contemporary readers of medieval theology may notice there a procedure which has become ubiquitous in analytic philosophy at least as far back as Frege. The medievals regularly solve theological problems by engaging in *semantic ascent*. The phrase is not medieval; so far as I know it was coined by W. V. O. Quine.[10] But it labels an ancient practice. We ascend semantically when we turn from talking about objects to talking about words, from talking about the world to heeding the grammar – seemingly obvious yet often elusive – of our own discourse. This the medievals often did, and quite explicitly. They ask whether a certain *dictio* or *locutio* is correct or incorrect, possible or impossible, true or false, and then set about analysing the term or utterance in question. Thus, in the case we will look at here, medieval trinitarian theologians not only ask whether the divine essence generates or is generated, but also whether the following *statement* is true: 'The essence generates the essence' (*essentia generat essentiam*), or whether it can be *said* that (*utrum possit dici*) *the essence generates the essence*.

With the strategy of semantic ascent goes a battery of grammatical and logical devices, sometimes quite technical, for analysing the words and sentences which ascent brings to our attention. In thirteenth- and fourteenth-century western trinitarian theology, these include the distinction between terms used *in recto* and *in obliquo*, between terms used in the masculine and in the neuter, between terms taken as substantives and as adjectives, between concrete and abstract *modi significandi*, between the signification and supposition of terms, and between formal predication and predication *per identitatem*.[11] So, for example, trinitarian theologians of the time practise semantic ascent not only by asking whether 'The essence generates' is true, but by asking whether or not the term 'essence' can 'stand for' (*supponit pro*) a divine person.

The practice of semantic ascent may, however, give the impression that substantive ontological issues are being ignored or distorted for the sake of trivial linguistic ones. Theology, after all, is supposed to be about God, not about the word 'God'. Nowadays we readily assume that the crucial issues in trinitarian theology, such as whether the three divine persons are really one God, need to be dealt with by a metaphysical analysis of matters like whether relations can subsist and constitute persons, whether relations in God have to involve origin, and whether (or how) the persons can be identical *in re* with the essence. Attending to semantic questions like whether it can be said that the essence generates the essence, and whether 'essentia' can stand for a divine person, at best simply stipulates a way of talking. It settles nothing about what God is really like. At worst semantic ascent amounts to a 'linguistic despoiling of the world', as Ruprecht Paqué says of Ockham.[12] It suggests that behind the words we so scrupulously analyse, the world, and *a fortiori* God, might be unknowably different than we suppose – or might not be at all. Perhaps because of such suspicions semantic ascent (and indeed analytic philosophy *tout court*) is almost entirely absent from the extensive discussions of the Trinity in modern theology. Perhaps this also has something to do with the relative inattention among historians of the period to the semantic dimension of medieval trinitarian theology.[13]

But semantic ascent need have no such dubious consequences. Its purpose is not to avoid ontological commitments, but to help us get clear on what our ontological commitments are, and on how vague or conflicting ontological commitments confuse discussion and block its progress. To use a well known example of Quine's: suppose that your ontology includes miles, and mine does not. So we argue: you say that the existence of miles is obvious; there's a mile wherever there are 1,760 yards. There aren't any yards either, I say, only bodies of various lengths. Are the earth and the sun separated by bodies of various lengths, you want to know. And so forth. But if we ascend from talking about miles to thinking about the word 'mile' and how it is used in sentences on whose truth value we agree ('The sun is 93 million miles from the earth'), we can use our common semantic commitments in order to get a grip on our ontological disagreement, perhaps to resolve it, perhaps to set it aside as not worth resolving.[14] Of course sometimes we disagree about which sentences are true. Precisely by having ascended to an explicit consideration of these sentences, we can bring to bear logical and semantic devices which enable us to be quite precise about the nature of our disagreements, and, more importantly, help us resolve them. We do not thereby abandon the question of what there is, but rather we answer it. If our sentences are true, then presumably there must be whatever objects and states of affairs it takes in order for them to be true.

By itself, therefore, semantic ascent entails no specific ontological commitments, whether stringent or extravagant. Frege uses it to artic-ulate and defend a flamboyant, at times Platonistic, ontology, Quine a relatively spare and nominalistic one. The ontologically generous Aquinas practises it in trinitarian theology at least as much as the ontologically parsimonious Ockham. Of course the extent to which Aquinas or other medieval trinitarian theologians exploit the resources of semantic ascent, and to what ends, we can only begin to tell by looking at a particular case.

The question 'Utrum essentia generet'

Readers of contemporary theology will quickly recognize the rele-vance of the question 'Does the essence generate?' Roughly since Barth and Rahner, Protestant and Catholic trinitarian theologies alike have often insisted on the need for a 'personalist' approach to trinitarian issues, in contrast with the 'essentialist' outlook long favoured, so it is often assumed, in western theology. The essentialist western 'starting-point', so the argument goes, at best plays down or makes unintelligible the distinctions among the persons of the Trinity. The three divine persons become mere 'relations within the essence', relations, somehow, of the one divine essence to itself. At worst trini-tarian essentialism takes the essence as pre- or supra-personal, and the source of the persons. This denies the personal causal role within the Trinity proper to the Father, subordinates the persons to the essence, and may end up denying the Trinity outright: the essence alone may become constitutive of the reality of the one God, above and beyond the personal distinctions.[15] Eastern Orthodox theologians have pressed these points with particular force, often under the heading of the 'monarchy' of the Father – for them the view that the Father, alone among the divine persons, is a causal principle with respect to the others.[16] But their criticism of the West's presumed 'essentialism' has won wide acceptance.

Even a brief examination of the extensive medieval discussion of the question whether the divine essence generates anything (in particular, whether it generates any divine person) may thus be of systematic as well as historical significance.

Systematically, it might help us with the difficult question of the relation between the persons and the essence, and thereby with the basic trinitarian problem of how the three persons can be the one God. That is: it's widely agreed (and certainly was in the Middle Ages) that there's one divine essence or nature, with which Father, Son, and Holy Spirit are in some way identical. On the numerical unity of the divine essence hangs the claim of Christians that there's only one God, not three. But while Father, Son, and Spirit are in some way the same as the one divine essence, they are not the same as each other. On this hangs Christian faith in the Trinity and, with that, in the divinity – and so the saving power – of Christ and the Holy Spirit. The question, of course, is how the numerical unity of the divine essence and the numerical distinction of the divine persons can both hold good. Scholastic theology in the Middle Ages paid a lot of attention to this problem, and took the question 'Does the essence generate?' to bear on it directly.

Historically, attention to this disputed question may help us decide whether the western trinitarian tradition really merits the label 'essentialist', especially at that point – scholastic doctrines of the Trinity after Lateran IV – where it is most readily assumed to apply.

The medieval locus classicus for the question whether the essence generates is Book I of Peter Lombard's *Sentences*, the fourth and fifth distinctions. At the outset of distinction five Lombard addresses the questions whether the divine essence is generated (by the Father) or generates (the Son).[17] Against these claims he develops three arguments. In a passage subsequently much discussed, Lombard summarizes the results of these arguments by invoking a premise drawn from Augustine which, he thinks, decides the issue: nothing generates itself. 'Therefore we say that the divine essence did not generate (*non genuit*) the essence. For since the divine essence is a certain single and highest reality (*res*), if the divine essence generated the essence, one and the same reality generated itself, which is entirely impossible. Rather the Father alone generated the Son, and from the Father and the Son the Holy Spirit proceeded.'[18] He is not, however, entirely happy with this. Augustine and Hilary often say or imply that 'what the Father is', or the essence, or the nature, generates and is generated, so Lombard spends the rest of the fifth distinction wrestling with a number of texts from these authorities, not always to his complete satisfaction: 'I am exceedingly agitated about these statements. I would rather hear from others how they are to be understood than hand on my own opinion.'[19]

In Lombard's treatment of this trinitarian question, over which he is obviously troubled, semantic ascent is almost entirely absent. At one point he does make an explicitly semantic argument, about the reference of relative terms.[20] But he seems not to notice this, and makes nothing of it. Most of the argumentative weight falls on the straight-forwardly metaphysical premise that nothing can be the cause of itself. No semantic recourse here. What clinches 'essentia divina non genuit essentiam' is, as it would later be put, an argument in first-intentional terms rather than second-intentional ones, an argument in terms of what can be rather than of what can be said.

The question whether the essence generates was regularly addressed in the second half of the twelfth century, but it acquired special prominence through Joachim of Fiore's attack on Lombard's view of the matter around the turn of the century. The Fourth Lateran Council (1215) rejected this attack on Lombard's orthodoxy, and instead condemned what it took to be Joachim's opinions on the unity and distinction of the persons of the Trinity, and their relation to the divine essence. It's difficult to get a fix on the precise relationship between the teaching of Lombard, Joachim, and Lateran IV, not least because Joachim's treatise against Lombard is lost.[21] But in the subsequent the-ological discussion of *utrum essentia generet* the standard view is that Joachim errs precisely in claiming that the essence does in fact beget or produce something. He becomes the routine polemical target on this question, the stock example of a theologian who gets it wrong. Joachim's error becomes that of taking the assumption of divine simplicity (in particular, that the three persons are in reality the same as the one essence) to license an inference from 'Pater generat' to 'essentia generat'.

On the basis of Lateran IV's description of his teaching one might equally well take Joachim to be arguing that since 'Pater generat' is obviously true, but 'essentia generat' cannot be, the Father and the essence cannot, contra Lombard, be the same *res*. Joachim's point would thus not be to affirm *essentia generat*, but to deny the simplicity of God (the real identity of essence and person). Evidently there was some unsettlement among later thirteenth-century theologians over which way to take Joachim. Aquinas, for example, attributes both views to him at different times.[22] The usual reading, however, is the first.

Besides drawing attention to the issue, Lateran IV's decision about Lombard and Joachim has two principal effects on the subsequent discussion of *utrum essentia generet*. First, it officially closes the substantive question. There is 'a certain single and highest reality', the 'divine substance, nature, or essence', which just is the Father, the Son, and the Holy Spirit, whether the three are taken together or one by one. But, closely echoing Lombard, 'this *res* does not generate, nor is it generated, nor does it proceed, but it is the Father who generates, the Son, who is generated, and the Holy Spirit, who proceeds, so that the distinctions are in the persons, and the unity in the nature'.[23] Henceforth the debate is not over whether the essence generates, but over what the best argument is to show that it does not. Second, Lateran IV bequeaths to later theology the task of making sense of the claim that while the essence is the same as the Father, it does not generate, even though the Father does (and, correlatively, that it is not generated, even though the Son is). On both counts thirteenth- and fourteenth-century theologians will often take semantic ascent to be their best recourse.

Aquinas on the modi significandi of trinitarian discourse

Aquinas treats the question 'Does the essence generate?' several times, including, naturally, his *Scriptum* on Lombard's *Sentences*, and a commentary on Lateran IV's rejection of Joachim of Fiore.[24] I will concentrate on his last discussion of the matter in *Summa Theologiae* I.39.5.

Initially Aquinas poses the question in a highly generalized form: 'Can [adjectives, verbs, or participles for characteristics of the divine persons] be predicated of essential terms taken abstractly?'[25] But 'The essence generates' is clearly the case which concerns him. Here 'generates' is a verb for a characteristic of a divine person (namely the Father) and 'the essence' is the essential term taken abstractly. In the *sed contra* of this article he recalls Augustine's argument, upon which Lombard depends, that nothing generates itself. This lets us know where the truth of the matter lies: the essence doesn't generate. That Aquinas puts this Augustinian and Lombardian commonplace in the *sed contra* indicates, however, that he doesn't expect it to bear any argumentative weight, at least not on its own. Instead he takes the argument necessary to meet Joachim's error to be semantic in character.

Others before Aquinas, like William of Auxerre, had already put their finger on why an explicitly semantic argument seems necessary in order to handle the problem of whether the essence generates. According to Lombard, 'The essence generates' is supposed to be false because nothing can generate itself. Now there is only one God, just as there is only one divine essence. So with apparently equal effectiveness Lombard's metaphysical premise rules out 'God generates God'. But this, since it's in the Creed, everybody naturally concedes ('God from God', spoken of Jesus Christ). So why does 'God generates God' go through, but not 'The essence generates the essence'?[26] We have little hope of answering this question unless we can get a reasonably systematic grasp on what our words refer to, and under what linguistic circumstances. To solve this theological problem, we need semantic ascent.

Aquinas's chief, though not sole, semantic recourse for dealing with the problem is to distinguish between the *res significata* and the *modus significandi* of terms – literally, between what a term signifies and the way in which it signifies. The idea is that different terms can refer to the same thing (the *res significata*), but do so in different ways (the *modus significandi*). So, to use the sort of example which became standard in modistic grammatical theory later in the thirteenth century, suppose Simo, Risto, and I see Vesa suddenly run out of the room. One of us exclaims, 'Cursus' ('Lo, a run.'), another, 'Currens' ('Lo, running.'), and the last, 'Currit' ('He runs.'). All of these statements refer to one and the same happening, namely Vesa's exit from the room. But each does so in a different manner, signalled by the grammatical distinction between noun, participle, and finite verb. We might roughly characterize the difference by saying that the first refers to what happens simply as a motion of a certain kind or quality, the second as an ongoing event, and the last as a human act, taking up time in the present.[27] That these modes of signifying are really distinct, and that the distinction matters, can be seen from the fact that these terms cannot necessarily be substituted for one another without changing the truth value of the sentences in which the substitution is made (though modistic grammarians usually tried to support the distinction on morphological grounds).[28]

Aquinas argues semantically against *essentia generat* by attending especially to this last point. 'When it comes to the truth of utterances, it is not only necessary to consider the things signified, but also the mode of signification.'[29] With regard to the utterance at hand, Aquinas takes over the standard distinction between concrete and abstract terms (in the very way the question is put), but interprets it in terms of diverse *modi significandi*. Thus 'Deus' and 'essentia' both signify or refer to the same thing, namely the one divine essence. But they do so in different ways. 'Deus' signifies the divine essence concretely, that is, as possessed by an individual person (*in habente*, as Aquinas says). 'Deus' is thus on a semantic par with 'homo', a term which signifies the human nature or essence as possessed by, or embodied in, an individual person.[30] 'Essentia' – or more precisely, since we're speaking of God's essence, 'deitas' – signifies the divine nature abstractly, or 'as an abstracted form' (*ut formam abstractam*).[31] 'Deitas', in other words, refers to the divine essence itself, and not to the persons who possess it. 'Essentia' and 'deitas' ('divinity') are thus on a semantic par with 'humanitas' ('humanity') and not with 'homo' ('human being').

Thus armed with clarity about the reference of 'Deus' and 'essentia/deitas', Aquinas can draw on a standard piece of medieval logical theory to show what's wrong with 'essentia generat'. In medieval logic, the 'supposition' of a term is what it stands for or refers to when it is actually used in a sentence. This is distinguished from the term's 'signification', which is what the term refers to on its own (as the medievals supposed), in abstraction from any particular use.[32] With regard to the case at hand, 'since it signifies the divine essence as possessed by an individual, the term "Deus" . . . can stand for a person' in a true sentence. More generally, 'the *propria* of the persons' – those characteristics which are unique to each of the divine persons – can be predicated of the term "Deus"'. Thus 'God is generated' and 'God is one who generates' come out true, since there is a divine person who is generated and a divine person who generates. Contrariwise 'essentia', since it has an abstract mode of signifying – since it refers to the divine essence alone, and not to its personal possessors – 'cannot stand for a person' in a true sentence. More generally, 'the *propria* of the persons, by which they are distinguished from one another, cannot be predicated of the essence'. Therefore 'The essence generates' comes out false, since there is only one divine essence, which does not produce a second.[33]

Semantic ascent thus helps us get a grip on how 'Deus generat Deum' and 'Essentia generat essentiam' can have different truth values, despite having the same surface grammar and despite being subject to the same stricture against anything generating itself. The same goes, of course, for 'homo' and 'humanitas'. 'A human being generates' is very frequently true, while 'Humanity generates' never is (taking 'humanity', that is, not for a collective noun but, in Thomas's sense, as referring to what all human beings have in common). Further background assumptions naturally come into play. One of these, equally applicable to 'homo/humanitas' and 'Deus/deitas', is that forms don't act, persons do: *actus sunt suppositorum*. Thus, given Thomas's semantic analysis, the action signified by 'generat' can be attributed to the first of each of these pairs, but not to the second. This tells us what to make of Augustine and other 'holy teachers' when they say things like 'Essentia de essentia' ('The essence [is] from the essence'). Their linguistic imprecision, Thomas gently insists, 'is not to be imitated, but explained' (*non sunt extendendae sed exponendae*), for example by supplying concrete terms when they misleadingly used abstract ones.[34]

The trinitarian reach of semantic ascent

On Thomas's analysis 'Deus generat Deum' turns out to be true, but not for all values of 'Deus'. The person for whom 'Deus' stands in 'Deus generat' is the Father; only the substitution of 'Pater' for 'Deus' makes 'Deus generat' come out true. Similarly, ' . . . generat Deum' comes out true only when 'Filium' is substituted for 'Deum'. So the question *utrum essentia generet* gives Aquinas the opportunity to consider one version of a basic trinitarian problem sharply presented, as we have observed, by Lateran IV: how can the divine persons be identical with the divine essence, yet the persons not be identical with each other? Here the question takes the form: how can the Father be identical with the essence, if the Father generates (another person) and the essence does not? If the two are really identical, it would seem that they have to have all the same properties. The identity of essence and person thus poses a problem even in the case of one person, the Father alone. Aquinas considers this problem from several points of view, and in each case offers an explicitly semantic solution to it.

Aquinas first takes up the objection that, since God is the divine essence, and God generates, the essence must generate.[35] His reply to this apparently devastating objection (not only to his denial of *essentia generat*, but to the identity, evidently necessary for monotheism, of essence and person) is almost astoundingly simple. While God and the divine essence are the same in reality (*secundum rem*), we still have to *speak* about them in different ways. The *res significata* of 'Deus' and that of 'essentia divina' is the same, namely the one divine essence, but the two terms have irreducibly distinct modes of signifying the essence (as possessed by a person, and abstracted from a possessor).[36] And that's it. Aquinas evidently thinks this brief semantic observation answers the objection.

We can see why by recalling that on the semantic analysis Aquinas employs, 'cursus', 'currens', and 'currit' can all refer to the same thing (Vesa's exit), but because they do so in different ways, they cannot necessarily be substituted for one another *salva veritate*: if Vesa leaves the room in an exceptionally good mood, 'Currens gaudet' ('The one running rejoices') will be true, but 'Cursus gaudet' ('The run rejoices') will obviously be false. Similarly, 'Deus' and 'essentia' refer to the same thing, but the different ways they refer, their different *modi significandi*, make it impossible to substitute them for one another without changing the truth values of the relevant sentences. Thus 'Deus generat' is true, and 'Deus est essentia' is true, but nonetheless 'Essentia generat' is false. Aquinas makes a cognate argument for the more concrete case of 'Pater est essentia' ('The Father is the essence'), with an added note about the way the abstract mode of signifying of 'essentia' blocks the possibilities for supposition (that is, substitution *salva veritate*) enjoyed by predicates in other cases.[37]

Thus Aquinas offers a remarkably straightforward semantic resolution of a basic trinitarian problem. The *modi significandi* of our terms make the truth values of our sentences fall out in just the right way. We can say that there is personal generation in God, and thus real personal distinction, and deny that there is numerical multiplication of the divine essence, and thus three gods, and be right each time.

It may seem as though this is far *too* simple. Surely we have to do more on this weighty subject than clear up referential confusions and block unwanted inferences. We need a metaphysical account of procession, origin, relation, and so forth in order to show, if we can, how the divine persons are distinct from each other and not from the essence. Aquinas of course offers such an account, based not least on the distinctive characteristics of 'relation', which alone among the categories of being includes neither substantial nor accidental *esse* in its very idea, and so eases the thought of identity with the divine essence accompanied by mutual distinction.[38] He develops this line of thought further in the next question of the *Summa*, following the semantic arguments we've been looking at.[39]

But it isn't entirely clear, even on Aquinas's own view, how much this metaphysical undertaking adds to the semantic explanation he offers. We have, after all, no *modus significandi* for the identity either of relation with person or of relation with essence – no *modus*, that is, for a subsistent relation.[40] Of course all of our words, and not just those whose home is metaphysical speculation, have a creaturely mode of signification which is inadequate to God. But surely we have at least as good a grip on the reference and meaning of 'God', 'generates', and 'essence' as we do on 'subsistent relation', or any of the other technical concepts we use to try to account for the identity of person and essence in God, and its compatibility with the real distinction of persons. We have, moreover, reliable ways of fixing the truth value of sentences which combine these familiar terms, at least as much as those which use the more speculative ones. From these combinations of familiar terms we can easily infer the identity of person and essence, and the distinction of person from person, in God. A metaphysical account of the same issue might serve many purposes, but it seems unlikely to tell us anything decisive about the triune God that we couldn't know more readily in another way.

Whether Aquinas gives a *convincing* semantic analysis of 'The essence generates' and cognate trinitarian statements is another matter, for another day. This was already much debated in the thirteenth and fourteenth centuries, when Aquinas was only one of many theologians who took reflection on *utrum essentia generet* as an occasion to consider the possible uses of semantic ascent in trinitarian theology.

There's irony here. Ockham, for example, offers a critical assessment of Aquinas's treatment of this trinitarian *topos*, in the midst of an extended semantic discussion devoted mainly to refuting Scotus's views on the matter.[41] But Ockham, decried (not least by Thomists) as a linguistic despoiler of the world – perhaps the inventor of that dark art – doesn't think semantic analysis really accomplishes much in this area. What's most telling against *essentia generat* is simply the way the saints talk: the truth of the matter can be gathered 'from the linguistic use of the saints and others'. But in rejecting *essentia generat* the saints evidently rely not on semantic analysis, but on the old-fashioned metaphysical assumption that the divine essence can't be multiplied.[42] What was enough for them should be enough for us, even if we also have a semantic argument on hand.

It's Aquinas, by contrast, who thinks semantic analysis does real work at this crucial trinitarian point. So on Thomas's own grounds – as Victor Preller was perhaps the first in our own day to see clearly – whether his semantic analysis is convincing is, at least, very much the right question to ask.

Notes

I'm grateful to Russ Friedman and Lauge Nielsen for their comments on an earlier version of this paper, and in particular for alerting me to some of the recent work on medieval semantics.

1. Victor Preller, *Divine Science and the Science of God: A Reformulation of Thomas Aquinas* (Princeton, 1967).

2. 'It will be argued, in short, that Aquinas is always in the *Summa* operating *qua* theologian, and that the philosophy quoted in his theology is neither necessary nor sufficient to establish the meaning or truth of any assertion made by Aquinas, from "God exists" to "God is Three Persons in One Substance"' (*Divine Science*, p. 33). When it comes to Christian theology's relationship with philosophy, Aquinas is interested not in synthesis, but in conquest – he wants to tame and subdue philosophy for theological ends, and so make of it something better than it could ever be on its own: 'when philosophy appears in [Aquinas's] theological treatises it has been so integrated into a theological structure as to lose its independent philosophical character' (Preller, *Divine Science*, pp. 26–7). Even in his commentaries on Aristotle, Preller argues in the Mascall Lecture published in this volume, pp. 253–67, 'Aquinas is always writing as *catholicae doctor veritatis*' (p. 262). Preller's section on 'The Theological Use of Philosophy' – the 'promissory note' in the opening chapter of *Divine Science* (pp. 22–34), which it is a chief point of the book to redeem – remains a frank and lucid call for a resolutely theological take on what Aquinas is doing. The Mascall Lecture reissues this call, in its own terms.

3. 'Those philosophical arguments concerning God which are quoted in theology can be seen by faith to have the God of theology as their referent' (*Divine Science*, p. 32). On this, as on the need for a radically theological interpretation of what Aquinas is up to, I'm very much with Preller in spirit, though I think these interpretive claims can best be argued in a somewhat different way. Cf. Bruce D. Marshall, '*Quod Scit Una Uetula*: Aquinas on the Nature of Theology', in Joseph Wawrykow and Rik Van Nieuwenhove (eds), *Aquinas as Theologian* (Notre Dame, 2004), and 'Faith and Reason Reconsidered: Aquinas and Luther on Deciding What is True', *The Thomist* 63/1 (1999): 1–48.

4. For a lively discussion of 'analytical Thomism', including a brief bibliography, see *New Blackfriars* 80 (April 1999): 158–216; *The Monist* 80/4 (1997) is devoted to a collection of essays under this rubric. The phrase 'analytical Thomism' seems to originate with John Haldane, but the enterprise itself is perhaps most closely associated with the 'Cornell school', that is, with Norman Kretzmann's students and associates. Among recent book-length studies of Aquinas from this quarter, Eleonore Stump, *Aquinas* (New York, 2003) and Robert Pasnau, *Thomas Aquinas on Human Nature* (Cambridge, 2002) are particularly wide-ranging. For a different take on some of the lessons to be learned from an analytic engagement with Aquinas, see John P. O'Callaghan, *Thomist Realism and the Linguistic Turn: Toward a More Perfect Form of Existence* (Notre Dame, 2003).

5. For a useful sample of some of this earlier material see Anthony Kenny (ed.), *Aquinas: A Collection of Critical Essays* (New York, 1969).

6. See, e.g., Brian J. Shanley, OP, 'Analytical Thomism', *The Thomist* 63/1 (1999): 125–39. Part of the problem here lies in the mistaken assumption, usually held at a distance, that analytic philosophers are committed to a more or less uniform set of substantive or procedural doctrines. As Dagfinn Follesdal observes, 'While it is fairly clear what Thomism is, it is far from clear what is meant by "analytic philosophy"' (*New Blackfriars* 80 (April 1999), p. 175).

7. There are exceptions. See, e.g., Geach's article on the trinitarian and christological consequences of the opposed theories of predication he finds in Aquinas and Ockham: P. T. Geach, 'Nominalism', in *Logic Matters* (Oxford, 1972), pp. 289–301.

8. To note one example: Thomas was well aware that the doctrine of the Trinity poses logical problems about identity which need to be addressed (cf. *Summa Theologiae* I.28.3 ad 1; 39.1 obj. 1–2. From here on I'll cite the *Summa Theologiae* by part number only, followed by question, article, and location within the article. I'll use the Latin text in the Blackfriars edition, which makes some modifications in the Leonine text). Medieval theologians after him, like Scotus, were even more keenly aware of it. But the contemporary theological discussion of Thomas on the Trinity has hardly taken note of this issue, still less of the possibility that the extensive debate about identity among analytic philosophers might provide resources for dealing with it, or pose problems that need to be met. It's been left to analytic philosophers of religion to seek a plausible notion of identity that can cope with Christian trinitarian and incarnational claims. Cf. Peter van Inwagen, 'And Yet They Are Not Three Gods but One God' and 'Not by Confusion of Substance but by Unity of Person', in *God, Knowledge, and Mystery* (Ithaca, 1995), pp. 222–79; Bruce D. Marshall, 'What Does the Spirit Have to Do?', in Matthew Levering (ed.), *Reading John with St Thomas Aquinas* (Washington, 2004). We'll return to this question in a different form when we look at Aquinas's application of semantic theory in trinitarian theology.

9. On this see Bruce D. Marshall, 'Theology After Cana', *Modern Theology* 16/4 (2000): 517–27.

10. See his *Word and Object* (Cambridge, Mass., 1960), pp. 270–6.

11. A considerable amount of work on medieval logic and semantics has been accomplished in the years since Preller published *Divine Science*, though a good deal evidently remains to be learned. For helpful introductions see Jan Pinborg, *Logik und Semantik im Mittelalter* (Stuttgart, 1972) and the articles in Norman Kretzmann, Anthony Kenny, and Jan Pinborg (eds), *The Cambridge History of Later Medieval Philosophy* (Cambridge, 1982), pp. 161–269. For a compressed but useful entry into the more recent discussions of grammar and semantics in particular, see Irène Rosier-Catach, 'Modisme, pré-modisme, proto-modisme: vers une définition modulaire', in Sten Ebbesen and Russell L. Friedman (eds), *Medieval Analyses in Language and Cognition* (Copenhagen, 1999), pp. 45–81.

12. Cited in Alain de Libera, *La philosophie médiévale*, 3rd edn (Paris, 1998), p. 430.

13. For exceptions to this generalization, see Stephen F. Brown, 'Medieval Supposition Theory in its Theological Context', *Medieval Philosophy and Theology* 3 (1993): 121–57, and Timothy L. Smith, *Thomas Aquinas's Trinitarian Theology: A Study in Theological Method* (Washington, DC, 2003), pp. 137–91.

14. See Quine, *Word and Object*, p. 272.

15. On the genesis of these claims in twentieth-century theology, with an assessment of their historical plausibility, see Bruce D. Marshall, 'The Trinity', in Gareth Jones (ed.), *The Blackwell Companion to Modern Theology* (Oxford, 2003).

16. Thus, classically, Vladimir Lossky (with the characteristic modern eastern link to the *Filioque*): 'relations of origin which [as in what Lossky calls "the western conception"] do not trace the Son and the Spirit immediately back to him who is alone the source, to the Father – the one as begotten, the other as proceeding – become a system of relations within the one essence, something logically posterior to the essence'. *Essai sur la théologie mystique de l'église d'orient* (Paris, 1944), p. 56 (my translation; cf. *The Mystical Theology of the Eastern Church* (London, 1957), p. 57). Lossky's 'logically' perhaps stops short of a maximally strong version of the final and most drastic claim, that western theology implicitly repudiates the doctrine of the Trinity altogether.

17. *Magistri Petri Lombardi Sententiae in IV Libris Distinctae*, 3rd edn (Grottaferrata, 1971), vol. 1, pp. 80.25–81.6.

18. *Sententiae* I.5 (p. 82.19–22).

19. *Sententiae* I.5 (p. 86.28–9).

20. *Sententiae* I.5 (p. 81.7–12).

21. On this see Fiona Robb, 'The Fourth Lateran Council's Definition of Trinitarian Orthodoxy', *Journal of Ecclesiastical History* 48/1 (1997): 22–43. Robb's informative presentation is marred by her assumption, perhaps prompted by some contemporary trinitarian theologians (p. 43), that because Joachim officially lost this western trinitarian battle he must have been right, and his opponents probably in the baleful grip of trinitarian essentialism.

22. In I.39.5.c, Aquinas says that Joachim (rightly) affirms divine simplicity but draws the wrong inference from it, namely *essentia generat*. But earlier (*Expositio super secundam decretalem*, nos 1190, 1194) he suggests that Joachim (rightly) denies *essentia generat*, but draws the wrong inference from *that*, namely that God is not simple. For the text of this *Expositio* see R. Verardo (ed.), *S. Thomae Aquinatis Opuscula Theologica*, vol. 1 (Turin, 1954), pp. 428–31.

23. The cited passages are from Heinrich Denzinger and Adolf Schönmetzer (eds), *Enchiridion Symbolorum Definitionum et Declarationum*, 36th edn (Barcelona, Freiburg, and Rome, 1976), 804.

24. R. P. Mandonnet, OP, and M. F. Moos, OP (eds), *S. Thomae Aquinatis Scriptum super Sententiis*, 4 vols (Paris, 1929–47), I.5.1.1, but most of the questions on distinctions four and five are pertinent. The commentary on Lateran IV is *Expositio super secundam decretalem* (above, n. 22).

25. This is Aquinas's own title for I.39.5, as given at the beginning of I.39. The

quite different formulation at the head of the article stems from a later editor. The bracketed phrase is from Aquinas's title for the closely related preceding article: 'Can adjectives, verbs, or participles for characteristics [of the divine persons] be predicated of essential terms taken concretely?'

26. Jean Riballier (ed.), *Magistri Guillelmi Altissiodorensis Summa aurea*, (Paris and Grottaferrata, 1980), Liber I, (tractatus) IV, (caput) VI, p. 56.91–104. According to William, Joachim of Fiore had already formulated this objection to Lombard.

27. The distinction between *res significata* and *modus significandi* thus *may* be similar to Frege's famous distinction between *Bedeutung* and *Sinn*, between the reference of a term and its meaning, that is, the way its reference is given. But here, as often, it is difficult to be clear about the extent to which medieval and modern concepts and distinctions can be mapped onto one another.

28. The 'modistic' grammatical theory which developed after 1260 is one of the main currents of medieval semantics, and has been extensively studied of late (cf. above, n. 11). On the ancient and medieval origins of a specifically theological use of the distinction between what is signified and the mode of signification, see Irène Rosier, '*Res significata* et *modus significandi*: Les implications d'une distinction médiévale', in Sten Ebbesen (ed.), *Sprachtheorien in Spätantike und Mittelalter* (Tübingen, 1995), pp. 135–68. As Rosier shows (cf. p. 136), the theological use of the *res/modus* distinction has its own history and motives, and to some extent predates the development of modistic grammar in the arts faculties. She concentrates on the semantics of the divine names (the sort of issue Aquinas treats in I.13), as a number of others have done (cf. her bibliography, pp. 163–8). The use of the *res/modus* distinction in trinitarian theology has not, so far as I am aware, been much studied.

29. I.39.5.c.

30. See I.39.4.c.

31. I.39.5.c. Cf. I.39.2.c: 'When it comes to the mode of signification, even in God the essence is signified as the form of the three persons.'

32. Medieval logicians develop the theory of supposition with considerable complexity, and vigorously contest both the theory's content and its application to cases. For a sample of representative views see Stephen Brown's article, cited above, n. 13.

33. All the quoted passages are from I.39.5.

34. I.39.5 ad 1. Interpreters who worry that Aquinas succumbs to an impersonal 'essentialism' – or that western trinitarian theology after the early fifth century is slavishly devoted to Augustine – perhaps ought to pay attention to such passages.

35. I.39.5 obj. 3.

36. 'God and the divine essence are the same in reality, but because of a different mode of signifying it is necessary to speak differently of each' (I.39.5 ad 3).

37. Cf. I.39.5 ad 4.

38. Relations are not predicated 'absolutely', but 'as a reference to another,

and therefore do not introduce composition into that of which they are said' (I.30.1 ad 3; cf. 28.2; 3 ad 1).

39. I.40, especially art. 1–2.

40. Our creaturely way of thinking inherently introduces basic types of distinction and composition which aren't in God, in particular the distinctions between form and matter and between subject and accidents. This has a direct impact on trinitarian theology: divine 'person and property' – specifically the property of having a person-constituting relation to another, like *paternitas* (for the Father) or *filiatio* (for the Son) – 'are identical in reality, but nevertheless they differ in our way of thinking about them' (*sunt idem re, differunt tamen secundum rationem*; I.40.1 ad 1). Language embodies the differences basic to our way of thinking: 'our mode of signifying follows our mode of understanding' (I.45.2 ad 2). So at the heart of trinitarian theology, as everywhere else, what we say of God composes what we have divided; its 'mode of signifying befits creatures', and not God (I.13.3.c). By the same token, thought cannot slip the bonds of language to know God in some way unfettered by our creaturely modes of signifying. 'Everything which is known (or just 'thought' – *cognoscitur*) can also be signified by a word' (*In Sent.* I.22.1.1 s.c., ed. Mandonnet (above, n. 24), p. 532. Cf. I.13.1.c: 'To the extent that our mind can know something, it can be named by us'). It's just the yen to leave behind the creaturely limits on our thought and speech, and think the identity of person, relation, and essence in God, that makes trinitarian faith seem impossible. If we try to identify in thought what's identical in reality, impersonal essentialism or polytheism – *essentia generat* can be taken either way – looks inevitable. For Aquinas it's precisely by accepting that what's identical in reality can't be identical in our thought and speech that we learn to avoid such problems: 'for this reason it's not necessary that when one is multiplied' – person, or relation – 'the other is multiplied' – relation or essence (I.40.1 ad 1).

41. See William of Ockham, *Scriptum in Librum Primum Sententiarum*, dist. 5, q. 1. Gerard Etzkorn (ed.), *Guillelmi de Ockham Opera Theologica*, vol. 3 (St Bonaventure, NY, 1977), pp. 25–48. On Aquinas see esp. p. 28.5–14, though Ockham's arguments against Scotus raise several points which are pertinent to Aquinas as well.

42. Cf. *Scriptum* I.5.1 (ed. Etzkorn, p. 34.5–11); the quoted phrase is from p. 34.6.

3. Connections Created and Contingent

Aquinas, Preller, Wittgenstein, and Hopkins

STANLEY HAUERWAS

A main source of our failure to understand is that we do not *command a clear view* of the use of our words. – Our grammar is lacking in this sort of perspicuity. A perspicuous representation produces just that understanding which consists in 'seeing connexions'. Hence the importance of finding and inventing *intermediate cases*.

The concept of a perspicuous representation is of fundamental significance for us. It earmarks the form of account we give, the way we look at things. (Is this a 'Weltanschauung'?)

Philosophical Investigations, §122

1. *The curious case of the missing footnotes: a not very mysterious mystery*

In *With the Grain of the Universe*, the Gifford Lectures delivered at the University of St Andrews (2001), I argue that natural theology is unintelligible divorced from a full doctrine of God.[1] Even more strongly I contend that if you could 'prove' the existence of God, if you had evidence that something like a god must exist, then you would have evidence that the God that Jews and Christians worship does not exist.[2] In support of these claims I suggest that Thomas Aquinas would agree with this understanding of the status of our knowledge of God. I therefore conclude that those who have appealed to Aquinas to justify the assumption that 'natural theology' is a necessary first step to sustain theology based on revelation have distorted Aquinas's understanding of Christian theology.

I did not claim that this understanding of natural theology or of

Thomas Aquinas was original. I had learned from George Hendry that the 'little coda' – 'and this everyone understands to be God' – that ends each of the proofs is an indication that Aquinas understood the 'proofs' were not proofs.[3] David Burrell was, however, my main teacher for this understanding of Aquinas. His analysis of Aquinas's philosophical moves made it clear, at least clear to me, that Aquinas was first and foremost a theologian.[4] But I had forgotten that it was neither Hendry nor Burrell who first shaped my reading of Aquinas on natural theology. It was Victor Preller. It is therefore with some embarrassment that I note that nowhere in *With the Grain of the Universe* do I acknowledge my indebtedness to Preller's *Divine Science and the Science of God: A Reformulation of Thomas Aquinas*.[5]

I am not sure when I first read *Divine Science and the Science of God*, but I am almost certain it was before I left graduate school in 1968. In graduate school I was allegedly being trained to be an 'ethicist', but 'ethics' only named for me a way to explore the challenge made at that time by some well-known philosophers who argued that it is not so much religious language which might be false; but rather that theological convictions are meaningless because they do not and cannot do any real work for informing us about the ways things are.[6] I am sure I read Preller because I had been told that the criticisms he develops in chapter 4 in *Divine Science and the Science of God* against the various strategies to 'save' the meaningfulness of religious language were very important, as indeed they were and are. I am also sure that at David Burrell's urging I re-read Preller in my early years at Notre Dame.[7]

This makes it all the more embarrassing that in *The Grain of the Universe* I failed to acknowledge my debt to Preller. I have always maintained that a 'creative idea' is just forgetting where you read it. So it is not surprising that I forgot Preller's influence on me. Such a 'forgetting', moreover, may be partly due to the success of Preller's argument (albeit its delayed success). You can now learn the main outlines of his account of Aquinas from many different sources, which makes it possible to forget that it was Preller who led the way.[8] But we should not forget that *Divine Science and the Science of God* was so against the grain of neo-scholastic interpreters of Aquinas that Preller had difficulty gaining a hearing.

The other reason that explains my failure to acknowledge Preller's influence is much more commonplace – I had lost or loaned my copy of *Divine Science and the Science of God* without it being returned. However, re-reading *Divine Science and the Science of God* for this essay made clear, at least to me, that I could have made the case I tried to make in *With the Grain of the Universe* more strongly if I had remembered Preller's more detailed arguments in his book. Preller thought and said better in 1967 what I was trying to say in 2001.

That I had forgotten how much I owed to Preller, however, provides an opportunity I want to exploit in this essay. My primary interest is not in defending the position I took in my Gifford Lectures, though I am not averse to that result. Rather, by calling attention to Preller's arguments, I hope to explore a problem I think he and I share in common. Put simply, I take the problem to be: given our arguments against natural theology, how does or can the worship of the God Preller and I worship display the truthfulness of those convictions? Though this is often seen as an apologetical task, I think it is a mistake to so limit the enquiry such a question produces. It is not just a matter of what we have to say to those who do not share our common worship, but equally it is a question that must be asked and answered by those who are internal to the practice of Christian worship, if we believe that what we believe is true. That is, are we ready to risk our lives for what we believe is true? I hope to show that Preller and Wittgenstein represent in different but complementary ways the recovery of the contingent character of all that is. Moreover, Wittgenstein and Preller school us how to recognize the contingent character of our lives without attempting to subvert the frightening character of the contingent through explanations.

In the 'Foreword' to *Divine Science and the Science of God*, Preller makes clear that his book is not an attempt to provide a philosophical defence or proof of theological language or propositions. Rather, 'at most I have stated some of the things that must be true of human thought and language if theological claims are not to be rejected out of hand' (p. vii).[9] Or as he puts it later in the book:

It is the program of natural theology to lead the intellect through a series of judgments which hopefully will result in a negative insight

77

productive of the further judgment that the intellect has encountered a non-intelligible level of experience incapable of formulation in a conceptually meaningful question. The conclusion of natural theology is then the paradox that the human intellect is ordered to a reality that it cannot know and is seeking an intelligibility that it cannot understand. In judging the world to be radically unintelligible, we are implicitly seeking God, and in talking about 'God' we are judging the world. All the language of natural theology is language about that which is sought after but unknown. It is incapable, therefore, of conforming the mind to that which is sought. It conveys no *knowledge* of God – even of an imperfect sort – and it terminates in the judgment that there is that of which we have no knowledge. (pp. 179–80)

These remarks beg for further elucidation; for example, does Preller want to deny, contrary to Aquinas, that the mind can be adequated to know that which cannot otherwise be known?[10] What could it possibly mean to say we have 'encountered a non-intelligible level of experience'? – non-intelligible, maybe, but how could that be an 'experience'? Rather than engage these questions directly, I first want to call attention to a challenge I believe Preller and I both face. That Preller claims to do no more in *Divine Science and the Science of God* than to say 'some things that must be true of human thought and language if theological claims are not to be rejected out of hand' is a background presumption necessary to sustain my contention in *With the Grain of the Universe* that God is known only through witness. Put differently, Preller and I argue that there can be no coercive argument to compel acknowledgement that God is God. Yet I worry that my argument, as well as Preller's, may fail to say all that needs to be said. It is one thing to argue that God cannot be proved. It is quite another matter to suggest that nothing more can be said about why belief in the God that cannot be proved may nonetheless 'make sense' in the world as we know it. Indeed, 'make sense' may be a weak way of putting the matter. Surely Christians have claimed and continue to claim that their faith is about the way things are. Preller's (and my) refusal to assume some knock-down arguments must exist to justify the Christian faith seems to suggest to those committed to more rationalistic accounts that we can say no more than 'Try it; you will like it.'

I think Preller (and I) have a response to this challenge. The response, however, requires me to re-narrate the case Preller makes in *Divine Science and the Science of God* in the light of some of the developments in Wittgenstein's work. When Preller wrote *Divine Science and the Science of God* he was obviously more influenced by Wilfrid Sellars than Wittgenstein. Of course anyone familiar with Wittgenstein's work cannot help seeing how many of the arguments Preller uses in his book can readily be described as Wittgensteinian. Preller could have easily been influenced by Wittgenstein through Sellars; or it may even be the case, as David Burrell has long argued, that Aquinas really anticipated some of the lessons we now attribute to Wittgenstein. So Preller appears Wittgensteinian because he is such an able reader of Aquinas. However, I am not so much interested in the question of influence. But I do hope to show that reading Preller through Wittgensteinian eyes provides some of the intellectual and moral tools we need to suggest why Christians rightly believe their faith in God is also a claim about the way things are, making possible continued conversation with those who do not share our faith.

I need to be clear about the character of what I am trying to do in this essay. I cannot pretend that what I am about can bear the grand description of 'an argument'. To be sure, I will report on arguments – quite good arguments I believe – that Preller and Wittgenstein develop. However, I cannot pretend that displaying the similarity between Preller's arguments against arguments for God's existence and the change in Wittgenstein's thought from the *Tractatus* to the *Investigations* is anything more than an attempt at illuminating a family resemblance. At best I try to make some connections that I hope some may find illuminating. In the final section of the paper, however, I will make a few suggestions about how one might go on if the resemblance between Preller's theology and Wittgenstein's philosophy works in the way I try to develop below. Finally, as I suggested above, I hope in the process of comparing Preller and Wittgenstein to illumine the position I developed in *With the Grain of the Universe* as well as to suggest why Christian witness necessarily involves the assertion of claims about the way things are. Indeed, the necessity of witnesses suggests that Christians must work to find ways to listen as well as talk with those who do not share our faith.

2. *Preller's argument in brief*

The heart of Preller's argument in defence of his understanding of what he takes to be Aquinas's views is quite simple.[11] 'God, for Aquinas, is "outside of the general category of intelligible things" because his "intelligibility" cannot be defined in terms of *our* conceptual system – it does not appear in the "light of reason"' (p. 155).[12] In short, if God is not part of the metaphysical furniture of the universe, then God cannot be made to function 'as an *intelligible* link – even the *first* link – in a conceptual progress or causal chain, [because if God so functioned] then of necessity any defect or problem associated with 'contingent reality' will be built into the concept of God' (p. 135).

Aquinas's use of the name 'God' is therefore determinatively theological, drawing its rationality from revelation (p. 144). But even revelation does not justify the presumption that we can speak of God unproblematically. Thus the five ways, which seek to tie God into the world by extrapolating a notion of causality or perfection from our conceptual system, cannot be successful. Preller's detailed analysis of the five ways is crucial for his overall argument. He must show (and I think he does) not only that the five ways fail but that Aquinas knew they must fail. Preller observes that, of all the categories introduced in the five ways, 'contingency and necessity' in the third proof are least removed from the 'creational notion' that informs Aquinas's use of the proofs. For it is Preller's notion – a contention that David Burrell has continued to develop – that Aquinas reads all the arguments for God from the viewpoint of creation: 'The human mind is ordered to God the *Creator* as to One Unknown. The intellect implicitly demands that the 'existence' of the world be measured and made necessary by a free *intentional or conceptual act*. It does not know, however, in what way that is possible' (p. 164). That is why Preller rightly notes that the 'contingency' implied in the third proof is not the 'contingency' implicit in the relationship between creator and creature. Preller acknowledges that the fifth way based on the governance of creation may not be 'finally incompatible' with Aquinas's doctrine of God, but

Aquinas elsewhere acknowledges that God's 'providence over all cannot be proved' (p. 134). Moreover Preller argues that the Aristotelian presuppositions of the first three ways are incompatible with the fifth.

In short, the 'proofs' cannot be successful because, according to Preller, the five ways are quite incompatible with Aquinas's doctrine of God. God chooses to place himself at man's disposal by grace, that is, by gift. 'Even that gift, however, becomes man's possession – at his disposal – only in the "light of Glory" when reality is seen in terms of God's intentions. In this life "God" remains a word in *another* language – a word *mentioned but not used in our language*' (p. 156).[13]

According to Preller the problem is not that reason can establish certain significant things about God but that evidence is lacking for other significant things that may be true of him. Rather, the problem is how we could ever think we might see the significance of any proposition about God, revealed or not. Preller notes that it is misleading to say this is merely a linguistic problem, though it no doubt involves the question of language. Human language is intentional because it is about things and expresses thoughts that are themselves intentional about things. 'Successful reference depends upon a meaningful intentionality or conceptual context. "God", however, is a name which can never occur within a conceptual context which is meaningful to us' (p. 183).

This means that our speech about God can only be, indeed must be, analogical. But we should not be surprised by this given that any act of knowing is analogical (p. 52).[14] Accordingly, any attempt to make 'being' or 'existence' privileged modes of talk about God are doomed to failure. Being and existence after all are also analogical terms,[15] which means at the very least that our talk of God's existence is radically different from speaking of the existence of tables and chairs (p. 152). Moreover, the demand 'Give me an explanation of the existence of everything,' a demand often assumed to get God-talk off the ground, is a pseudo-demand,

> since we cannot conceive of anything which could be such a explanation except in terms of *our* use of "exists" – which is the use needing, for Aquinas, further justification. If we grant to Aquinas that

existence *must* be 'intelligible' and that 'intelligibility' means 'necessity', and if we further grant to him that 'necessity' in this instance means 'measured by the free intentional activity of some "intelligent" agent', then it follows analytically that there must exist some 'intelligent' entity from whose intentional point of view the *esse* of the world is seen to be intelligible *because* it follows from his own immanent powers of 'conceiving' reality. (p. 171)

Only God's existence is, therefore, self-evident, because only in God is there no distinction between essence and existence (p. 173). The only reason to apply the term 'existence' to God is that the world would remain radically unintelligible if there did not 'exist' that from which the world derives its hypothetical necessity. But God's existence does not only mean that God is the source of all other existence. That is why the term 'exists' is radically unintelligible when applied to the world. 'Exists' is intelligible only when it signifies God himself (pp. 174–5). This led me to claim in *With the Grain of the Universe* that the problem is not whether God exists, but in what sense it can be said that anything other than God exists. Of course, once it is acknowledged that all that is exists by God's grace, then it is equally true that only God exists necessarily.[16]

But where does that leave us? According to Preller it means 'in terms of the natural universe of human discourse, the claims of faith must remain unintelligible, as must also the claim to possess a new mode of understanding in terms of which the claims of faith are intelligible' (p. 225). Was Preller an early representative of Wittgensteinian fideism? I do not think so, but then I do not think anyone is a representative of Wittgensteinian fideism.[17] Rather, I think Wittgenstein provides those who believe in God – a God who, as Preller so carefully demonstrates, cannot be proved – a way to go on which challenges the assumption that if God cannot be proved then belief in God is subjective and not susceptible to being either true or false.

3. Wittgenstein on act and wonder

As I suggested above, I believe Preller may well have been far too modest when he suggested that all he has done in *Divine Science and the Science of God* is to show some of the things that must be true of human thought if theological claims are not to be rejected out of hand. Moreover, I am not at all sure he is right that the claims of faith must always remain unintelligible in terms of the 'natural universe of human discourse'. I do not deny that may often be the case; but I do not see why we must assume in advance that we will know what form the 'natural universe of human discourse' will take. Surely we will simply have to wait and see; or, to draw on Wittgenstein, we will first have to look.[18]

In order to make my case I want to focus on two remarks made by Fergus Kerr in his *Theology After Wittgenstein*. Kerr observes that Wittgenstein's appreciation of William James is a bit odd because Wittgenstein in his later work 'strives to show that neither feeling nor reason but *action* is the foundational thing'.[19] Secondly, Kerr suggests that the later Wittgenstein

> moves from wonder at the world as such, in its logical structure, to an attitude of wonder towards particular things, in their individual-ity – 'this blossom, opening!' More to the point, Wittgenstein seems to fear that it is only with difficulty that a mathematician can main-tain a sense of awe once he begins to treat a 'miracle of nature' as a *problem*.[20]

In the far too brief remarks on Wittgenstein that follow, I want to show that Wittgenstein's discovery that our saying is action, that practices are necessary for our ability to understand one another, and what Kerr calls his wonder towards things particular, are interrelated. Moreover, I think their interrelation is an indication of, and a witness to, the created character of all that is. In short I want to suggest that the movement in Wittgenstein's thought from the *Tractatus* to the *Investigations* parallels Preller's account of Aquinas's understanding of the character of our knowledge of God. Put differently, I want to at least suggest that when Wittgenstein's and Preller's works are read together they each confirm the necessary acknowledgement of what David Burrell, drawing on Robert Sokolowski, calls 'the distinction'. That is the distinction between God and the world, which is unlike any other distinction we use 'since we mean thereby to distinguish God from everything else that is, in such a way that God is the source of all-that-is'.[21]

One might be able to sustain an account of 'the distinction' from the perspective of the *Tractatus*; but I hope to show that 'the distinction' appears in a quite different light given Wittgenstein's work in the *Investigations*. I am not suggesting that there are not profound continuities between the *Tractatus* and the *Investigations* – indeed, I think the continuities are deeper than the discontinuities. Rather, I want only to suggest that in the *Investigations* Wittgenstein discovered that 'the world' could not be comprehended or explained in the mode exemplified by the *Tractatus*.[22] In both the *Tractatus* and the *Investigations* Wittgenstein saw that explanations must come to an end. But, as John Churchill suggests,

> in the *Tractatus* the disembodied pure intellect, picturing the world of facts in the frame of logical form, achieves a pure, will-less wonder at the existence of the world. But in the later philosophy it is not that bare fact of the world's existence that excites our wonder. It is the intricate attunement of human being to the world in all its detail and complexity.[23]

In short, in the *Investigations* we see that 'the world' is constituted by making connections between contingencies that make it possible for us to see the beauty of what is.

That Wittgenstein was content in the *Investigations* to do just that – investigate – I think has to do with his recognition that 'words are also deeds', or, as he was later to put it in *On Certainty*, quoting Goethe: 'In the beginning was the deed.'[24] In the *Investigations* he no longer thought his task was to provide an end to philosophical enquiry, but to show why philosophical enquiry can have no end.[25] All of this is but a recognition that neither we, nor the world, nor our relation to the world exists by necessity. To 'look behind', to 'look inward' are temptations fuelled by our desire to secure our existence through the discovery that what exists does so by necessity.[26] The private language argument as well as his contention that intentions are embedded in their situations set by human customs and institutions reflect his recognition that there is no 'deeper reality' than that found in the everyday.

In the *Tractatus* language functions to depict facts through a single logical structure. That is, in the *Tractatus* Wittgenstein thinks of language as 'a great crystalline structure of sharp logical precision, mirroring a world of facts, at the logical limit of which is a vanishing metaphysical and ethical subject'.[27] But in the *Investigations* language is a 'logically multifarious jumble of practices thoroughly contingent upon and interpenetrating with human social activities of bewildering variety'.[28] Accordingly there is no place for monolithic wonder. Just as Preller helps us understand that the 'five ways' cannot 'prove' the existence of God, so Wittgenstein helps us see that the ambition of philosophers to comprehend the 'world' cannot but fail. Enquiry, investigation, goes all the way down and is never ending.

Wittgenstein's animosity toward science is at least in part a reflection of how science can dull our sense of the wonder at the particular. 'Man has to awaken to wonder – and so perhaps do peoples. Science is a way of sending him to sleep again.'[29] His work is the attempt to help us rediscover the particular without providing an explanation or explanations that reduce the particular to an instance of a more general condition. 'The insidious thing about the causal point of view is that it leads us to say: "Of course, it had to happen like that." Whereas we ought to think: it may have happened *like that* – and also in many other ways.'[30]

John Churchill argues that Wittgenstein's understanding of what it means to follow a rule best reveals his understanding in the *Investigations* of what it means for explanation to come to an end. In particular Churchill calls attention to the so-called 'paradox of rule-following' in the *Investigations*, the paradox quite simply being that anything and nothing can count as a successful following of a rule.[31] The temptation this presents is to believe that an interpretation can help us understand a rule whose application is unclear. But this can only result in endless interpretations. Thus Wittgenstein's conclusion in the *Investigations* is that there must be 'a way of grasping a rule which is *not* an *interpretation*, but which is exhibited in what we call "obeying the rule" and "going against it" in actual cases'.[32]

For every specific rule, Churchill argues, there must be some underlying practices. For Wittgenstein the possibility of rule-following, as well as all language and other rational behaviour, rests on commonalities of behaviour that are not given by necessity. Thus Wittgenstein throughout the *Investigations* conducts thought experiments that explore our understanding or lack of understanding between people and animals with which we share little or nothing. The point is that 'all matters of getting it right and getting it wrong rest finally on shared behavior. Commonality of behavior is the analogue to logical form in the *Tractatus*: it is that upon which the possibility of language depends.'[33]

In the *Tractatus* wonder at the existence of the world is inspired by the fact that, absent an explanation, there is a world at all.[34] In the *Investigations*, Churchill suggests, wonder before the unexplained lies in matters of fact about our lives that make rule-governed practices possible. 'At the root of every practice is a way of operating that we learn not by having it explained and justified to us, but by simply doing it, or by being trained into it. *This* is how it goes, though there is no reason for that!'[35] The temptation to look for inner processes that allegedly take place in 'the mind' is an attempt to avoid the recognition that the way we learn to follow a rule is by training. We crave an explanation to show how a student has of necessity learned to go on, but there can be no explanation more compelling than the training itself.[36]

Churchill summarizes his case:

In the *Tractatus* what is shown is shown to a vanishing metaphysical subject. In the later philosophy our insight into the end of explanation lies in our discovery of the inclination of humans for seeing *this* as *that*, taking *this* as the natural continuation of a practice, and so on; that is, in our awareness of typical human perceptions and reactions in their role as making possible any rule-governed activity. In the *Tractatus* the talk is of a single, unified and eternal sense of things – a grand ineffable meaning. But in the later philosophy the loci of the possibility of wonder are small, local, various, and mundane. They will lie in such unspectacular facts as the ability humans have to recognize threatening gestures as such, or to respond spontaneously, without training, to the expression of others, or to get the hang of this or that practice. The loci of wonder in the later philosophy are the products of time and contingency –

how we happen to have evolved, what our cultural practices happen to be like, rather than the grand atemporal necessity of logical form.[37]

Preller's observations in the 'Conclusion' of *Divine Science and the Science of God* are therefore all the more interesting. He begins by noting that no language springs full-blown from the head of any human being. Rather, learning to use a language well is an ongoing lesson in pain and frustration. Indeed, ultimately to use a language well we must submit to the 'syntactical laws' which make the language a source of intelligibility and light. This means we must often respond without understanding to the 'darkly disapproving countenances of those who lay down the pedagogical laws of semantic association. We learn to make the material moves justified by the syntactical laws of our common human language before we learn ourselves to obey those laws' (p. 266). It is hard not to believe that Preller, drawing on what he had learned from Sellars, was thinking with Wittgenstein when he wrote these words. He even gives as his example of how we are constituted by the languages that we speak (and which speak us) the way we learn to make the sound of 'red' at certain times and to avoid it at others.

Preller observes that there is a further consequence of this account of language. When a child 'makes the leap' forward into the intentional realm of self-consciousness, he becomes something that he was not previously. Preller then observes that if we ever ceased using the language we now use, we would cease being the same 'persons' we now are, which leads him to the claim:

> If our language is distorted – if it does not truly and adequately reflect the intentions of God in creation – then I am not, at the level of conscious self-awareness, what I am intended by God to be, and what I therefore really am as known only to him and expressed only in his Word. It is, I think, a central thesis of the language of faith that I shall only *become* at the level of reflective self-awareness that which I really *am* as a creature of God when my intentional being is constituted by an intelligible 'Word' addressed to me and confirmed by my intentional response in kind. (p. 270)

I take Preller's point to parallel the argument I tried to make in *With the Grain of the Universe*, drawing on William James's *The Will to Believe*, that there are some realities that to be 'known' require the transformation of the agent.[38] This is why my account of James's understanding of 'the will to believe' was shaped by my prior reading of Wittgenstein. The latter, of course, helps us see the role of language in such a transformation that was missing in James.[39] But Preller did see the significance of language. He not only saw the significance of language, but Preller helps us see how Aquinas intended the *Summa* to provide the kind of training necessary for the recognition that we are creatures who must receive our very ability to speak as a gift. Such a recognition does not compel the acknowledgement of a creator, but it does suggest how the failure to live with humility, a failure common to Christian and non-Christian alike, results in a distorted understanding of the way things are.[40]

Put in the terms I use in *With the Grain of the Universe*, any account of Christianity that does not make witness constitutive of the practice of the faith cannot be true. Not to be true not only means to be unfaithful to Christian practice, but also means to belie the contingent character of all that is. Witnesses witness our contingency. But Christians believe that God has given us life-forming practices that enable us to live without seeking false comforts in a world of contingency we do not and cannot control. That we must be trained to be human, that we must be trained to communicate with one another so that we make the connection between ourselves, others, and this and that, indicates that the God we worship as Christians is the same God who has created the sun, stars, and this petunia.[41] That Preller helps us in *Divine Science and the Science of God* to recognize why all that is does not exist by necessity enables us to see that all that is witnesses to the God that created what is.

4. Contingency, connections, and beauty

I fear I have already tested the patience of any reader who has made it this far in this essay. Is there any pay-off that comes from my attempt to show a resemblance between Aquinas's and Preller's and Wittgenstein's (and Hauerwas's) understandings of the contingent character of all that makes up our world? I cannot pretend that what I am about to suggest amounts to a pay-off, but I hope it is at least suggestive. In the last chapter of *Divine Science and the Science of God* – in which Preller explores the various attempts to show how the language of faith may be compatible with 'the natural universe of human discourse' – he has a fascinating discussion of poetry and, in particular, the poetry of Gerard Manley Hopkins.[42] Preller notes that poets do more than create new meanings – farmers and bureaucrats do that as well – but poets see possibilities of interpretation not suggested by straightforward descriptions of the everyday.

Preller uses Hopkins's poetry, noting that Hopkins not only calls attention to what things do, but to the way things are.[43] According to Preller, Hopkins suggests each thing *is* what it *does*: 'what a thing does constitutes its "self" – it is its "selving forth". Hopkins sees the *esse–operatio* of nature as a mode of self-expenditure. What things *do* in the world is to blaze forth in a more or less lavish and expensive display of their potency, and then die out in a brilliant trail of "blue-bleak embers" which "fall, gall themselves, and gash gold-vermilion"' (pp. 222–3).

Preller observes that Hopkins introduces no new 'facts' into his description of reality, and another poet might even disagree with him. But they would not be disagreeing about the empirical fact that objects come into being and disintegrate. Rather they would be disagreeing about the proper mode of *taking* that fact. Moreover, how 'that fact' is taken by the reader of Hopkins's poem tells us something about how the world is – for example, we learn why 'the reader' and 'the fact' are not two independent entities. Rather, as Preller suggests, just as Hopkins thinks the world is saying something to our longing for the permanence of beauty, so also Aquinas believes the contingency of the world says something to our desire for the good.[44] 'Our desire' is constitutive of the way things are.

Preller, however, thinks that Hopkins's use of religious language in his poetry confirms his contention that the language of faith cannot share the same form as other human language. Preller notes that Hopkins

can *assert* that self-expenditure is sacrifice – a yielding by nature of beauty back to God – to be understood only in the light of Christ ('my chevalier!'). Hopkins suggests that the flux of the world can only be understood, that is, in the light of faith. He cannot produce that faith or exhibit the meaning of religious language – he must depend upon the meaning of the language of faith when he uses it in his poetry. (p. 224)

Yet again I wonder if Preller has done justice to the significance of his own analysis of Hopkins's poetry. That the world can only be understood 'in the light of faith' does not in itself tell you that the language of faith fails to tell you anything about the way the world is. Indeed Preller's account of Hopkins's poetry suggests that as readers of Hopkins we would know less about the world than we do if his poetry did not exist. Of course even if such is the case, given the low epistemological status generally given to poetry in our time, to compare the language of faith to poetry may not seem to many to be doing the language of faith any favours.[45]

There is, however, a remarkable passage in *Culture and Value*, which I believe supports my suggestion that Preller's remarks about Hopkins advance the case for the way the language of faith can tell something about the way the world is. Wittgenstein reports that one of his friends, Engelmann, told him that when he discovers a drawer full of his old manuscripts, he first thinks they are splendid and that he should make them available to other people. But when he imagines publishing some of them, the whole business loses its charm and becomes impossible. Wittgenstein comments that when Engelmann looks at his work and finds it good, but cannot publish it,

> he is seeing his life as a work of art created by God, and, as such, it is certainly worth contemplating, as is every life and everything whatever. But only an artist can so represent an individual thing as to make it appear to us like a work of art; it is *right* that those manuscripts should lose their value when looked at singly and especially when regarded *disinterestedly*, i.e., by someone who doesn't feel enthusiastic about them in advance. A work of art forces us – as one might say – to see it in the right perspective but, in the absence of art, the object is just a fragment of nature like any other.[46]

Wittgenstein's work I believe to be the ongoing attempt to help rediscover the frightening beauty of the particular. That is why he thought philosophy must finally be a form of poetry. In the *Investigations* he asks, 'Could there be human beings lacking in the capacity to see something *as something* – and what would that be like? What sort of consequences would it have? – Would this defect be comparable to colour-blindness or to not having absolute pitch? – We will call it "aspect-blindness".'[47] 'Aspect-blindness' turns out to name our normal condition. Faced by the sheer variety of the world, we seek to control the variety through theory, that is, we try to demonstrate that the way things are is the way things have to be. That is why it is so frightening for us to see 'the object' as a fragment of nature, which can only be related to other fragments of nature by narratives that help us see the connections between contingent things and events without losing their contingent and particular beauty.[48]

I think we have no way to know whether Wittgenstein was or was not a Christian. I certainly do not think much hangs on whether he was or was not in terms of his significance for theology.[49] What I do think is that the kind of exercises he developed to help us see the particular are not unlike the kind of exercises Christians must go through – the kind of exercise that Preller rediscovers in Aquinas – to see in the sheer 'thereness' of what is: God's work. In 1947 Wittgenstein wrote a set of remarks that now appear on the same page of *Culture and Value*. Though I am sure it is sheer contingency that they appear on the same page, I am equally convinced that they are interrelated:

> The truly apocalyptic view of the world is that things do *not* repeat themselves. It isn't absurd, e.g., to believe that the age of science and technology is the beginning of the end for humanity; that the idea of great progress is a delusion, along with the idea that the truth will ultimately be known; that there is nothing good or desirable about scientific knowledge and that mankind, in seeking it, is falling into a trap. It is by no means obvious that this is not how things are.

> The miracles of nature.
> One might say: art *shows* us the miracles of nature. It is based on the *concept* of the miracles of nature. (The blossom, just opening

out. What is *marvellous* about it?) We say: 'Just look at it opening out!'[50]

Notes

1. Stanley Hauerwas, *With the Grain of the Universe: The Church's Witness and Natural Theology* (Grand Rapids: Brazos Press, 2001; London: SCM Press, 2002), p. 15.

2. Hauerwas, *With the Grain of the Universe*, p. 29.

3. Hauerwas, *With the Grain of the Universe*, p. 26; George Hendry, *Theology of Nature* (Philadelphia: Westminster Press, 1980), p. 14.

4. The first book by Burrell that forever changed how I read Aquinas was his *Analogy and Philosophical Language* (New Haven: Yale University Press, 1973). His *Aquinas: God and Action* (London: Routledge and Kegan Paul, 1979) is his most sustained defence of his understanding of Aquinas. I think the 'natural theology' reading of Aquinas was persuasive to many only because they forgot his account of why charity is the form of the virtues. What Aquinas says about the virtues cannot be abstracted from his understanding of our knowledge of God.

5. Victor Preller, *Divine Science and the Science of God: A Reformulation of Thomas Aquinas* (Princeton: Princeton University Press, 1967).

6. The issues raised in *New Essays in Philosophical Theology* (London: SCM Press, 1961), edited by Anthony Flew and Alasdair MacIntyre, were never far from my attempt to reintroduce the language of the virtues in ethics.

7. For Burrell's appreciation of Preller's book see his 'Religious Life and Understanding', *Review of Metaphysics* 22/4 (June 1969): 681–90. I also had the honour of meeting Victor several times when I was visiting Princeton.

8. I am thinking in particular of Eugene F. Rogers, Jr, *Thomas Aquinas and Karl Barth: Sacred Doctrine and the Natural Knowledge of God* (Notre Dame: University of Notre Dame Press, 1995), and William Placher, *The Domestication of Transcendence: How Modern Thinking about God Went Wrong* (Louisville: Westminster/John Knox Press, 1996).

9. Toward the end of an article written in 1989 entitled, 'Sexual Ethics and the Single Life', Preller makes a quite similar claim about the status of the arguments he develops in the essay which defend a more 'traditional sexual ethic' on the basis that all human actions gain their moral intelligibility by being ordered to God. He observes that he does not expect his arguments to be convincing to those who accept the description of actions based on the individualistic and naturalistic presumptions of our culture. He observes, 'there are no hard rules of rationality to which I can appeal. All that I, or any other supporter of traditional morality can do is ask the new reformers and modern libertarians to look again at their model and ask themselves seriously if it can be used to justify the pursuit of a just and peaceful society which is anything other than a context for the unbridled pursuit of human gratification and pleasure. And I can also ask them if they honestly believe that such a pursuit of gratification is conducive to the sort of character they

themselves would like their friends and neighbors to possess. The model of human nature they use to justify their demands for radical change in traditional sexual ethics may be in some sense compatible with virtuous character, loving relations, and a just social order, but it is in no way conducive to such goods.' The essay appears in *Men and Women: Sexual Ethics in Turbulent Times*, edited by Philip Turner (Cambridge, Mass.: Cowley, 1989), pp. 143–4. I hope it is not self-serving to observe that I could wish for no better account of the kind of argument found often in my own writings.

10. It is very important that anyone trying to answer this question notice that Preller says that 'natural theology' is incapable of so adequating the mind. Yet Preller shows quite well how natural theology may prepare us for acknowledging the limits of our knowledge of God. It is important that 'nature' and 'grace' be distinguished, but not bifurcated. For my attempt to think through these matters see *Sanctify Them In the Truth* (Nashville: Abingdon Press, 1998), pp. 37–59.

11. Some may object I am conflating Preller's views with those of Aquinas, but I see no alternative. *Divine Science and the Science of God* is appropriately subtitled 'A Reformulation of Thomas Aquinas'. In his review of Preller's book David Burrell observes that whether Preller's linguistic reformulation of Aquinas is 'Aquinas may be endlessly discussed' (p. 682). As far as I can see, however, given the argument Preller makes in the book there is no way to distinguish his views from his reformulation of Aquinas.

12. I have wondered if Preller's understanding of Aquinas, which was so much against the grain of the Thomism of his day, may have at least been made possible by his reading of works of Aquinas other than the *Summa*. For example, the internal quotation comes from Aquinas, *De Trinitate Boethii Commentarium*. The structure of *Divine Science and the Science of God* could be a subject in itself. I think, for example, the first two chapters can be read as an attempt to retrain the readers' habits in order to prepare them for the work done in chapter 3. That Preller began with questions about the 'name' of God seems to be the necessary preparation for his overall argument.

13. In *With the Grain of the Universe* I suggested that by attending to Barth's argument in his *Göttingen Dogmatics* we see that Aquinas is closer to Barth than perhaps even Barth recognized (pp. 164–7). I certainly would not suggest that Preller is providing a Barthian reading of Aquinas, but I think there is no question that his understanding of Aquinas brings Aquinas quite close to Barth. For example, Preller observes that the followers of Barth who try to make him assert that God is finite because of the Incarnation fail to see the implications of their claim, that is, either God ceased to be God in the Incarnation, or every predicate that applies to Christ applies to God as he always was and will be. Preller observes, I think quite correctly, 'Barth's point is that there is no *deus absconditus*, the nature of which is not known by faith, lying behind the *deus revelatus*' (p. 215).

Preller seldom refers to Barth in *Divine Science and the Science of God*, but it is hard not to read the theological remarks he makes in the last chapter in a Barthian fashion. For example, he quotes Aquinas's claim that 'the Mystery of Christ's Incarnation and Passion is the way by which men come to beatitude' in support of his contention that the central empirical referent of Sacred Doctrine is the humanity of Christ (p. 249). A few pages later he observes, 'What is primarily meant by "the image of God in man" is the imperfect image in the believer. As Karl Rahner remarks, since the Incarnation, all theology has become anthropology – and, we might add, all anthropology has become Christology' (p. 260). Barth's favourite quote from Aquinas was, 'Deus est non genre', which Preller also highlights (p. 11) and is clearly at the heart of the argument of *Divine Science and the Science of God*. Richard Church, however, rightly reminds me that to read Aquinas in a Barthian fashion remains controversial to say the least.

In *With the Grain of the Universe* I, like Preller, was so intent on showing the 'proofs' were not proofs, I failed to suggest why Aquinas discussed them. Of course one answer (and it is too quick an answer) is that they were in the tradition. Just as Aquinas used everything in the tradition to his own ends, so he used the 'proofs'. For Aquinas, I believe, the proofs were his way of saying, 'Given the God of creation we should not be surprised the world looks like this.' As Richard Fern puts it, the proofs should be read 'as efforts to identify generally accessible features of the world in which religious believers experience the sustaining presence of a sacred reality. What makes these reasons in support of religious belief is that the features identified constitute "otherwise anomalies", aspects of our common experience that make good sense, arguably, only on the supposition reality, at rock-bottom, is sacred' (*Nature, God, and Humanity: Envisioning an Ethics of Nature* (Cambridge: Cambridge University Press, 2002), p. 122). Fern suggests, for example, that the cosmological argument is the attempt to suggest that the existence of anything makes little sense unless something exists necessarily.

14. Preller quite rightly, I think, argues that Aquinas had no 'doctrine of analogy', because the so-called 'doctrine' is not a means of knowing God but: 'a meta-linguistic analysis of the state of certain words and propositions to *name* God. From God's point of view there is undoubtedly an "analogy of being"; from our point of view, however, there is only an "analogy of 'being.'"' The proofs for the existence of God are our way of confessing our ignorance of the "analogy of being". We do not know the principle which might unify all aspects of our awareness of "that which is"' (p. 170).

15. I suppose that Preller's account of these matters is sufficient to make him an anti-foundationalist, though I am not sure how such a label helps us better understand him. Given his understanding of analogy he rightly maintains that reality is '*entirely* reconceivable' (p. 69), but he certainly does not think that all conceptions count equally. He acknowledges that it is quite possible for two necessary and incommensurable language systems to exist, but there is no neutral language available to overcome such incommensurability (p. 60). This is complicated by the fact that to have one concept in a language means, at least if Wilfrid Sellars is right, we must have them all (p. 43). It is a mark of Preller's good sense that he does not try to say more than can be said about these matters.

16. I am grateful to Rob MacSwain for reminding me of this important point.

17. See, for example, the response of D. Z. Phillips to the charge he is a

Wittgensteinian fideist in his *Faith After Foundationalism: Critiques and Alternatives* (Boulder: Westview Press, 1995), pp. 236–7. John Berkman has brought to my attention an article by Donald Evans on Preller's book that argues that in developing his argument for the 'absolute opaqueness' of God Preller must maintain some minimal understanding of what human language means as applied to God. In particular Evans calls attention to Preller's claim in *Divine Science and the Science of God*, 'While the believer does not understand the propositions of Sacred Doctrine, he nevertheless believes that his mind is being conformed by God to himself when he assents to the truth of the propositions in a state of real or infused faith. He not only believes that there exist in the language or Word of God analogical counterparts of the propositions of faith, and that, in the Word of God, those counterparts are intelligible; he also believes that, when he is in a state of real or infused faith, he possess a special sort of "intention" which gives to his affirmations of the language of faith a real referential and descriptive power that is apparent to God and the *beati*' (p. 262) (Donald Evans, 'Preller's Analogy of "Being"', *The New Scholasticism* 45/1 (Winter 1971): 1–37. I am indebted to John Berkman not only for calling attention to Evans's article, but also for helping me see what I am trying to do in this essay.

18. I am, of course, referring to Wittgenstein's famous remark in the *Investigations* (§66), 'To repeat: don't think, but look!' This command comes in the context of his discussion of games in which he is trying to admonish us not to develop a theory of games but rather look for family resemblances that help us see not only their similarities, but their differences. His later remark, 'One cannot guess how a word functions. One has to *look at* its use and learn from that' is perhaps more relevant to the point I am trying to make (*Investigations*, §340). Wittgenstein observes that prejudice stands in the way of our 'looking', but he says such a prejudice is not a stupid one. I think he is right to suggest that such a prejudice is not stupid, but rather draws on our hunger to control the variety of objects through theory in order to show that things must be this way or 'this is the way things must have happened'. Such a desire is not stupid, but I believe is very dangerous.

19. Fergus Kerr, *Theology After Wittgenstein*, 2nd edn (London: SPCK, 1997), p. 158. Ray Monk reports that one of the few books Wittgenstein insisted that Drury should read was James's *Varieties of Religious Experience*. 'Drury told him that he had already read it: "I always enjoy reading anything of William James. He is such a human person." Yes, Wittgenstein replied: "That is what makes him a good philosopher; he was a real human being."' Ray Monk, *Ludwig Wittgenstein: The Duty of Genius* (New York: Free Press, 1990), p. 478. Russell Goodman has now shown in his *Wittgenstein and William James* (Cambridge: Cambridge University Press, 2002) how deeply Wittgenstein read James, and in particular the *Principles of Psychology*.

20. Kerr, *Theology After Wittgenstein*, p. 204.

21. David Burrell, *Friendship and Ways to Truth* (Notre Dame: University of Notre Dame Press, 2000), pp. 92–3.

22. I am quite frankly not sure whether I can defend this claim or even that it

can be defended, depending as it does on how one reads the *Tractatus* as a whole. However, I am thinking of these propositions in the *Tractatus*:

> 6.44 It is not *how* things are in the world that is mystical, but that it exists.
> 6.45 To view the world *sub specie aeterni* is to view it as a whole – a limited whole.
>
> Feeling the world as a limited whole – it is this that is mystical.

(Ludwig Wittgenstein, *Tractatus Logico-Philosophicus*, trans. D. F. Pears and B. F. McGuinness (London: Routledge & Kegan Paul, 1963)).

23. John Churchill, 'Wonder and the End of Explanation: Wittgenstein and Religious Sensibility', *Philosophical Investigations* 17/2 (April 1994): 389. Kerr expresses his appreciation for Churchill's fine article in *Theology After Wittgenstein* (p. 204). My dependence on Churchill's article will be apparent. I am not sure why, but I always find it easier to write 'about' Wittgenstein by using work that has been written on Wittgenstein rather than making a direct appeal to his work. I think one of the reasons is that I am not sure you can ever write about Wittgenstein because he did not want you to write about him; he wanted you to know how to go on in your own way. I am, of course, not denying that there are quite wonderful books written on his work, such as David Pears's *The False Prison: A Study of the Development of Wittgenstein's Philosophy*, 2 vols (Oxford: Clarendon Press, 1997). But even Pears's work tends to betray the character of Wittgenstein's mode of work just to the extent that Pears writes in a traditional philosophical genre. For those interested in how my own work has been shaped by Wittgenstein I can commend no better book than Brad Kallenberg's *Ethics as Grammar: Changing the Postmodern Subject* (Notre Dame: University of Notre Dame Press, 2001). I confess I was at first embarrassed even to be compared to Wittgenstein, but then I realized on reading Kallenberg's book for the third or fourth time that Kallenberg just needed me as a stand-in for Christianity. I am indebted to Kallenberg, not only for teaching me much about Wittgenstein, but for teaching me about myself.

24. Ludwig Wittgenstein, *Philosophical Investigations*, trans. G. E. M. Anscombe (New York: Macmillan, 1953), §546. The quote from Goethe is found in *On Certainty*, §402.

25. Many read Wittgenstein's remarks about philosophy in the *Investigations* as a demeaning of the philosophical task. He certainly wanted to help his readers understand when philosophy should come to an end, but I do not think that means he thought the work of philosophy was without importance. 'To show the fly the way out of the fly-bottle' (*Investigations*, §309) is surely a task worth doing and never ending. Wittgenstein clearly thought most people, or at least people not corrupted by bad philosophy, did not need philosophy in order to live well. But that does not mean that philosophy has no role in helping us avoid the lies that grip our lives. That philosophy 'ought really to be written only as *poetic composition*' suggests he assumed philosophy, like poetry, is to help guard our language from going on a holiday and extend our ability to see the world (*Culture and*

Value, p. 24e). But to write philosophy as poetry is no easy task and explains Wittgenstein's own sense that he cannot quite do what he thinks he should do. At the very least Wittgenstein's attitude toward philosophy embodies the kind of humility exemplified in Aquinas's understanding of the role of the philosopher. Finally, the problem is not with philosophy but, as Wittgenstein well knew, with the prideful use of philosophy. For an account of Wittgenstein's work that stresses the role of learning 'to see' see James Edwards, *Ethics Without Philosophy: Wittgenstein and the Moral Life* (Tampa: University of South Florida Press, 1985). Few have taught us better how to think with Wittgenstein than James Edwards. However, Kallenberg criticizes Edwards, perhaps rightly, for assuming a self free from all communal, historical, and religious influences (*Ethics as Grammar*, pp. 59–71).

26. Wittgenstein's remarks on 'descriptions' in the *Investigations* I think indicate the importance of the movement of his thinking from the *Tractatus* to the *Investigations*. Thus his claim in the *Investigations* (§291) that descriptions are instruments for particular uses like the machine-drawing which an engineer has before him. Moreover, he is acutely aware how difficult it is to rightly and exactly describe because, as James noted, 'Our vocabulary is inadequate' (*Investigations*, §610). For an extremely informative article that helps us understand how Wittgenstein's engineering background shaped his understanding of the task of description see Kelly Hamilton's 'Wittgenstein and the Mind's Eye', in *Wittgenstein: Biography and Philosophy*, ed. James Klagge (Cambridge: Cambridge University Press, 2001), pp. 53–97. For a book that develops in great detail the importance of description for ethics see Charles Pinches, *Theology and Action: After Theory in Christian Ethics* (Grand Rapids: Eerdmans, 2002).

27. Churchill, 'Wonder and the End of Explanation', p. 398.

28. Churchill, 'Wonder and the End of Explanation', p. 399.

29. Wittgenstein, *Culture and Value*, p. 5e. The hostility expressed in some of Wittgenstein's objections to science can give the impression that he had no use for science, which I do not believe is the case.

30. Wittgenstein, *Culture and Value*, p. 37e.

31. Wittgenstein, *Investigations*, §§198–202.

32. Wittgenstein, *Investigations*, §201.

33. Churchill, 'Wonder and the End of Explanation', p. 401.

34. I am well aware that many who have given up any practice of a faith still find provocative the question, 'Why is there something, when there could have been nothing?' For example, Jared Diamond in a review article of David Wilson's *Darwin's Cathedral: Evolution, Religion, and the Nature of Society*, recalls as a 'hyper-rational' undergraduate at Harvard in 1955 he was challenged by Paul Tillich's use of that question to show that science cannot provide an answer. He ends the article noting that religions will thrive as long as the question has no answer. The problem with the apocalyptic use of the question is that it is not apparent why the question should be asked at all. As a result Christian convictions are distorted because they are made to answer a question that makes little sense. Indeed I suspect such a question is the breeding ground of deism. See Jared

Diamond, 'The Religious Success Story', *New York Review of Books* 49 (7 November 2002): 30–2.

35. Churchill, 'Wonder and the End of Explanation', p. 401.

36. Churchill makes the nice point, which Kerr obviously thinks interesting, that Wittgenstein's admiration of James's *Principles of Psychology* is puzzling given James's tendency to psychologize verbs such as 'think', 'interpret', 'construe'. As Churchill points out, if the function of verbs is not to refer, then there is no arena for an intrinsically intelligible phenomenon called 'mind' (p. 403). Churchill's point applies equally to Wittgenstein's reading of James's *Varieties of Religious Experience* which 'internalized' religious experience. Surely it is religious behaviour on which Wittgenstein should have focused. Of course the puzzle is deeper just to the extent that James's focus on action in the development of his pragmatism put him in tension with the significant role he gave 'experience' in the *Varieties*.

37. Churchill, 'Wonder and the End of Explanation', pp. 406–7.

38. Hauerwas, *With the Grain of the Universe*, pp. 50–61.

39. However, see the footnote on pp. 54–5 of *With the Grain of the Universe*. In that footnote I suggest that James's account of habits could provide a context for understanding the role of language for avoiding the 'myth of the given'. Wittgenstein's admiration for James is well known, but exactly what he thought he learned from James remains unclear. In *On Certainty* (§422) we do find the remark: 'So I am trying to say something that sounds like pragmatism. Here I am being thwarted by a kind of *Weltanschauung*' (Ludwig Wittgenstein, *On Certainty*, ed. G. E. M. Anscombe and G. H. Wright, trans. Dennis Paul and G. E. M. Anscombe (New York: Harper & Row, 1969)).

Edwards provides a very helpful account of Wittgenstein and pragmatism in *Ethics Without Philosophy*, pp. 225–30. He concludes that, though there are some quite strong similarities between Wittgenstein and pragmatism, Wittgenstein's concern with human understanding 'originates in a dissatisfaction with the tradition deeper than that which motivates the pragmaticist' (p. 230).

40. In *Culture and Value* Wittgenstein observes, 'The *edifice of your pride* has to be dismantled. And that is terribly hard work' (p. 26e). I do not take this remark to be about 'ethics', but rather as an indication that for Wittgenstein pride is one of the factors that makes it impossible to see objects as they are. The *Investigations* I think should be read as a form of training in humility. For an account of the *Tractatus* as Wittgenstein's attempt to be 'godlike', see Edwards, *Ethics Without Philosophy*, pp. 68–73. Anyone familiar with John Bowlin's book *Contingency and Fortune in Aquinas's Ethics* (Cambridge: Cambridge University Press, 1999) will recognize the influence Bowlin's work has had on what I have tried to do in this paper. Bowlin wonderfully illumines the relation between knowledge and the acquisition of virtue by calling attention to the challenge presented in dog training. He observes, 'Training dogs well is hard because it is difficult to become the sort of person who can command them with just authority, obey them when appropriate, distinguish false kindness from true respect, and love some thing or activity in a way that will generate a community of common loves with a dog' (p. 156).

41. The kind of training Wittgenstein and Preller gesture toward is wonderfully described in Marjorie Hunt's *The Stone Carvers: Master Craftsmen of the
Washington National Cathedral* (Washington, DC: Smithsonian Institution Press,
1999). Her book focuses on Vincent Palumbo and Roger Morigi, who spent a lifetime carving the stone for the National Cathedral. They were each brought up in
the 'trade'. Vincent describes it this way: 'When you come from a traditional
family you learn from the talking. What happened to me, we was in that trade. We
was talking about work anytime; at breakfast, dinner, supper, most of the subject
was work. Think about this stone, how we gonna do this, who was gonna do that,
we gotta use this trick. So you're growing, and you listen, and your mind, it gets
drunk with all those things, and then when it comes time, you remember' (pp.
20–1). Hunt notes that the family was the key institution for this training, laying
the crucial foundation early through informal periods of learning. Hunt observes,
'Like a child learning language, he [Vincent] began to acquire a grammar of stone
carving; he began to piece together knowledge of the various elements of the craft
and the underlying principles that governed them. Sitting around the dinner table
listening to his father and grandfather tell stories and discuss work, he became
familiar with the names of the tools and the different types of stone. Little by little,
he became acquainted with the work processes and specialized terminology of the
trade' (p. 21). To 'acquire a grammar of stone carving' nicely suggests how the
exercises Wittgenstein develops in the *Investigations* are meant to cure the philosophical disease associated with the epistemological presumption we must choose
between idealism and realism. A wonderful way to present Wittgenstein's work
would be to write a Wittgensteinian commentary on *The Stone Carvers*.

42. James Edwards also uses Hopkins's poetry to exemplify Wittgenstein's
endeavour to enable us to 'see through' what we see. For example when Hopkins
speaks of the falcon as 'kingdom of daylight's dauphin', Edwards suggests he is
trying to help us see through what we ordinarily see. 'If we suddenly see the
dauphin of the kingdom of daylight sailing there in the heavens, if that image takes
hold of us and for a moment disappears as a "mere" image, then upon our return
to our everyday conceptions we become newly aware of *their* status. By means of
the extraordinary image, we are forcefully reminded of the role of those everyday
conceptions in determining what we see; thus we can see through the ordinary
objects of our sight. The temporary appropriation of the poetic image deliteralizes
all our seeing, at least for a time. And in that deliteralization is a corresponding
expansion. Once it is brought home to us that the world is much richer than our
everyday conceptions of it, we can never be quite so complacent in our ordinary
ways of seeing, feeling and acting. There are words yet unconceived in our familiar
forms of life' (*Ethics Without Philosophy*, p. 212).

43. I am indebted to Brad Kallenberg for his critical reading of this paper. He
has saved me from a number of mistakes that are the result of a lazy mind. Too
often I let my language be captured by a dualism Wittgenstein tried to help us
overcome. For example, in my effort to suggest how the language of faith tells us
about 'the way the world is', I may give the impression that language is something
that 'depicts' 'reality' 'out there'. The language of faith does convey the way the

world is for those whose lives are shaped by that language, but that it does so only makes it possible for the way the world is to be exemplified in their lives. Kallenberg rightly notes that Hopkins's claim that each thing 'is what it does' is at the heart of the attempt by Wittgenstein to overcome the 'realism-scepticism' problem. In a letter to me Kallenberg observes, 'we inhabit a world that is internally related to language/form-of-life/communal practices'. Accordingly the claims Christians make about the way things are does not draw on representational accounts of how we know, but rather such claims are meant to help us discover how the language we speak creates conditions for its own felicity. But those conditions also provide the context for conversations with those who do not speak our language of faith.

44. I note that Preller says that Aquinas believes the contingency of the world says something to our longing for 'complete intelligibility' (p. 223). I substituted 'good' for 'complete intelligibility' because I think it closer to Aquinas's own understanding.

45. For an attempt to help us see the interrelation between the 'signatured' character of artistic truth and the kind of truth characteristic of religious speech see George Dennis O'Brien, *The Idea of a Catholic University* (Chicago: University of Chicago Press, 2002), pp. 33–45, 80–7.

46. Wittgenstein, *Culture and Value*, p. 4e. I do not believe Wittgenstein had a theory of art because I do not think Wittgenstein had a theory about anything. It is certainly the case, however, that he had fascinating remarks about art and aesthetics throughout his work. In particular see *Lectures and Conversations on Aesthetics, Psychology, and Religious Belief*, ed. Cyril Barrett (Berkeley: University of California Press, 1967). The 'motto' Wittgenstein liked so much – 'Everything is what it is and not another thing' – appears in his 'Lecture on Aesthetics', p. 27.

47. Wittgenstein, *Investigations*, p. 213e.

48. This sentence obviously has resonances I have learned from the work of Iris Murdoch, who may well have learned them from Wittgenstein. In his biography of Murdoch, *Iris Murdoch: A Life* (New York: Norton, 2001), Peter Conradi tells us Murdoch never had the opportunity to listen to Wittgenstein lecture, but she was in constant conversation with people who had studied with Wittgenstein. In what manner Murdoch's increasing Platonism may or may not have transformed what is clearly Wittgenstein's influence on her would make a fascinating study. However, Charles Pinches has anticipated what such a comparison might look like when he says, commenting on Murdoch's Platonism: 'Platonism pulls us, finally, beyond this world to a god above it. Christianity, while terribly attracted by this upward motion, must resist it. It must reenter the world – which it can never see as in some sense "unreal". I do not know if there is such a thing as distinctly Christian art, but if there is, it must include this return. Great art must always challenge our lived perceptions of what is real. In addition to this challenge, Christian art may need to include a re-representation of the lived world, as real' (*Theology and Action*, p. 187). Earlier (p. 185) Pinches suggests that my later work is not as determined by my earlier emphasis on how art can provide the way

to see truthfully. That may be the case, but if so all it means is that I have failed to say what I should have been saying.

49. I, therefore, differ from my good friend James McClendon, who argues that Wittgenstein was a Christian. See his *Systematic Theology*, vol. 3: *Witness* (Nashville: Abingdon Press, 2000), pp. 227–70. Norman Malcolm certainly makes a strong case that, whether Wittgenstein was or was not a Christian, the point of view he develops in the *Investigations* is analogous to a religious point of view. Malcolm argues that there are 'four analogies between Wittgenstein's conception of the grammar of language, and his view of what is paramount in a religious life. First, in both there is an end to explanation; second, in both there is an inclination to be amazed at the existence of something; third, into both there enters the notion of an "illness": fourth, in both, *doing, acting*, takes priority over intellectual understanding and reasoning.' See Norman Malcolm, *Wittgenstein: A Religious Point of View*, edited with a response by Peter Winch (Ithaca: Cornell University Press, 1993), p. 92. Winch rightly questions whether Malcolm's analogies are as revealing as Malcolm thinks, but obviously the case I have tried to make in this essay shares some features of Malcolm's account. Winch observes that Malcolm's argument that explanations have to stop does not mean we are required to regard acceptance of things as they are as a gift (pp. 113–14). Winch, for example, calls attention to Wittgenstein's remarks in *Culture and Value* (p. 71e) about the sheer 'cussedness of things' which he thinks describes an attitude diametrically opposed to gratitude. Winch observes, however, that the significance of such expressions for Wittgenstein depends not on the words used but on the difference their use makes in the lives of users. But that seems to be Malcolm's point, namely, that Wittgenstein thought the failure to live with gratitude is a failure to recognize the way things are. Unlike Malcolm, however, I am less confident that I know what I am talking about when I talk about a 'religious point of view'. I have also refrained from appealing to Wittgenstein's well known remarks on religion, Christianity, and theology. I think his remarks on these matters are, like everything else he said, well worth pondering, but I do not think they add or subtract from the position I have tried to develop in this essay. I do think, however, that the remarks in *Culture and Value* concerning the resurrection are among his most important: 'Perhaps we can say: Only *love* can believe the Resurrection. Or: It is *love* that believes the Resurrection. We might say: Redeeming love believes even in the Resurrection; holds fast even to the Resurrection. What combats doubt is, as it were, *redemption*' (p. 33e).

50. Wittgenstein, *Culture and Value*, p. 56e. Another way of approaching what I have tried to do in this essay is through an account of 'negative theology'. Alex Sider, for example, in an essay commenting on Denys's account of our knowledge of God, stresses the importance of Denys's understanding of hierarchy as the necessary context for his account of negative theology. Sider notes, 'For Denys, all creation is ordered with respect to and by God, so that it is harmoniously structured and reflective of God's glory. Much of Denys' work is devoted to detailing how God can be accurately reflected by a harmony of parts. Because for Denys, God is the sole single principle, no one aspect of created reality could

approach an adequate manifestation of God. Creation, therefore, witnesses to God's glories precisely in virtue of its multiplicity. Aspects of creation are divided and subdivided into parts that, when taken in concert, tell us something about what God is like. For example, we can infer from Denys that the differentiation of the virtues is an instance of this: by cultivating the virtues in their variety, we come to see how courage requires temperance, justice, prudence, and so on. Moreover, in seeing how the virtues are interconnected we come to know something about their unity in God. This goes as well for the basic structure and order of material things. One basic task for theology is therefore to reflect on the interconnections among objects in creation in order to begin to see how God's glory surpasses the wonderful intricacy of the world. Thus, on Denys' view, the life of stones as such is less revelatory of God than that of humans, but both are necessary – because we must reflect on how stones are like and unlike humans and vice versa – to approach more fully our knowledge of God. The importance of hierarchy for Denys lies not in the ranking of humans above stones, but in the way that the created hierarchy as a whole displays how creation is intrinsically ordered to reflect God' ('The Hiddenness of God and the Justice of God: Negative Theology as Social Ethical Resource' (unpublished), pp. 5–6). I am indebted to Sider for a critical reading of an earlier version of this paper. His criticism has made it a much better paper. I am also indebted to Jeff Stout and Rob MacSwain for their close reading and editing of this paper.

4. 'Real Knowledge' or 'Enlightened Ignorance'

Eric Mascall on the Apophatic Thomisms of Victor Preller and Victor White

FERGUS KERR, OP

1. *Mascall on Preller's book*

Eric Mascall reviewed Victor Preller's book, *Divine Science and the Science of God*, in *Theology* 71, 1968.[1] 'This extremely interesting book', Mascall said, 'takes for granted in the reader an acquaintance with the fundamental attitudes of both Thomist and linguistic epistemology.' While noting that the book offers no special difficulty for 'anybody possessing this minimal philosophical equipment', Mascall warns that it nevertheless 'will require careful and persistent attention'.[2] Given that the review appeared in a journal that favours brevity, Mascall confines himself to two main points, one fairly technical, the other of much wider significance.

First, Mascall contends that Preller's interpretation departs in certain details from Aquinas's epistemological theory. The exposition would have been helped, he suggests, 'by an explicit recognition that the whole *apparatus* of perception, both psychological and physiological, is an *objectum quo* or a system of *objecta quibus*, by means of which the percipient apprehends the trans-sensory *objectum quod*, which is the actual intelligible entity'. What this hints at, no doubt, is Mascall's suspicion that the account of Aquinas's epistemology is much too influenced by Preller's enthusiasm for the philosophy of mind advanced by Wilfrid Sellars.

Second, and more important for our purposes here, Mascall claims that, while Preller notes 'the "agnostic" emphasis' in Aquinas which leads him to say that we do not know what God is but only what God is not, and likewise for our knowledge of how God is related to the world (see *Summa Theologiae* (*ST*) I.3 prologue), Preller 'interprets these remarks in the most literal and extreme way'. This claim takes us to the heart of Mascall's reservations about Preller's interpretation of Aquinas. It locates Mascall's position in the variety of twentieth-century versions of Thomism. And it relates directly to the (then and still) highly contentious question of the knowledge of God available in this life.

Mascall also hints at other difficulties. For example, Preller holds the 'highly original' view that Aquinas's famous 'Five Ways' (*ST* I.2.3) were not regarded by Aquinas as 'ways by which, on the basis of his philosophy, he could demonstrate that God exists' – they were only 'five typical ways by which philosophers had traditionally argued for the existence of God'. That is to say, according to Preller, Aquinas was not out to demonstrate God's existence by arguments of his own but merely reminding his students of types of argument that had been current for centuries. He was not even interested in improving them, let alone espousing them.

For Preller, all that Aquinas thought it possible to argue is that 'the existence of the world would remain radically unintelligible if there did not exist something from which the existence of the world derived its hypothetical necessity'. 'God' is defined, according to Aquinas, so Preller contends, in terms of a relationship to something the nature of which is unknown. Mascall does not have the space to explain how Preller arrives at 'this minimal conclusion'. Nevertheless, he allows himself to suggest that 'the actual metaphysical relation between God and his creatures provides an access to God of which Professor Preller's radically logical and linguistic approach is unable to take adequate account'. In short, Mascall allies himself with the 'many critics', who would, he is sure, 'wish to raise the question whether either natural or revealed knowledge of God is quite as minimal as Professor Preller asserts'.

So much for Mascall's review. His main worry, clearly, is that Preller exaggerates the apophatic element of Aquinas: the negativity in

Aquinas's conception of the knowledge of God which we may obtain or be granted in this life. Appearing as it did at a low point in interest in Thomism, and anyway never easily available in the United Kingdom, Victor Preller's book made little impact on other British students of Aquinas. The Oxford Blackfriars library did not even have a copy. When it was listed in a second-hand bookseller's catalogue ten years ago I immediately wrote for it: judge of my surprise when it turned out to have been Mascall's own copy!

No comments whatsoever appear in the margins. On the other hand, over thirty passages in the book have been marked and indexed. In addition, Mascall had inserted a brief letter on the book from his colleague and friend at King's College, London, the distinguished philosopher of religion H. P. Owen.[3] Owen writes that, like Mascall, he is 'baffled' by the book. He is clearly well aware of Mascall's views and seems confident that they are in agreement with one another. This private correspondence helps to define the difference between Mascall and Preller on Aquinas's doctrine of our knowledge of God.

In a postscript, Owen notes that he is particularly grateful for seeing the book, since it has 'an obvious interest' in the post-Vatican II climate. Owen and Mascall take it for granted that the book was written by a Roman Catholic (which in fact Preller was at the time). After all, Preller says in the Foreword that he will be using the writings of Aquinas as a model of religious language, 'not because I feel that Thomistic theology either is or ought to be a model for contemporary theologizing, much less philosophizing, but simply because Aquinas holds a place of extraordinary authority both within the official circles of contemporary Roman Catholicism and within the less official discussions of contemporary philosophers, both religious and antireligious'.[4]

Whatever about the philosophers, Aquinas had just lost much of his authority in the wake of the Second Vatican Council's retrieval of biblical and patristic theology. Preller's remark, in fact, might suggest that he was not exactly on the inside of Roman Catholic discussions.[5] In 1968, anyway, Owen and Mascall were no doubt shaking their heads, as many both inside and beyond the Roman communion were at that date, about the decline of Thomism and the flourishing pluralism in Catholic theology.

The chief point Owen makes is that Preller twists Aquinas towards an 'almost Barthian' preference for *analogia fidei* over *analogia entis* and saddles Aquinas with an 'unqualified' apophatic theology. Assuming that Owen's letter is an echo of what Mascall himself would have said, though neither would have been so blunt in print, we can (I think) re-read Mascall's review in light of the thirty passages he marked in his copy of the book, to which Owen says he has paid special attention.

2. Preller on contemporary Thomists

We cannot go through these passages in detail. In sum, they all relate to Preller's insistence that no knowledge of the divine nature is available in this life. In one passage, for instance, Preller contends that 'many Thomists have failed to see that the "doctrine of analogy" is not a means of knowing God, but a meta-linguistic analysis of the state of certain words and propositions used to *name* God' (*Divine Science*, p. 170). He then puts it pithily in one of the many fine formulations in the book:

> From God's point of view there is undoubtedly an 'analogy of being'; from our point of view, however, there is only an 'analogy of "being."'

Cajetan is mentioned here, the only time in the book, while in a footnote Preller aligns himself with Battista Mondin, Ralph McInerny, and especially Hampus Lyttkens, 'a ground-breaker in the field'.[6] Decoded, what this means is that, on the question of analogy, Preller rejects the standard Thomist interpretations at the time, which, however varied in detail, nevertheless took their stand on Cajetan's theory of analogy.[7]

Preller mentions Réginald Garrigou-Lagrange, the pre-eminent Cajetanian Thomist of the day, charging him, in connection with analogy, of supposing that 'one can get some idea of the nature of God by "cleaning up" a human concept – by denying those aspects of a human concept that cannot apply to God, until all that is left is a perfect and formal "idea" that corresponds to something in God' (*Divine Science*, p. 210). That is to say, Garrigou-Lagrange believes that we can, in this life, have '*some* idea of the *nature* of God' (my italics), whereas, so Preller wants to say, Aquinas completely excludes the possibility that we could have *any* idea of the divine nature.[8]

The problem with 'the Neo- and Paleo-Thomists', indeed with most of 'his defenders and his detractors', is that they fail to take seriously Aquinas's 'explicit denial of any attempt to tell us what God is like or how he exists' (*Divine Science*, p. 26).[9] These interpreters do not understand that the purpose of 'natural theology' is 'not to convey information about God, but rather to empty the mind of any pretension of possessing concepts in terms of which to judge the nature of the "final intelligibility" of reality – the intelligibility of God'. The result of natural theology, putting it a little differently, is not 'to render man's experience intelligible here and now, but to draw conclusions from the non-intelligibility of that experience' (*Divine Science*, p. 30).

The exceptions among the admirers of Aquinas who understand his apophaticism, Preller says in a footnote, are 'Sertillanges, Victor White, Karl Rahner, and, in general, the continental theologians who utilize the categories of phenomenology or existentialism to interpret Aquinas' (*Divine Science*, p. 30, n. 45).[10] The only English-speaking figure mentioned in this list is Victor White.[11] According to Preller, White maintains that, since the proof of the existence of a being must deliver some concept of the *esse* of that being, the Five Ways cannot be arguments towards knowledge of God. They are only arguments for asserting the proposition 'God exists.' This fits with Preller's insistence that Aquinas's theistic proofs do not, and were never intended to, deliver as much about God as many commentators have believed, admirers and adversaries alike. In another neat formulation Preller sums up what he takes to be White's position: 'the conclusions of natural theology . . . are notable for their utter lack of specific content – for their sentential vacuity' (*Divine Science*, p. 32). Clearly, this matches even more with Preller's reading of Aquinas's apophaticism.

3. Victor White's apophatic Thomism

But Preller's reference is wrong: White's book is not *The Unknown God* but *God the Unknown and Other Essays*; and it came out not in 1948 but in 1956. The essay which he quotes is, however, cited correctly as 'The Unknown God' (it first appeared in 1952). Like most of White's published work it is very short, running to ten pages; a sketch rather than a fully worked-out interpretation, almost bare of footnotes.

From the opening paragraph White locates Aquinas in the tradition of John of Damascus and the Pseudo-Dionysius. Frequently citing or alluding to the former's statement that it is impossible to say of God what he is, and the latter's that the most perfect union with God is union with the utterly Unknown, Aquinas insists over and over again not only that 'we *do not* know what God is – the essence, nature and "whatness" of God – but also that we *cannot* know it: *non possumus*'.[12] That certainly sounds like a theme insisted upon throughout Preller's book: no real knowledge of the divine nature or essence is available in this life.

White goes on to say that 'all saints and sages of any consequence, whether in East or West, whether Christian or non-Christian, are in full agreement with St Thomas on this point' – an assertion he supports with references to Plotinus, the *Upanishads* and the *Tao Te Ching* – yet 'many of his own professed disciples seem to have watered down his teaching to some extent'. Whether Preller would have happily endorsed White's first claim is perhaps doubtful; but he was in complete agreement with White that 'many' Thomists 'watered down' Aquinas's apophaticism. In particular, as White says of these 'professed' Thomists, 'they will tell us that although it is true that we cannot of course fully know the essence or nature of God in this life, we can and do have a vague, inadequate or (as they call it) a "non-quidditative" knowledge of the Divine Nature, and they hold that this is what St Thomas really means'. In the next sentence White appeals to 'Père Sertillanges and others' in support of this assessment of Aquinas's 'categorical and unqualified language, which says quite clearly that we do not know the Divine Nature at all, and that it is utterly (*omnino*) unknown to us'.

White argues, very strongly, that we can say nothing positive about God at all. The famous Five Ways, he contends, begin from our acquaintance with 'all sorts of happenings, changes, productions, things, values, strivings', setting out to show that none of these could exist, indeed nothing at all could happen, unless something with which we have no direct knowledge existed – 'something people call divine' (*ST* I.2.3). We can no more know the existence, *esse*, of God than we can know God's nature, *essentia*. According to the doctrine of the divine simplicity there is no distinction in God between nature and being (*ST* I.3). The Five Ways, White summarizes, 'enable us to know, not the being or existence of God (*Dei esse*), but only that what men call God is, or exists (*Deum esse*)' (*God the Unknown*, p. 18). Unless there is some such unknown ground[13] on which everything ultimately depends, then nothing would have ever happened at all.

As White is well aware, this sounds like agnosticism. White argues that, while the agnostic says, 'We do not know, and the universe is a mysterious riddle,' those who understand Aquinas properly say, 'We do not know what the answer is, but we do know that there is a mystery behind it all which we do not know, and if there were not, there would not even be a riddle. This Unknown we call *God*. If there were no God, there would be no universe to be mysterious, and nobody to be mystified' (*God the Unknown*, pp. 18–19).

Mascall would not have dissented from that. He would, on the other hand, have been suspicious of White's reading of Aquinas's argument to the effect that, even 'with the revelation which is of grace, we do not know in this life what God is, and so [even by grace] we can be united to him only as to one unknown to us' (*ST* I.12.13 ad 1). What this comes to, according to White, is as follows: 'God is thus no less of an Unknown God to the believer than to the unbeliever, to St John of the Cross than to Shankara or Plotinus, and we may say that to the Christian believer he is more, rather than less, mysterious' (*God the Unknown*, p. 22). What the Christian has to go on, Aquinas says, are 'more and better effects' – meaning the entire dispensation of grace, the Incarnation and the outpouring of the Spirit, the Gospel on which our ultimate happiness depends – which are nevertheless still only 'effects' (*ST* I.12.13). White cites in support of this minimalist reading of the passage Aquinas's commentary on the Pseudo-

Dionysius: 'The utmost achievement of which we are capable in this life in knowing God is the realisation that he is beyond anything we can think, and so the naming of God which is by way of denial is supremely appropriate' (*De Divinis Nominibus* 1.3).

4. Eric Mascall's 'dynamic' Thomism

Victor White's apophatic reading of Thomas Aquinas coincides with Victor Preller's, and so calls in question Mascall's claim that (for example) Preller's reading of the Five Ways is 'highly original' – by which Mascall really means 'without precedent'. Both White and Preller agree that in this life we have no positive knowledge of God; we are related to the divine nature as something absolutely unknown. But Eric Mascall was not comfortable with such unqualified apophaticism, no more with White's than with Preller's interpretation of Aquinas.

In his magisterial survey, *Twentieth-Century Religious Thought*, John Macquarrie refers to Mascall, along with Austin Farrer, as 'distinguished representatives' of Thomism in the Anglo-Catholic wing of the Church of England.[14] As he says, from *He Who Is* (1943) onwards, 'the Thomism expounded by Mascall had a decidedly dynamic character'.[15] Although the book was subtitled, 'A Study in Traditional Theism', Macquarrie says 'Mascall's dynamic understanding of God' was already going beyond standard Thomism. Macquarrie seems to identify mainstream Thomism with 'traditional theism' which, in turn, evidently has a distinctly un-dynamic conception of God. He cites Mascall speaking of Aquinas's God as 'not a static perfection but the absolutely unlimited Act and Energy'. For Macquarrie, this shows that Mascall was anticipating 'Transcendental Thomism'[16] – but that cannot be right. Mascall's sympathies with Transcendental Thomism were extremely limited, as his 1970–1 Gifford Lectures, delivered in Edinburgh and published as *The Openness of Being*, surely show. Throughout his writing on Aquinas, it is nearer the truth to say that Mascall aligns himself with the Existential Thomism, so-called, associated with Etienne Gilson,[17] and, even more, with Jacques Maritain.[18] If he had little sympathy with Transcendental Thomism, Mascall had even less with the apophaticism defended by the likes of Sertillanges and Victor White.

Mascall and White seem never to have discussed their radically different readings of Aquinas's negative theology. True, they lived in Oxford, at either end of Cornmarket, from 1945 when Mascall arrived from Lincoln until 1954 when White departed for California. True also, in the original edition of *He Who Is*, Mascall noted a debt to White about a tricky textual problem in the Third Way argument (*ST* I.2.3): the intrusive 'semper' in the printed texts; but that was probably an exchange by letter.[19] It seems likely that the relationship between Mascall and White never went beyond formal scholarly contacts over such matters of detail. Mascall was a shy man; and perhaps the Dominicans at the time were somewhat in awe of what appeared then as the Anglican redoubt of Christ Church, where he lived. There seems, anyway, to have been no venue where Mascall and White could have teased out their very different understandings of Aquinas's doctrine of God. And, lamentable as it seems in retrospect, Mascall was never invited to deliver the annual Aquinas Lecture at Blackfriars, Oxford.[20]

The second (1966) edition of *He Who Is* discloses Mascall's unhappiness with White's apophatic reading of Aquinas. He refers in the Appendix to the first three chapters of *God the Unknown*, including the paper which Preller cites.[21] What Mascall picks out, however, is White's remark in the third chapter, 'Talk about God', to the effect that, despite himself perhaps, Karl Barth agrees with Aquinas in contending that while God is personal, he is 'personal in an *incomprehensible* way, in so far as the conception of his personality surpasses all our views of personality' (*God the Unknown*, p. 32).

In the original (1943) version of *He Who Is* Mascall inveighs strongly against theologians of the 'neo-Protestant' school, the 'irrationalism' of the 'neo-Calvinists' who contend that 'the only knowledge of God that man can have – or, at any rate, the only knowledge of him that will not be hopelessly perverted and distorted – is given to us by the deliberate and unilateral action of God in Jesus Christ, and that man is an entirely passive recipient of it, accepting it by a pure act of faith as something which his own powers are totally inadequate to approach' (*He Who Is*, p. 23). He cites Karl Barth's Gifford Lectures,

The Knowledge of God and the Service of God, disapprovingly – the very text that White quotes in support of his claim that Barth is closer to Aquinas's position than Barth thinks.

Mascall, like most commentators in the 1940s writing from a Catholic perspective, fears that Barth denigrates reason and indeed human beings altogether. Over against this Mascall insists: 'all truth is ultimately from God, and something more needs to be said than that in comparison with the action of God, the acts of man are as nothing. It is that, man and his natural powers being themselves the work of God, there must be an organic relation between what man can find out about God and what only God can make known to him' (*He Who Is*, p. 25). It is for this reason, Mascall notes, that 'Catholic theology has distinguished between the sciences of natural and revealed theology, and has also maintained that the two are intimately connected'.

In support, Mascall here cites Maritain, Gilson, and Sertillanges. Whatever the differences among them, these Thomists appeal to the axiom that 'grace perfects nature', in the sense that 'grace not only supplies perfections that lie above the level of nature, but also restores nature to its own proper integrity: *gratia* is not only *elevans* but *sanans* too'. The implication of this is that, 'while in principle there is a certain limited knowledge of God which is accessible to the human reason as such, in practice it is only in the light of revelation that the human reason can function adequately and obtain, even within its own proper limits, a knowledge of God which is free from error'. That is to say: 'Natural and revealed theology are thus in the abstract autonomous, being concerned respectively with the sphere of reason and nature and with the sphere of revelation and grace, but in the concrete a true natural theology can only be developed in the light of the Christian revelation.' Finally, Mascall cites Gilson, writing of 'those rational truths . . . which did not enter philosophy by way of reason' – specifically, as Mascall soon mentions, the conception of God in terms of *being*, the metaphysical theism which Gilson saw as originating in God's self-revelation to Moses at the burning bush (*He Who Is*, p. 25).

Mascall returns to the assault against Barth, quoting Maritain and, more mischievously, Gilson: 'God speaks, says Barth, and man listens and repeats what God has said. But unfortunately, as is inevitable as soon as a man makes himself God's interpreter, God speaks and the Barthian listens and repeats what Barth has said.'[22] Such views of Barth may still be found today. It is not surprising that Mascall should endorse them in 1943. By 1966, however, in the Introductory Essay of the revised edition of *He Who Is*, he notes work by Roman Catholics which is quite positive about Barth – though he still cannot accept Victor White's apophatic Thomism.

By the 1960s a number of Roman Catholic scholars were engaged in reconsidering various issues in the light of Barth's theology. Hans Urs von Balthasar's book on Barth came first, as early as 1951, containing discussion of analogical discourse about God; but Mascall seems unaware of it (the first English translation dates from 1971). As already noted, Victor Preller cites Battista Mondin's rejection of the standard Thomist accounts of Aquinas's supposed doctrine of analogy (*Divine Science*, p. 170). While endorsing Mondin's view, albeit describing it as 'in some respects the less valuable as being the more common', Mascall regards his discussion of analogical predication in Protestant theology as 'specially interesting' (*He Who Is*, p. xv).

Mondin discusses Luther, Calvin, Kierkegaard, and Tillich, among others, and of course Barth, in connection with Aquinas. Mascall quotes him as follows: 'Barth is understood to give such priority to grace as to make nature just an instrument of grace. Apart from grace, nature is meaningless. . . . Aquinas, on the other hand, is understood to stress the consistency of creature and its self-sufficiency in such a fashion that its relation to grace is purely accidental. Nature has ontological priority over grace, it can exist and be known apart from grace' (Mascall, *He Who Is*, p. xvii – citing Mondin, *Principle of Analogy*, p. 171). These are both caricatures, Mondin contends:

Actually neither Aquinas nor Barth maintains the rigid views described above. Barth knows that such an extreme supernatural-ism is impossible. He knows that without some connection between nature and grace, man would not be able to recognize that grace has any meaning for him. . . . As to Aquinas, he knows that in the present historical situation, nature and grace are inseparable. He knows that nature is not an end in itself, but is subordinated to grace as to its superior end. He knows that true knowledge of nature comes from grace. (Mascall, *He Who Is*, pp. xvii–xviii – Mondin, *Principle of Analogy*, p. 171)

In short, by 1966 Mascall is happy to cite Mondin's 'remarkably ironical conclusion'. While recognizing that Barth and Aquinas differ in emphasis, Mondin writes that 'instead of maintaining two conflicting doctrines, Aquinas and Barth simply emphasize different aspects of the same reality. . . . In the description of the God–creature relationship Aquinas's and Barth's views are much closer than in the interpretation of the meaning of theological language' (Mascall, *He Who Is*, p. xviii – Mondin, *Principle of Analogy*, p. 171). Mascall concludes this part of his Introductory Essay by citing a throwaway line by Herbert McCabe to the effect that, in his opinion, 'too much has been made of St Thomas's alleged teaching on analogy'.[23]

5. Real knowledge of God in this life

Whether Mondin's comparison of Barth and Aquinas would have modified Mascall's suspicions of Victor White's remarks seems doubtful. In the end, Mascall wants 'a real knowledge of God in this life' (*He Who Is*, p. 226), which on White's view Aquinas did not admit.

Victor White's 'Talk about God' is devoted to the use of analogical predication in theology. This is how theologians steer 'between the Scylla of agnosticism and the Charybdis of anthropomorphism' (*God the Unknown*, p. 26). He recapitulates familiar points in Aquinas's discussion, focusing principally on 'the philosophical absurdity', the 'theological blasphemy', of 'putting God in a category'. God cannot be even the highest specimen of the class of existents (cf. *ST* I.3.5).

'There are many more or less frank evasions of the problem,' White says. First, there is straightforward agnosticism: 'if God there be, then from the very nature of things we can know nothing and say nothing about him'. Second, there is quasi-agnosticism ('rightly or wrongly associated with oriental mysticisms'): 'the only thing we can know about God is that we know nothing about him, that we can progress in the knowledge of him only by ridding our minds of all human ideas until they become what can only be called a sheer blank'. Third, there are various symbolist theories: 'any attribute we apply to God is necessarily an anthropomorphism, and taken in its inherent meaning, is false as applied to him'. Fourth, there are medieval-scholastic theories: 'these divine attributes do not really and strictly apply to God, but only mean that God is the *cause* of those qualities in his creatures'. Fifth, coming to Barth, White understands him to mean that 'we may apply to God only those terms explicitly applied to him in Scripture, without seeking to justify them rationally'. Here, as we have seen above, White believes that Barth's practice belies and is 'sounder' than his theory. According to White, Barth would agree with Aquinas that God is 'personal in an *incomprehensible* way, in so far as the conception of his personality surpasses all our views of personality' (*God the Unknown*, p. 32).

White cites Barth's claim that 'the Thomist employment of analogy' is 'almost the mark of antichrist' (*God the Unknown*, p. 28). So far as he can see, however, Barth confused Aquinas's use of analogy with Erich Przywara's 'speculations regarding the *analogia entis*' (*God the Unknown*, p. 33).[24] In support, White quotes Aelred Graham, the Ampleforth Benedictine scholar, from as far back as 1935, clearly stating that Przywara's position, whatever its merits, is 'peculiar to himself' and in no way a satisfactory lens through which to read Aquinas on analogy.[25] White's chief interest – his 'only purpose' – in his paper is, however, to indicate what 'the Thomist theory of analogy' actually '*claims* to do for the theologian': that is to say, to suggest 'just how much, and just how little, the Thomist theologian claims for his affirmations about God' (*God the Unknown*, p. 32).[26]

White concludes his paper much too rapidly, saying no more than this: 'The doctrine of analogy itself makes the Thomist acutely conscious of his ignorance of God, it might almost be said of his agnosticism; but it is, as Père Penido, O.P., has said, an "enlightened ignorance," "an agnosticism from excess of light."'[27] In other words, White is surely saying that the grand claims most Thomists would make about the knowledge of the divine nature obtainable by analogical predication have to be abandoned – but unfortunately he does not spell out 'just how much' we may expect from Aquinas's resort to analogical predication in what may be affirmed about God. As his trump card, however, White cites the passage we noted above, where Barth recognizes the applicability of analogy in discourse about God, allows 'some possibility of a relationship between the creature and the Creator inherent in the creature as such', and is thus not after all on the other side of a 'gulf' from Catholic theology (*God the Unknown*, p. 32).

Mascall dislikes the general tenor of White's remarks. He agrees that we know that the God whose proper name is 'He Who Is' exists (*Deum esse*): 'we know this from our consideration of finite beings' (the Five Ways). 'But how much does this tell us about him? What content of *Ipsum esse* does it disclose to us?' (*He Who Is*, p. 225). Our knowledge of God in this life is only knowledge of what God is *not* – but Mascall wants to know 'the extent to which St Thomas thought this knowledge *de Deo quid non sit* covers'. About this, he says, Aquinas's interpreters 'differ very greatly'. And here he cites Victor White and Jacques Maritain as contrasting examples. So far as Mascall is concerned, evidently even in the Five Ways, without advancing deep into the questions about divine simplicity, goodness, infinity, and so forth, Aquinas believes that the discussion discloses some 'content' to the identification of God as 'Being itself'.

For Victor White, Mascall says, what is included in our knowledge of what God is not – its 'content' – is 'very small indeed'. As we saw above, White would surely have insisted that this knowledge is not just 'very small indeed' but actually non-existent. Worse still, this alleged knowledge would already be verging on the 'non-quidditative' knowledge of God which White regards as 'vague, incomplete, or inadequate' – the view of the self-styled Thomists which agree that while for Aquinas there is no 'quidditative' knowledge of the divine nature in this life, there is nevertheless some worthwhile 'non-quidditative' knowledge. We have no possibility of attaining or being granted positive knowledge of the divine nature in this life: all the interpreters agree that this is what Aquinas maintains. Whether this means, as Sertillanges famously asserted, that 'We do not know God *in any way, in any thing, in any degree*' is another matter.[28] Preller and White are clearly attracted by this apophaticism; Mascall is not.

Mascall cites a remarkable passage from Maritain:

the divine nature is not known to us in itself, agreed – yet 'it communicates a created participation of itself to what is not itself –

that word "participation" expresses in the ontological order the same thing expressed by the word "analogy" in the noetic order. . . . The Divine Nature remains veiled, not revealed, to our metaphysical gaze. It is not objectivised according to what it is in itself. And yet, thanks to ananoetic intellection, it is constituted the object of an absolutely stable knowledge, of a science which contemplates, and delineates in it, determinations which imply negation only in our mode of conceiving.' (*He Who Is*, p. 225, citing Maritain, *The Degrees of Knowledge* (London: Geoffrey Bles, 1959); the French original came out in 1932)

Seeming not to baulk at how high the seas of language run there, Mascall observes that Maritain is 'nearer the truth' than White as regards knowledge of God.

Recalling the doctrine of creation 'as Christianity understands it', Mascall insists that since 'God is the direct cause of everything that a creature has and is, to know God "in his effects" is to know him in a very close and intimate way'. After all, he says, 'Aquinas goes on to deduce a very large number of facts about God once he has proved that God exists.' In any case, 'it is extremely difficult to draw a sharp line between what we know by reason and what we know by grace, since the two are in practice normally concurrent and co-operative'. Grace is experienced, Mascall notes, primarily by the 'knowledge of connaturality, or *per modum inclinationis*, which is "felt" rather than reasoned about' (referring us to *ST* I.1.6 ad 3 and again to Maritain).

But, Mascall contends, even if we set aside whatever contribution grace may be making, although we can know God (whether by nature or grace) only through his effects, 'this knowledge need by no means be trivial or sketchy'. On the contrary, because Aquinas's theology is 'rooted in the act of being which is analogically common to God and his creatures', we have access to 'a process by which we can transform the *via negativa* into the *via eminentiae* and, without trying to escape our creaturely status, can achieve a real knowledge of God in this life' (*He Who Is*, p. 226).

White's claim, in connection with what he says about Barth, to the effect that there is 'some possibility of a relationship between the creature and the Creator inherent in the creature as such' (*God the*

Unknown, p. 32), is surely a claim that Barth would vehemently have rejected ('inherent in the creature as such'!). On the other hand, if White means something like Mascall's assertion that Aquinas's talk of God is 'rooted in the act of being which is analogically common to God and his creatures', then White is surely much closer than he thinks to Mascall and indeed to the Thomists who believe in the possibility of real – though of course not quidditative – knowledge of God in this life. Preller, by comparison, goes all the way with Sertillanges: 'In this life God is and remains *ignotum*' (*Divine Science*, p. 265).

There is a direct connection, Mascall argues, citing Maritain once again, between the fact that we can talk about God using language analogically and the fact of our ontological dependence upon God in the real metaphysical order. In short: 'if we experience finite beings as they really are we experience them as God's creatures and so we mediately experience him, not, of course, *sub ratione deitatis* but *sub ratione creatoris*, as the loving Creator of both them and us' (*He Who Is*, p. 226).

We have no experience of God as God, Mascall is saying; but we do have experience of God as Creator, mediately in the created. Mascall has slipped from 'knowledge' to 'experience', which would need some discussion; but we may say that, on his reading, while Aquinas denies that we have knowledge of the divine essence or nature in this life, he allows a mediated knowledge of God as Creator (and *a fortiori*, no doubt, as Redeemer).

6. Conclusion

The most generous review of Victor Preller's book, by Sr Louise-Marie Antoniotti, appeared in the most eminent of all Thomist journals – *Revue Thomiste*.[29] As is customary in that journal, most of her review is given over to a summary of the argument, but she concludes approvingly with an extension of the above quotation from Preller: 'In this life God is and remains *ignotum* – the Unknown God whom we cannot grasp or control in terms of the forms of intelligibility created by our intellects' (*Divine Science*, p. 265).

In her critical reflections on the book, Antoniotti expresses gratitude for the way in which Preller has 'resituated St Thomas in the tradition of the great contemplatives, St Augustine and the Pseudo-Denys'. She cites the lengthy quotation from Aquinas's Commentary on the *Sentences* with which Preller's book concludes (*Sent.* 1.7.1.1):

> When we proceed toward God by the way of remotion (*remotio*), we first deny of him anything corporeal; and then we even deny of him anything intellectual, in the sense that it may be found in creatures, such as 'greatness' and 'wisdom'; and then there remains in our minds only that God *is*, and nothing more; so he exists as it were [for us] quite bewilderingly (*in quadam confusione*). Lastly, however, we remove from God even this 'being' itself (*hoc ipsum esse*), as that is found in creatures; and then God remains in a kind of darkness of unknowing (*in quadam tenebra ignorantiae*), the unknowing in which, as regards the state of this life, we are most conjoined to God – as Denys says, this is the cloud (*caligo*) in which God is said to dwell.

Here Sertillanges, White, and Preller would all converge: the knowledge of God in this life can at most be 'an enlightened ignorance', in the phrase White quotes from Penido. As Aquinas says, 'we cannot know the essence of God in this life as it is in itself' (*essentiam Dei in hac vita cognoscere non possumus, secundum quod in se est*). But that is only half the sentence, the rest of which reads 'but we know it [the divine nature or quiddity] to the extent that it is represented in creaturely perfections' (*sed cognoscimus eam secundum quod repraesentatur in perfectionibus creaturarum – ST* I.13.2 ad 3).

Victor Preller, Antoniotti says, centres his book on the epistemological status of a knowledge which takes God as its object. This explains why she thinks he neglects a complementary truth. She cites the following 'particularly dense' passage from Aquinas's *De Veritate* (18.1 ad 1): 'It is clear that fallen man, to see God, needs a threefold medium: the created itself (*creatura*), from which we ascend into divine knowledge (*in divinam cognitionem*); secondly, the image of God which we receive from the created; and thirdly, the light in which we are perfected for being directed toward God, either the natural light of reason or the light of grace, that is of faith and wisdom.'

Antoniotti's point is that Preller attends only to this third condition. She wishes he had noticed that Aquinas includes, in our approach to God, the mediation, not only of the 'light', but also of the image of God which creatures bear in themselves (the second condition), as well as the world itself, from which we ascend into knowledge of God (the first condition). Aquinas, she argues, recognizes the capacity of our minds to have a certain *cognitio divina* as we come to see the likeness of God in the created order. In effect, the world itself offers a certain knowledge of God: albeit we are indeed directed toward God by the 'light' of nature as well as of grace, the light of reason as well as the light of faith and wisdom.

Victor Preller, as well as Victor White, not to mention Père Sertillanges, insist so strongly on the famous statements by Thomas Aquinas according to which we know what God is *not*, but not what God *is*, that they play down his equally plain statements that we can know something about God by reflecting on the world which is God's doing. Antoniotti treats Preller's book like a glass that is half full, Mascall as if it were half empty; but they would both agree that, for Aquinas, the world tells us a good deal about the God 'to whom we are united as the Unknown' (*ST* I.12.13 ad 1).

Notes

1. Eric Lionel Mascall (1905–93), an Anglican priest of the Oratory of the Good Shepherd; taught at Lincoln Theological College 1937–45; and Christ Church, University of Oxford 1945–62; Professor of Historical Theology at King's College, the University of London 1962–72; published among much else *He Who Is: A Study in Traditional Theism* (London: Longmans, Green, 1943; rev. edn London: Darton, Longman & Todd, 1966); *Existence and Analogy* (London: Longmans, Green 1949); *The Openness of Being: Natural Theology Today*, Edinburgh Gifford Lectures 1970–1 (London: Darton, Longman & Todd, 1971); as well as his autobiography, *Saraband: The Memoirs* (Leominster: Gracewing, 1992).

2. *Theology* 71 (1968): 467–8.

3. Huw Parry Owen (1926–96), Professor of Christian Doctrine at King's College, London; published *Revelation and Existence: A Study in the Theology of Rudolf Bultmann* (Cardiff: University of Wales Press, 1957); *The Christian Knowledge of God* (London: Athlone Press, 1969); *Concepts of Deity* (London: Macmillan, 1971); *Christian Theism: A Study in Basic Principles* (Edinburgh: T. & T. Clark, 1984).

4. Victor Preller, *Divine Science and the Science of God: A Reformulation of Thomas Aquinas* (Princeton: Princeton University Press, 1967).

5. According to Anthony Kenny, the collapse of Thomism by 1968 had cleared the way for philosophers in the analytic tradition to read Aquinas for themselves; see his *Aquinas* (Oxford: Oxford University Press, 1980), p. 28: 'Since the Second Vatican Council Aquinas seems to have lost something of the pre-eminent favour he enjoyed in ecclesiastical circles, and to have been superseded, in the reading-lists of ordinands, by fashionable authors judged more relevant to the contemporary scene.'

6. Battista Mondin, *The Principle of Analogy in Protestant and Catholic Theology* (The Hague: Martinus Nijhoff, 1963); Ralph McInerny, *The Logic of Analogy* (The Hague: Martinus Nijhoff, 1961); and Hampus Lyttkens, *The Analogy Between God and the World* (Uppsala: Almquist, 1952).

7. Thomas de Vio (1469–1534), born in Gaeta, hence Gaetano/Cajetan, Dominican friar, Master of the Order of Preachers, delivered fiery address in 1512 at the Fourth Lateran Council demanding extensive church reform; named Cardinal in 1517 and sent by Pope Leo X to reason with Martin Luther, unfruitfully; but set aside his massive commentary on Aquinas's *Summa Theologiae*, composed between 1507 and 1520, to concentrate on biblical studies; nevertheless the critical (Leonine) edition of the *Summa*, inaugurated in 1888, is accompanied throughout by Cajetan's commentary, a straightforward attempt to provide the correct hermeneutic.

8. Réginald Garrigou-Lagrange (1877–1964), trained at Le Saulchoir (then in Belgium) but for fifty years the leading Dominican theologian in Rome, with influential books in philosophy and spirituality as well as dogmatic theology, very much in the tradition of Cajetan; supervised Karol Wojtyla's doctorate on Aquinas and St John of the Cross; among the first to attack *la Nouvelle Théologie*, indeed coining the phrase: Henri de Lubac, Jean Daniélou, Karl Rahner, Hans Urs von Balthasar, and many others.

9. By 'Neo-Thomists' Preller probably meant the Louvain University school (as distinct from the Louvain Jesuits); by 'Paleo-Thomists' he undoubtedly meant (supposedly) literal expositors like Garrigou-Lagrange.

10. Antonin Dalmace Sertillanges (1863–1948), French Dominican friar, taught at Le Saulchoir 1929–39 but mostly in Paris; prolific writer, best known for his interpretation of Aquinas's doctrine of creation and especially his radically apophatic interpretation of Aquinas's theology of God. And Joseph Maréchal (1878–1944) was a Belgian Jesuit who spent most of his life at Louvain; trained as a psychologist; a student of religious experience and mysticism; composed *Le point de départ de la métaphysique* in five *cahiers* of which the fifth (1926) seeks to rethink Aquinas's epistemology in light of Kantian transcendental philosophy, hence Transcendental Thomism. In the Select Bibliography, Preller lists a book by Stanislas Breton which owes a good deal to Husserlian phenomenology, the two relevant books by Rahner which show some influence of Heidegger, and articles by Maurice Corvez and Cornelio Fabro, auguries of the much more explicit post-Heideggerian study of Aquinas which would engage them later. But there is

something odd about this list. It must have been obvious to Preller that Sertillanges was completely at variance with Rahner and whoever else he had in mind as 'continental theologians' engaged in re-reading Aquinas in the light of 'phenomenology or existentialism'. Indeed, in another footnote, he instances 'Père Sertillanges and the followers of Maréchal' as holding quite different interpretations of an important point in Aquinas's epistemology from 'all the "traditional" commentators' (*Divine Science*, p. 42, n. 18). Here, clearly, he sees the radical difference between Sertillanges and the Maréchalian or Transcendental Thomists, but also, rightly, the equally radical difference between them and 'traditional commentators' and 'Paleo-Thomists' such as Garrigou-Lagrange.

11. Henry Gordon Victor White (1902–60), English Dominican, taught dogmatic and moral theology at Blackfriars, Oxford, 1930–54; died of cancer; important correspondence with C. G. Jung; published three books: *God and the Unconscious* (London: Harvill Press, 1952); *God the Unknown and Other Essays* (London: Harvill Press, 1956); and *Soul and Psyche: An Enquiry into the Relationship of Psychotherapy and Religion* (London: Harvill Press, 1960).

12. White, *God the Unknown and Other Essays*, p. 16.

13. White says: '*causa* is St Thomas's word, but this does not of course mean "cause" in the restricted sense in which it is used in modern science', a message still by no means accepted by many readers.

14. John Macquarrie, *Twentieth-Century Religious Thought* (first published 1963; London: SCM Press, 2001), p. 290. Austin Marsden Farrer (1904–68) spent most of his career in Oxford: Chaplain and Tutor at St Edmund Hall 1931–5; Chaplain and Fellow of Trinity College 1935–60; and seventh Warden of Keble College from 1960 until his death. His most important work in the philosophy of religion was *Finite and Infinite* (Westminster: Dacre, 1943).

15. Macquarrie, *Twentieth-Century Religious Thought*, p. 386.

16. Joseph Maréchal and his followers: see n. 10 above.

17. Etienne Gilson (1884–1978), French Catholic layman, medievalist, utterly opposed to Cajetanian Thomism as well as Transcendental Thomism; his reading of Aquinas as the discoverer of God as 'act of being' in the light of God's self-revelation to Moses at the burning bush (Exod. 3.14) is traceable in the revisions of *Le Thomisme* (1919 and onwards).

18. Jacques Maritain (1882–1973), French Catholic layman, continued the tradition of Cajetan, and the other sixteenth-century Thomist commentators.

19. *He Who Is*, p. 47. The pagination of 1943 is retained in the 1966 edition, expanded by an Introductory Essay and a substantial Appendix.

20. Mascall was, however, delighted at being invited by the American Dominicans in 1974 to take part in the 700th anniversary celebrations of Aquinas's death: see *Saraband*, pp. 333–4.

21. *He Who Is*, p. 224.

22. Gilson, *Christianisme et philosophie* (Paris: Vrin, 1936), p. 151. Cited by Mascall in *He Who Is*, p. 28.

23. Herbert McCabe (1926–2001), studied chemistry then philosophy at Manchester, where he was taught by Dorothy Emmett; entered the Order of

Preachers in 1949; studied theology with Victor White; edited *New Blackfriars* from 1964 to 1979 (apart from a three-year gap); taught Aquinas at Blackfriars, Oxford, from 1968 until his death; wrote *Law, Love and Language* (London and Sydney: Sheed & Ward, 1968; due for reissue with a preface by Stanley Hauerwas); *God Matters* (London: Geoffrey Chapman, 1987); *God Still Matters* (London and New York: Continuum, 2002); volume of sermons forthcoming. The quotation to which Mascall refers is from 'Knowing and Naming God' (Blackfriars Summa Theologiae, vol. 3, London and New York, 1964), p. 106. Mascall devotes the rest of this Introductory Essay to suggesting that, 'with splendid works' by John Meyendorff and Vladimir Lossky, it is clear that Gregory Palamas's doctrine of the divine energies has 'little in common' with the 'sophiology of the Bulgakovian school', which means, Mascall thinks, that it would have not surpassed 'Thomas's ingenuity to reconcile Gregory's doctrine of the divine energies with his own conviction of the divine simplicity' (p. xviii). In short, Gregory Palamas and Thomas Aquinas have 'a great deal in common'.

24. Erich Przywara (1889–1972), Polish/German Jesuit theologian, whose highly creative, not to say idiosyncratic conception of *analogia entis* as the fundamental form of Catholicism seems to have fascinated Karl Barth; his *Polarity: A German Catholic's Interpretation of Religion*, trans. A. C. Bouquet (Oxford: Oxford University Press, 1935) made a considerable impression in British theological circles during the pre-war years. (Mascall calls it 'this difficult but most illuminating book', *He Who Is*, p. 126, n. 3.)

25. See Aelred Graham, 'A Catholic Interpretation of Religion', *Blackfriars* (October 1935): 746ff.

26. Herbert McCabe was among Victor White's best students, but White was dead before McCabe published his dismissive remark about 'St Thomas's alleged teaching on analogy'.

27. Despite the 'O.P.' appellation in White's quote, Maurilio T. L. Penido, who taught at Fribourg, was not a Dominican. His *Le rôle de l'analogie dans la théologie dogmatique* (Paris: Vrin, 1931) – 'perhaps the best exposition', according to Mascall – is a great book for sure, but basically in line with Cajetan, very hostile to Sertillanges's apophatic interpretation of Aquinas (see pp. 170–1).

28. A. D. Sertillanges, *Agnosticisme ou Anthropomorphisme* (Paris: Bloud, 1908), p. 60.

29. *Revue Thomiste* 69 (1969): 651–6.

5. Religious Life and Understanding

Grammar Exercised in Practice

DAVID B. BURRELL, CSC

Introduction

To gain some perspective on Victor Preller's contribution to my quest for understanding how to execute philosophical theology, I revisited a piece published in 1969, entitled 'Religious Life and Understanding', where I had attempted to show how his linguistic recasting of Aquinas's venture to understand matters divine could help us recover the assistance of that master in seeking to understand such things ourselves.[1] In this essay, composed at a time when *hermeneutics* was the rage, I wanted to show how Victor Preller's re-reading of Aquinas offered us a way to render him contemporary, and especially (at that time) to expose the construction of 'classical theism' as an egregious anachronism. By employing linguistic tools constructively to show how Aquinas could never have been a 'Thomist', these efforts helped us all recover an Aquinas deftly engaged in the paradoxical effort to say something about that One 'when all of our affirmations have the effect of signifying *to us* how God is *not*'.[2] Engaging in that effort would demand an extraordinary degree of semantic sophistication, and it may have seemed improbable to some that a 'pre-modern' like Aquinas could have mastered such delicate manoeuvres. Yet as I sought to exploit these semantic moves in my exposition *Aquinas: God and Action*, the work of Marie-Dominique Chenu showed clearly how twelfth-century work on the senses of Scripture had prepared Aquinas to move adroitly among various uses of language.[3] Even though he seldom adverted explicitly to differences in linguistic usage, Aquinas's capacity to exploit them displayed his grasp of the semantic structures at work. In short, Victor Preller's sustained efforts not only helped us re-read Aquinas, as he had, but allowed us to apprentice ourselves to Aquinas as a working master, for we could then recognize him grappling with issues which baffled us, and doing so with semantic tools as sophisticated as our own.

What Preller's work helped me to deconstruct was the neat division between 'philosophy' and 'theology' which had indeed fuelled the Thomist revival during the twentieth century, for he argued that the affirmations in *Summa Theologiae* I.3–26 are vacuous when regarded as philosophical assertions; yet Aquinas is within his rights to assert them in the *theological* context in which he does.[4] We are misled, then, only when we fail to recognize that Aquinas's project is explicitly theological, and doubly misled if we expect philosophy to do more than he himself demanded of it. We must call upon all the philosophical skill we can muster to display the semantics of faith-statements, but we still need faith to assert them. The key lies in his reading of question 2, the schemata for 'proving' God's existence, which have always suggested that Aquinas expected too much from reason. Preller helps us to see the way Aquinas pushes each schema – motion, contingency, order, and the rest – beyond the question at issue to broach the existential one, as if to say: if there were a God (which I believe there is) our way of introducing that One would be as the explanation for anything's existing. Yet the fact that something exists normally imposes itself on us; it is hardly the result of explication. So an enquiry seeking to explain things' existing must escape standard paradigms for *explanation*, so what explains their existing will not itself exist in the same fashion.[5] Yet for all the oddities of this move, we are able to expose its logic:

> Thus, to say that God 'exists' is to say that there is another conceptual system (an ideal language) in terms of which a syntactical move isomorphic in usage with our syntactically significant existential assertion ('_____') could be used in conjunction with an entity radically unlike the entities which are existentially assertable in our language. . . . If our analysis of the essentially analogous status of 'exists' was correct, we could know that the word could in theory have uses other than those which are significant in terms of our

conceptual system. To say that God 'exists' in some unknown sense of the word is not necessarily irrational.[6]

Thus far can logic carry us; though the assertion itself must needs be one of faith.

Practising praise: Preller, Hadot, and Pickstock

A useful way to celebrate my appreciation of this early guidance, so as to track the intervening thirty years, is to utilize the work of Pierre Hadot to move us a step further to scrutinize the kind of practice required to put such astute use of language at the service of faith.[7] Largely implicit in Preller's seminal work, to which he referred as the 'green and yellow monster', the role of practices would become clearer to Preller himself as his own life took the turns it did; so focusing on such practices here should help us flesh out the implications which close attention to grammar can have in our lives. My mother's heartfelt endorsement of Ezra Pound's dictum – 'when language corrupts crime abounds' – may well have prepared me to recognize how demanding a practice it is to use properly grammatical speech: what Wittgenstein displayed as the normativity proper to language. Indeed, when we focus on that role of language proper to expressing how things are, it becomes clear how proper discourse already embodies a form of life with taxing demands. For it will not permit us to shape the world to our words, as our own desires so yearn to do. So executing properly grammatical statements not only requires 'spiritual exercises', to adopt Pierre Hadot's way of characterizing philosophy itself, but will itself be such an exercise.[8] Moreover, as my own experience has revealed (and Hadot's extensive work must have corroborated for him), the activity of translating puts the disciplines needed for proper grammatical use to the severest possible test.[9] Yet daring to make assertions of faith can be more taxing still.

But how can that be, if pastors are called upon to do just that every week, while Eucharistic presiders may do so even daily? The telling response would be to ask those who must listen, to see whether they are nourished or not by what has been enunciated. Another tack would be to ask pastors how they prepare for this appointed task.

Certainly those who realize just how daunting the commission is will have spent time reflecting on their own incapacity to say anything properly, and that reflective moment could well add the key note of 'unknowing' to their words which might make them credible. This is a sample of the kind of practice which will invariably accompany a personal appropriation of Aquinas's distinction between 'thing signified' and 'manner of signifying' which attends any use of human language for God (*ST* I.13.3). That is, the way we employ expressions from our language, like 'compassionate', to address or to speak of God, will invariably connote our 'manner of signifying'. So we must offer some signal to remind ourselves and others that we are not using these expressions as they ought to be used when God is the 'thing [we intend] to signify'. Indeed, that is a use which we can never claim to have mastered! The practices we have adopted should allow us to signal that we appreciate just how improperly we are speaking in such matters; yet, as should be clear, such practices will not simply be called for in preparing sermons, but will have to be engaged any time we call upon God, either in prayer or in attempting to interpret our lives.

Yet how can we identify such practices? Liturgy comes immediately to mind, of course, though each of our traditions – speaking now of the Abrahamic faiths – will find itself layered with diverse liturgical practices. Yet that remains the challenge of participating in any tradition: to sort out what is best and allow oneself to be formed by it. We are never dispensed from critical appropriation. My guide here is Catherine Pickstock, in her memorable and ground-breaking probe, *After Writing*, where she displays at once how philosophical awareness provides the necessary basis for effective liturgy, while liturgical practice supplies the *telos* needed for philosophical enquiry.[10] (It is quite doubtful whether Preller himself would have espoused her way of proceeding, employing the highly intellectualist view of modern history that it does, yet in the space he opened up, conversation will ensue with quite disparate interlocutors.) Writing in an expressly 'postmodern' milieu, she shows how bereft philosophy can become when it no longer serves a transcendent *telos*. Indeed, without exercising that capacity for praise, to which we humans aspire but into which we must be initiated, the constructed 'objects' of Cartesian topography will conspire with the vanishing 'subject' of modernity to lead us into the wasteland of postmodernity, where discourse can only subserve power. In an extended argument reminiscent of George Steiner's *Real Presences* (London: Faber and Faber, 1989), we are reminded that discourse can only be meaningful if it has a point; yet since we are incapable of fabricating that point (out of nothing), such a point can only be assured by an originating act which gives our actions their point. For George Steiner, we cannot be creators without a creator; for Catherine Pickstock, we need the pedagogy of divine liturgy to keep us aware of our creaturely presence to that creator. Without that quality of awareness, cultivated through liturgical performance, discourse cannot but be pointless, as Jacques Derrida (the high priest of post-modernism) and others poignantly remind us. In the alternative sketched here, however, Pickstock maintains that liturgy offers philosophy its consummation by providing us with a school of praise. Yet liturgy is not so much a fact as it is a performance, so those performing it will have to become conscious of the specific ways in which the language we employ has been debased, lest using that same language deprive faithful worshippers of the very resources of the liturgy itself.

The thirty years separating Catherine Pickstock from Victor Preller, most notably the challenge to discourse issued in the name of 'post-modernity', will force her to articulate what he could let remain implicit: the loss endemic to the very semantic turn which he espoused and encouraged, once 'epistemology' succeeds in dominating the scene. What she identifies as 'the Cartesian fulfillment of ontology in epistemology [will inaugurate] an immanentist construal of reality as the "given", [which will give rise] to the possibility of an object' (p. 57). That is, 'objects, whose "being" does not exceed the extent to which they are known. Representation is now prior to ontology' (p. 63). Yet this strategic move effectively 'assumes a prior ontology which, by defining being as the unvarying, clear, and distinct, subordinates it to the measure of the knowing subject, and finally places its objectivity in doubt. But this new ontology . . . consummates a movement which separates being from its donating source by taking Being to be, first of all, not the divine *gift* of a participation in a plenitude of infinite actuality, but rather the mere inert *given* of a contentless "notion" of existence univocally common to the finite and the infinite' (p. 64).

Here Descartes capitalizes on a legacy from Duns Scotus, as we shall see, but radicalizes it by reducing a univocal 'being' to 'objects [which] subsist only within the abstract realm of mathematics' (p. 65). 'Spatialized' in this way, 'the given is no longer in excess of what can be known by means of method' and is even 'denuded of [its] corporeality by being purely an epistemological projection' (p. 65). Noting this paradoxical result leads the author to show us 'how the Cartesian object is contradictory insofar as it is purportedly part of physical *extensio* and yet its materiality is seen to be reducible to immanentized ideality, equivalent to the *nihil*' (p. 70). It will take a postmodern retrospective to lay bare that equivalence, yet that must be the logical result of reducing 'being to the "object" whose existence does not exceed the extent to which it is known by the subject' (p. 70).

Such an unremittingly severe indictment of the language of modernity, once its syntax has been unveiled to postmodern scrutiny, can certainly be faulted for making of 'modernity' one thing, yet those of us who (like Preller) would lead students to a fresh appreciation of the power and precision of medieval semantics can testify, from student objections to even entering that world, to the abiding grip of the mindset she exposes. Moreover, the deft ways in which Catherine Pickstock exploits postmodern 'conclusions' to identify the lacunae crucial to modernity allow her to offer an antidote as well. For if 'the systematic exaltation of writing over speech has ensured within Western history the spatial obliteration of time [which] is equally a suppression of eternity, . . . time can only be affirmed through the liturgical gesture which receives time from eternity as a gift and offers it back to eternity as a sacrifice' (p. 118). And here we have the utterly simple thesis of this complex critical essay. Modern thought was expressly post-medieval in its determination to sever the ties of the universe with its creator, of time with eternity, of human being with God. Yet as history has played out the logical issue of that deliberate severance, the very reality which the creaturely side claimed for itself as autonomous withered into nothingness once it could no longer regard itself as created. So the only way to reclaim one's own reality and that of the universe is to receive it rather than claim it; indeed, to recover oneself by recognizing the creator as the gracious source of one's being, and the One to whom that being longs to return in order fully to be. This is, of course, nothing short of a reversal of the dynamic which impelled modernity beyond the medieval synthesis, yet it is a movement called for by the dialectic of history, for if 'modern' can be parsed as 'post-medieval', then 'postmodern' = 'post-(post-medieval)'. So the obverse side of the apparently perverse conclusions of postmodern thought will have to be an astute retrieval of what modernity denied.

Here is where one glimpses the necessity for analogous discourse: something which Preller's linguistic analysis presumed and expressly defended, as he pointed to ways in which our astute use of language about God must effectively display the presence of a crucial 'distinction' between the creator and creatures.[11] For if modernity had found that *distinction* unintelligible (as testified by the quite disparate counter-stances of Pascal, Kierkegaard, and Karl Barth), late medieval thought had prepared the way for its denial, specifically in John Duns Scotus's rejection of the ground of the entire medieval symbolic universe: Aquinas's analogical appreciation of creatures' participation in the very being of the creator. In properly conceptualist fashion, 'Scotus asserted the metaphysical priority of Being over both the infinite and the finite alike. Thus God is deemed "to be" in the same univocal manner as creatures, and although God is distinguished by an "intensity of being", [God] nonetheless remains within, or subordinate to the category of Being (which now becomes the sole object of metaphysics)' (p. 122). Unwittingly, however, 'Scotist univocity unmediably separates the creation from God, [as it] paradoxically gives rise to a kind of equivocity, for the difference of degree or amount of Being disallows any specific resemblance between [God and creature], and excludes the possibility of figural or analogical determinations of [God's] character' (p. 123). Furthermore, 'the abandonment of participation in Being encouraged the establishment of *contractual* relations between the creature and God. For despite an apparently pious humility, which stressed one's radical distance from God, a secret proximity to, or "covenantal bond" with the Creator, was nevertheless smuggled in. This was combined with an increased emphasis upon the sovereignty of God's will, which, because the universe had now been desymbolized, becomes the only explanation for the way things are' (p. 123).

Pickstock traces the metaphysical roots of Scotus's insistence on univocity to his denial of Aquinas's 'real distinction between existence and essence [which forms] the inner kernel of both *analogia entis* and participation because it permits essence to be realized as essence only through the Being from which it always remains distinct: essence forever simply participates in that which alone realizes and fully determines it. Thus, ontological difference invites the possibility of likeness and proximity, whereas univocity of Being produces unmediable difference and distance' (p. 129). The transition to modernity, together with its outworking into postmodernity, lies latent here; while that theoretical transition is given practical expression in the socio-political transformations of late medieval / early modern society. Indeed, it is these transitions in social life and civic society which will effect 'the historical decline of the liturgical order' (p. 140). How, then, is that order to be reclaimed in practice, so that a philosophical theology of the sort which Victor Preller envisaged can become operative? We can only point to communities which have rooted themselves in a prayer tradition, like the evening prayer of the Communità di Sant'Egidio in Santa Maria di Trastevere in Rome, or that of the Communauté de Jérusalem in Paris; or numerous monastic settings, like the Monastery of the Annunciation in Nazareth. Here one learns how to punctuate one's day and one's work regularly with a nourishing prayer, learning silence by participating in a rhythm of praise following patterns received rather than concocted. If this sounds nostalgic, it only reflects an abiding need for ways of learning how to return everything to the One from whom we have received everything. That rhythm suffuses Aquinas's architectonic work, and that imperative gives body to Victor Preller's semantic turn, which at once obscures and reveals a participatory way of being and of speaking. So I have had recourse to Catherine Pickstock's acute analysis of the transition to modernity and on to postmodernity, to glimpse how necessary such a participatory metaphysics is to executing Preller's programme. But executing that metaphysics turns out to be as much a matter of liturgical practice as it is of grammatical analysis, for that analysis – thanks to Preller – has led us to the very limits of discourse. Beyond discourse lies silence, yet the communal human mode of silence is praise.

Material moves: Rogers and Bowlin

Less provocatively, we may flesh out the legacy of Victor Preller's work by identifying contemporaries mining the veins which he identified. I shall limit myself to two who studied with him at Princeton: Eugene Rogers (as an undergraduate) and John Bowlin (as a doctoral student). In his *Thomas Aquinas and Karl Barth: Sacred Doctrine and the Natural Knowledge of God*, dedicated to Preller and reflecting the immediate guidance of George Lindbeck, Rogers seeks to delineate the precise ways in which Aquinas's work can be read as contributing to a way of doing theology which displays a rigour never displayed in a 'foundational' paradigm.[12] How better than to read the opening question of the *Summa Theologiae* on 'sacred doctrine' in dialogue with Karl Barth, to illuminate the ways in which Scripture offers the directive context for its fine conceptual outworking? Rogers's argument focuses on 'theology as *scientia*', where the Latin term must be left untranslated to avoid deadly ambiguity. Since the entire project is derivative from Aristotle, however, the task is to show why and how Aquinas needed to transform Aristotle on *scientia*. The reason Aristotle's scheme had to be transformed was the revelational fact of creation, while the manner involved trying to show how all things must then be knowable in a new way, once their intrinsic intelligibility is owed to a principle beyond them and beyond our proper ken as well. Josef Pieper had remarked how creation is the 'hidden element in the philosophy of Aquinas'; Rogers shows in illuminating detail how that faith-assertion demands that Aristotle's very conceptions of knowledge needed to be remoulded from within, for Aquinas to utilize them so skilfully. His strategy is to focus on the *sed contra*, a brief introduction to the body of the argument, often a verse from Scripture, which more philosophical Thomists had relegated to window-dressing. To watch Rogers take these key texts, and elucidate them from Aquinas's own commentaries on the scriptural book in question, is to underscore the theological context of the *Summa* in a way which also displays the author's philosophical acumen.

John Bowlin, in his recent *Contingency and Fortune in Aquinas's Ethics*,[13] is not content with a formal treatment of virtue imbedded in a 'natural law' tradition, which had been the stock-in-trade of Thomistic ethics, but moves closer to the bone in focusing on the *difficulty* of acting virtuously, and so bringing fortitude or courage to the fore. This approach to Aquinas brings out the humanness of virtue as well as the sheer contingency of human good. Aquinas will not try to escape that contingency, with its inevitable reliance on fortune. Rather than pretend to provide moral guidance, his 'remarks on the natural law [function] as a description of human agency, created by God and governed by Providence . . . [so] his treatment of the ends that we apprehend and will with nature's necessity is his account of creation and Providence as they pertain to human beings and human actions' (p. 121). Yet Aquinas never loses sight of the way in which virtues are embedded in distinct human passions, though (as the citation above notes) he will have recourse to a more formal Stoic account of virtue, derived through Augustine, which focuses on the will as such to the detriment of distinct human powers (p. 162), as a way of anticipating a freedom to which we aspire and which grace holds out to us.[14] The resulting tension marks the advent of a free creator into Aristotle's world, as Bowlin deftly displays how such a presence in no way simplifies but rather intensifies human action. One thinks of this work as displaying the legacy of Victor Preller in the way it encourages its readers to apprentice themselves to an intellect and sensibility as nuanced as Aquinas's to improve their skills in ethical analysis. To follow Bowlin's dialectical strategies of appropriation is to recapitulate Aquinas's own attempts to apprentice himself to Aristotle's sinuous analysis of human action, yet do so as a person of faith must do it, whose human goals had been transformed beyond our imagining, thereby intensifying the complexities of acting.

Conclusion

I have tried to delineate what might be called Victor Preller's legacy to students of philosophical theology. His book is at one level a narrowly focused contribution to the scholarship on Thomas. But it also raises abiding questions about the proper way to pursue theological enquiry. Rogers and Bowlin obviously carry forward Preller's interpretive enterprise in one way by showing that an approach consistent with his can be extended to other aspects of Thomas's theological writings; there is a recognizable trace of Preller in their work. One could indeed say that they have succeeded in making Preller's approach to Aquinas central to contemporary theological discussion, far beyond what Preller himself achieved in the late 1960s. Furthermore, while Pickstock goes far beyond anything Preller himself endorsed back in 1967, one can also see her work as occupying a space that his enquiry helped open up. Since his work was at once profound in its questioning of received tradition yet cryptic about what theologians should make of his conclusions, we can see Pickstock as operating in a discursive space Preller opened up, despite the disparity in temper between their modes of discourse.

Indeed, we have yet to spy the further reaches of what Preller, along with others like Victor White, set in motion several decades ago.[15] Yet by employing the work of Catherine Pickstock (as an expressly 'radical' example), as well as that of Eugene Rogers and of John Bowlin, I have tried to illuminate ways in which Victor Preller emboldened others to proceed. He encouraged us to claim for ourselves writers whose enquiry is suffused with faith, by exploring how the reaches of that faith must be limned by semantic sophistication. Blazing these trails should teach us to show how faith can be a mode of knowing; and we need only contrast that phrase with Descartes to realize how startling an assertion it is. Moreover, merely asserting that faith can be a mode of knowing alerts us to ways in which 'postmodern' and 'pre-modern' modes of enquiry can converge; while attempting to articulate the semantics of faith-statements, together with the practices required to assert them with as little distortion as possible, displays the philosophical acumen implicit in asserting them. Aquinas is unmistakably one who understood these subtle matters, as Preller showed so clearly, yet each of us can continue in that vein if we allow ourselves to benefit from an apprenticeship that is as demanding as it is fruitful.

Notes

1. *Review of Metaphysics* 22 (1969): 676–99; Preller review at 681–90.
2. *Divine Science and the Science of God* (Princeton, NJ: Princeton University Press, 1967), p. 175.
3. (London and Notre Dame, Ind.: Routledge and University of Notre Dame

Press, 1979); M.-D. Chénu, *Le théologie du douzième siecle* (Paris: Vrin, 1957).

4. See my contribution entitled 'Philosophy and Theology' in the *Cambridge Companion to Modern Theology* (Cambridge: Cambridge University Press, 2002).

5. For a contemporary look at this vexing question, see Barry Miller, *The Fullness of Being* (Notre Dame, Ind.: University of Notre Dame Press, 2002).

6. *Divine Science*, p. 173.

7. For an illuminating introduction to the work of Pierre Hadot, see Arnold Davidson's translation and collection of some key articles: *Philosophy as a Way of Life* (Chicago: University of Chicago Press, 1995).

8. See his *Exercices spirituels et philosophie antique* (Paris: Etudes Augustiniennes, 1987), and also *Qu'est-ce que la philosophie antique?* (Paris: Gallimard, 1995).

9. His *Plotinus or The simplicity of Vision*, trans. Michael Chase (Chicago: University of Chicago Press, 1993) offers the fruits of a lifetime spent rendering Plotinus into French.

10. *After Writing: On the Liturgical Consummation of Philosophy* (Oxford: Blackwell, 1998).

11. See Robert Sokolowski's crucial study of the centrality of 'the Christian distinction' for philosophical theology, in his *The God of Faith and Reason: Foundations of Christian Theology* (1st edn, Notre Dame, Ind.: University of Notre Dame Press, 1982; 2nd edn, Washington, DC: Catholic University of America Press, 1995), as well as my attempt to show its interfaith implications: 'The Christian Distinction Celebrated and Expanded', in John Drummond and James Hart (eds), *The Truthful and the Good: Essays in Honor of Robert Sokolowski* (Dordrecht and Boston: Kluwer Academic, 1996), pp. 191–206.

12. (Notre Dame, Ind.: University of Notre Dame Press, 1995.)

13. (Cambridge: Cambridge University Press, 1999.)

14. For an exploration of this Augustine-derived Stoic influence on Aquinas's ethics, see the essay by Douglas Langston in this volume. [Editors' note.]

15. For a discussion of Victor White's Thomism in relation to Preller's, see Fergus Kerr's essay in this volume. [Editors' note.]

6. The Eclipse of the Spirit in Thomas Aquinas

EUGENE F. ROGERS, JR

Aquinas is suspicious of mystical experience because it seems to displace grace with glory, and Wittgenstein is suspicious of mystical experience because it seems to displace communal with incommunicable experience. Their concerns largely overlap. I begin with a concrete case.

I

Victor Preller usually liked not so much to conceal the complications of his life from students, as to confuse us with them. I remember my great surprise, as a sophomore at Princeton in the autumn of 1981, in seeing a long, white strip of celluloid peeping out of Vic's shirt pocket. At that point I knew Vic chiefly as the teacher of a lecture-course on approaches to the study of religion, a course that struck fear into the hearts of certain conservative Christians as a 'faith-breaker', and therefore of interest to me.

'What's that?' I asked, nodding at the plastic strip.

'It's a collar,' Vic replied coyly.

'What for?' I returned.

'For celebrating the Eucharist, of course.' Vic often used some phrase such as 'of course' to indicate that he knew a student was going to be surprised, but to pay him or her the unacknowledgeable compliment of pretending that he or she could not be. Or to forestall any more questions before surprise should dissipate.

Such distancing manoeuvres as the Prelline 'of course' were conspicuous by their absence when Vic told me[1] after his bout with throat cancer that he had experienced being lifted up on the prayers of his congregation into the prayer of the Spirit that prays for those who on account of weakness do not know how to pray as they ought, with sighs and groanings too deep for words (Rom. 8.26). He described this experience as the indwelling of the Spirit, not on his own account (he was too weak, he said, to form the words of the Lord's Prayer, or even the intention to pray), but on the account of others – on account of the faith of the Church – and as a proleptic participation in the life of the Trinity, whereby the Spirit catches us up into the relationship of the Father and the Son by crying 'Abba!' on our behalf (Gal. 4.6; cf. Rom. 8.15–16). Prayer is possible because a certain bidding and graciousness and gratitude takes place already among the persons of the Trinity, and the Spirit incorporates us into that non-Maussian exchange.[2]

We did not discuss how such an experience might be articulated in the terms of the end of Preller's *Divine Science and the Science of God*, where he speaks of the intellect as being 'seized by God',[3] and beatitude as a being seized by the love of the Trinity[4] – or how that seizure makes no exception to the rule that prayer and experience happen through the 'ordinary' practices of the Church, such as teaching and preaching, since 'faith comes by what has been heard' (Rom. 10.17).[5]

Nor did we discuss how such an experience might change one's reading of Thomas Aquinas or one's use of Wittgenstein. Certainly Vic would have continued to agree that such an experience was possible (without ceasing to ascribe it to the Spirit) only on the basis of a social practice already well under way, and therefore a mental, linguistic, and bodily one, or in Thomistic terms, habit. It was Vic who first pointed out to me Thomas's suspicion of experiences of rapture, 'experiences' that, because they took the soul out of this world – out of the shared world of society and language – were *in principle* incommunicable to others and therefore of little or no use to sacred teaching in this life.[6] If Aquinas did not deny them outright, that was not only because of his high regard for Scripture, but also because he believed such 'experiences' produced nothing stably linguistic enough to merit a denial. Accordingly, Vic did not experience this being caught up as a rapture in the incommunicable sense but as something for which the community and its scriptures and practices had given him language in advance – language and experience being one integral gift – and one that depended on the community not only for its expression but also for its very existence. For it was on the prayers of his friends, whether in or abstracted from words, that the Spirit lifted him up. That Victor Preller practised the life of the Spirit already and habitually before, after, and apart from that experience; that such a life was constituted in a linguistic, communal, bodily practice, including bowing and kneeling and 'that funny bit of business on your chest'[7]; and that such a life was fleshed out in the sacraments, the collar playing hide-and-seek in his breast pocket: those features were no source of conflict with quasi-mystical experience, but prevenient and incarnate grace. They confirmed his dictum that grace, as a gift that does not violate human nature, is always habitual. Even infused grace, which does not (logically) originate in a habit, nevertheless *issues* in a habit. From Vic's experience, too, a habit emerged seemingly *de novo*: Vic said that the years after his recovery from throat cancer were filled with a sense – a habitual sense, a more or less settled, if waxing and waning disposition – of grateful delight, a delight in (for example) springtime flowers, and thus somewhat at odds with a previous sense (I might add) of burden, unease, and winking cynicism. It was as though he found himself no longer a *Preller* (in German, a fraud, cheat, humbug),[8] if not yet a victor. – Now I have just said both that this transformation of Vic's habits had roots in communal practice, and that it emerged seemingly *de novo*: how can that be? I don't think Vic would have found that much of a paradox: in the work of the Spirit, the practice of gratitude was a habit of others before it was a habit of Vic's.

We did not discuss, as I said, how such an experience, one excellently susceptible of Wittgensteinian analysis, might have changed or deepened Vic's reading of Aquinas on the Spirit.[9] And yet the conversation leaves some clues about how to go on. For Aquinas, as for Wittgenstein and for Vic, the work of the Spirit is to be sought in the practices of the community, not because the Spirit is *reduced* to matter or community, but because the Spirit could not be received by human beings, for whom nothing can be in the mind not first in the senses, except in matter. Indeed one might think that for Aquinas as for much of the western tradition such a reduction threatens. For Aquinas, as for many other western theologians, the main treatment of the Spirit does not mention the Spirit much, but proceeds under a lower-case, common noun: I mean the tractate on grace. And yet Aquinas leaves the way wide open to read the tractate on grace as one about the Spirit, because he names it 'The New Law', the one Paul calls 'the law of the Spirit of life in Christ Jesus' (Rom. 8.2), the one that the Spirit writes on the fleshy tablets of the heart (2 Cor. 3.3) – biblical tags that open and set up Thomas's account.[10] This phrase of Paul's, adopted so prominently and so programmatically by Thomas, also introduces the very chapter, Romans 8 – astute readers will already have noticed – in terms of which Vic described the Spirit's intercession. And this phrase of Paul's, in accord with the emphasis common to Thomas and to Vic, frames the apparently non-linguistic 'too deep for words' activity of the Spirit in terms of 'law' and 'life', terms that recall the rules and forms of life in which alone such an experience can come about. What would it mean to interpret Aquinas's account of grace generally, and not just quasi-rapturous experiences, in terms of the Holy Spirit's dwelling in the heart, catching the human being up into the intratrinitarian life through concrete, bodily – that is, habitual – experience? What if, that is, we recast the tractate on grace without the use of that word, in order to display the Spirit come to rest on a body, and issuing therefore in habit?

II

I call the reformulation in this essay an eclipse, not by way of critique but as an interpretation *in optimam partem*. An eclipse is among other things a rendering visible of an otherwise all-too-dazzling source of light by the interposition of dark matter, so that finite human observers, who 'blink at the most evident things like bats in the sunshine',[11] can learn something from the penumbra. So the apparent reification of grace can show us the Spirit. As the carol commands, 'Veiled in flesh the Godhead see!' That the reference is christological counts more as explanation than objection, since the Spirit characteristically comes to rest upon matter, Christians suppose, *just because* the Spirit narratively and liturgically comes to rest upon and shines out from the Son.[12]

At the risk of explaining the obscure by the more obscure, I note a point of comparison between post-Augustinian talk of grace and post-Fregean talk of meaning. Like meaning, 'grace, for the Christian believer, is a transformation [of a form of life] that depends in large part on knowing yourself to be seen in a certain way: as significant, as wanted'.[13] Only, grace is the meaning that God bestows, by which God arranges not primarily words, but states of affairs (*res*) or forms of life (*logoi*) to signify.[14] Like 'meaning' in Wittgenstein's account, 'grace' is also a concept that took on a life of its own as its function of helping in controversy or clearing a space for debate was forgotten. In Kathryn Tanner's analysis of the 'plain sense' of a text, for example, meaning becomes a sociological space that makes room between the words of the text and the possibility of claiming their authority for a community purpose: so far from being restrictive, the plain sense allows a critic or reformer to claim the authority of the text against – that is, renegotiate – communal interpretation.[15] So too the language of grace allows the theologian to claim divine authority for human action, or to renegotiate communal ascription. As analysis of meaning went endlessly round and round after Frege's attention to *Sinn* and *Bedeutung*, so too grace arose as a subject of analysis after the Pelagian controversy in the West.[16] After Pelagius, 'grace and liberty . . . are transformed into two mutually exclusive concepts which then have to be reconciled, as if they were two objects exterior to one another'.[17] One might almost say the same about *Sinn* and *Bedeutung* after Frege. After Frege, meaning, too, seemed (falsely) to be a thing exterior to the discourse that enacted it. In both cases, grace and meaning, the way forward is sometimes to omit rather than focus on the troublesome term.[18] In both cases, we have a possibly suspect *tertium quid*. In both cases we have a question about the rules of a language-game, or to put it in more traditional terms, about the *modus loquendi theologorum*.[19]

Robert Jenson has recently posed the alternative, 'grace or the Spirit', with renewed urgency. Quoting Augustine, Jenson notes that 'The Holy Spirit's gift is nothing other than the Holy Spirit.'[20] Noting that 'It is, to be sure, an audacious doctrine,' Jenson quotes Augustine again joining the indwelling of the Holy Spirit to charity in the heart:

'Therefore the love (*dilectio*) which is of God and which is God is properly the Holy Spirit; by him that love of God (*Dei caritas*) is diffused in our hearts by which the whole Trinity indwells us.'[21] With odd exceptions like Luther and Edwards, Jenson finds that 'The doctrine was *too* audacious for subsequent theology,' becoming an 'option' in Peter Lombard's *Sentences*, which asked (rather than affirmed) whether 'the Holy Spirit is himself the love . . . by which we love God and the neighbor'.[22] Although Jenson admits the point of it,[23] Thomas's insistence that charity must (also) be our own possession, rather than the Holy Spirit *and nothing else*, becomes suspect. Is the alternative 'grace or the Spirit' a useful distinction, or a failure of nerve?[24] Does the language of grace 'betray an impersonal conception of the Spirit'?[25]

III

In Thomas Aquinas, the discussion of the Holy Spirit and the human being proceeds mostly in terms of grace, but the scheme is still visible by which the Spirit is interior to ('indwells') the bodily habits that enact it. Indeed, the more Latin, less King James word for the Spirit's interiority to the body is even more telling: the Spirit quite precisely and explicitly in-habits it.[26] Can you do without the language of grace altogether? Not quite. As with the language of meaning, sometimes you need it to get around certain other problems. Are there places in the discourse where it distracts? Yes, on the evidence of centuries of controversialists who have been so distracted. Can Thomas get along without it for long periods where he might otherwise use it? Yes, in his biblical commentaries.

A

In the *Summa* Thomas describes the 'missions' of the Son and the Spirit as movements that begin in eternity with a sending by the Father, and end in time with respectively the incarnation of the Son in Jesus and the sanctification of human beings by the indwelling of the

Spirit.[27] 'Grace' is the temporal end of the Holy Spirit's eternal mission, by which the Spirit comes to rest in the human heart and issues in habitual acts of faith, hope, and charity. Thomas deploys a comparative, a reflexive, and a superlative to insist that the New Law is 'principally the grace itself of the Holy Spirit'[28] because that is *potissimum* in it.[29] The passage does not contemplate the possibility that there might be anything stronger to say. Its multiple tropes of emphasis leave no impression of a failure of nerve; rather the opposite: they leave the impression that 'the grace of the Holy Spirit' functions almost as an appositive genitive, tending to identify rather than distinguish the two terms. Here we discern an Augustinian *trajectory*, never finally completed, toward identifying grace and the Holy Spirit.

But Thomas sometimes insists on the language of grace precisely as a middle rather than appositive term. He sometimes resists the move immediately from Spirit to habit. The contexts are very instructive. It is always to avoid some kind of misunderstanding of the relation between Spirit and habit, always solving some problem in the tradition, always therapeutic to the discourse. As 'meaning' preserves a space for argument and clarification, so 'grace' preserves a space for human voluntariness. Grace is not a kind of magic that moves the limbs directly, and it is not a kind of possession that elides the will. Rather grace involves or engages the will, so that grace redounds to affect the body through the soul both here and in the next life.[30] It is in order to avoid those kinds of *mis*understandings that Thomas insists upon grace.

Similarly, Thomas insists that charity is the Holy Spirit dwelling in the soul *in such a way* that charity can be really a human habit, against Lombard, who would omit the qualification; here, too, the 'medium term' clears a space for a purpose; it preserves the voluntary nature of the human act.[31] As a space-clearer, a place-holder, 'grace' does not call attention to itself, but to the 'courtesy' (in the word favoured by Julian of Norwich) that God pays to the creature in honouring her dignity. Grace is here an index of God's disposing all things *suaviter*,[32] of the divine tact or *politesse*, of the Holy Spirit's characteristic voice, 'still' and 'small' (1 Kings 19.12).

One of Thomas's most explicit considerations of this problem happens in two paragraphs in the article 'Whether grace places anything in the soul', an objection and its reply. Here, grace serves to mark a distinction between God as primary agent and the soul as secondary agent: 'an agent does not determine an object by means of his own substance'. God does not *replace* our substance with God's own; God does not eliminate or violate human nature: to put the danger in graphic terms, Thomas is worried about a scheme in which God would rub out human beings, or turn a gift into a rape. Rather, Thomas checks the Augustinian tendency with an Aristotelian distinction. An agent does not produce an effect by replacing the matter with herself. An agent effects by moulding or building according to a model, generally, by providing a form – even if this form is the form of herself, her image. God is an agent; grace is the form.[33]

There is indeed explicit mention of a third thing, a 'medium', in this passage. As Jenson's 'audacious' theologians might wish, the third thing is denied. But the third thing, surprisingly, is not 'grace'. What the passage denies is a medium (if you like, a *further* medium) between grace and the human being, between form and matter. The agent uses a form, but the form doesn't use anything: it forms. The view that Jenson attributes to Augustine appears in the objection:

> As the soul vivifies the body, so God vivifies the soul, whence Dt. 30.20 says, 'He is your life.' But the soul vivifies the body immediately. *Therefore also no medium comes between God and the soul.*[34]

The answer does not exhaustively deny the italicized phrase: only in one sense.

> God is the life of the soul by means of an efficient cause: but the soul is the life of the body by means of a formal cause. Now between form and matter does not fall anything in the middle (*non cadit aliquod medium*): since form by itself informs matter or subject. But an agent informs a subject not by her own substance, but by a form which she causes in the matter.

The danger that Thomas hereby avoids is an anthropological one. God is not a form. More specifically, God is not a *human* form. God can cause, and therefore also *have* a human form. But God is not *reducible* to a human form. In this context, Thomas's distinction need not be read as a failure of nerve. It may be read, instead, as a defence against Feuerbach before his time.

The difficulty comes when these spaces for clarification become an object of attention in their own right, *distracting* from the Spirit of God in the heart, or human acts arising therefrom. Much harm has been done to the transparent pneumatology of this scheme by controversies among later Thomists over 'created' and 'uncreated' grace. Protestants dislike the distinction because 'created grace' sounds to them at best a contradiction in terms, and at worst a descent into Pelagianism, the sort of grace the human being possesses as if by right, or even herself creates by the practice of habit. I was once told that the phrase 'created grace' never in fact appeared in Thomas. Although that turned out to be not quite true, the exception proves the rule. The solitary mentions of 'created grace' occur in christology, where Thomas has constructed the phrase to parallel quite precisely that other, more famous contradiction in terms, 'incarnate God', and in reference to the biblical phrase 'created in Christ Jesus',[35] dependent on that paradox. For the whole tractate on grace can also be read christologically, as the incarnation of God in other people, or their re-creation in the image of Christ, by which human lives become christoform *logoi*, God's own arguments.[36]

Human lives become *logoi* in the Logos, or receive christoform meaning, because grace catches them up into the trinitarian life. When it is at home, grace names the human participation in the divine nature already in this life, deification begun.[37] 'Gratia est participatio divinae naturae' in many, many places.[38] It is 'nothing else than the beginning (*inchoatio*) of glory', that is, life with God, 'in us'.[39] For grace 'on the way', or *in via* or 'at home', *in patria*, are the same grace, *idem numero*.[40] Grace is the gift of God, and the gift of participation in God, because what grace does – i.e. what God does in us – is deify.[41] As *God's* gift, it is appropriated to the Holy Spirit; as the *gift* of God, it is habitual.[42] These habits are not only those of virtue, but also the practices that define the community, namely the sacraments; the first bring the divine life formally, so that we become like God, the second effectively, so that the humanity of Christ works in us.[43] As in the humanity of Christ, so in his members; in grace the Holy Spirit does not bypass but rests upon and shines out from the body.

B

In his *Commentary on Romans*, chapter 8, Thomas comments in context upon the verse from which the so-called tractate on 'grace' takes its structural place and its proper name. Thomas actually entitles his treatment in the *Summa* the '*Nova Lex*', or New Law. Structurally, therefore, he places it at the end of the tractate on law, the external regulation of human acts, as apparently opposed to their internal source, or the virtues. But since the New Law is the law of the Spirit (Rom. 8.2) which is written on the heart,[44] the New Law caps the treatise on law by overcoming the distinction between the interior and exterior springs of human action. The Spirit moves the heart *from the outside* and *most internally*, since it is a feature of God's transcendence of creatures to be more internal to them than they are to themselves. Historically, it may be in commenting or preparing to comment upon this passage that Thomas hit upon the placement and title of the so-called treatise on grace: a placement and title that display the possibility of seeing the Spirit as the rule or form of the new life.[45]

The chapter in Romans is about the Spirit from beginning to end. It opens with the identification of 'law' with the 'Spirit', so foreign is it to Augustinian and Lutheran oppositions between those terms, which owe much, of course, to other bits of Paul. But here Paul has cast the law not as the *nomos* or *Gesetz* that accuses the conscience but as Torah, the law that the righteous 'delights to walk in'.[46] The chapter in Thomas's commentary begins with talk of grace, because Thomas can hardly help but think of grace as counterpart to 'law', and he is perhaps working out how well the Augustinian discourse about grace can be eliminated in favour of the Romans 8 discourse about the law of the Spirit by which one prospers, by which the Spirit 'inhabits' the heart (Rom. 8.9, 11). For the Pauline chapter from which Thomas takes the title and structure of his so-called tractate on grace never uses the word. By the middle of Thomas's commentary on the chapter – by the time he comes to the passage about the Spirit praying for those who cannot form even the words of the Our Father – he has accordingly so conformed his exposition to Paul's language that the language of grace disappears.[47]

Romans 8 begins as follows:

Vulgate	English of Vulgate	NRSV from Greek
1. Nihil ergo nunc damnationis est his qui sunt in Christo Jesu, qui non secundum carnem ambulant.	1. For there is now nothing of damnation for those who are in Christ Jesus, who do not walk according to the flesh.	1. There is therefore now no condemnation for those who are in Christ Jesus.
2. Lex enim spiritus vitae in Christo Jesu liberavit me a lege peccati et mortis.	2. For the law of the spirit of life in Christ Jesus has liberated me from the law of sin and death.	2. For the law of the Spirit of life in Christ Jesus has set me free from the law of sin and death.

The Vulgate of Romans 8.1 unavoidably lands Thomas in Augustinian controversies about grace. For it translates the Greek *katakrima*, RSV 'there is now no condemnation in Christ Jesus', as the technical term *damnatio*. Thomas finds himself squarely in the tradition of commentary according to which 'having' grace makes the difference between salvation and damnation – even if Paul's own context is Jews and Gentiles and the justification of the ways of God by the faithfulness of Jesus Christ. Paul is in fact not here in the midst of a technical, post-Augustinian treatise in which 'grace' has become a term of art and a centre of dispute.

Thomas emerges fairly quickly, however, from the Augustinian context in which the Vulgate's '*damnatio*' has placed him. Already by the middle of his commentary on the second verse he has found the plain air of a discourse in which the Trinity meets the Torah without the mediation of a third term:

Lex enim spiritus, etc., quae quidem lex potest dici uno modo Spiritus Sanctus, ut sit sensus: Lex spiritus, id est, lex quae est spiritus; lex enim ad hoc datur, ut per eam homines inducantur ad bonum; unde et Philosophus dicit, quod intentio legislatoris est cives facere bonos, quod quidem lex humana facit, solum notificando quid fieri debeat; sed Spiritus Sanctus mentem inhabitans non solum docet quid oporteat fieri intellectum illuminando de agendis, sed etiam affectum inclinat ad recte agendum.
Paracletus autem Spiritus Sanctus, quem mittet pater in nomine meo, ille vos docebit omnia, quantum ad primum, *et suggeret vobis omnia*, quantum ad secundum, *quaecumque dixero vobis* [John 14.16].

In 'For the law of the spirit', law can mean in one way the Holy Spirit, in this sense: The law of the spirit means the law, which is the Spirit; for law is given for this, that by it human beings be led to the good, whence even the Philosopher says, that the intent of the lawgiver is to make the citizens good, which indeed human law accomplishes, only announcing what ought to be done; but the Holy Spirit inhabiting the mind not only teaches what ought to be done by illuminating the intellect about things to be done, but also inclines the affect toward acting rightly.
'For the Paraclete, the Holy Spirit, which the Father will send in my name will teach you all things,' with respect to the first point, 'and urge you to all things', with respect to the second, 'whatsoever I will have told you' [John 14.16].

Alio modo lex spiritus potest dici proprius effectus Spiritus Sancti, sc. fides per dilectionem

In another way, 'the law of the spirit' can mean the proper effect of the Holy Spirit, namely faith

operans, quae quidem et docet interius de agendis. . . . Et haec quidem lex spiritus dicitur lex nova, quae vel est ipse Spiritus Sanctus, vel eam in cordibus nostris Spiritus Sanctus facit. *Dabo legem meam in visceribus eorum, et in corde eorum superscribam eam* [Jer. 31.33].	operating by love, which of course also teaches interiorly about things to be done. And according to this reading the law of the spirit is called the New Law, which is either the Holy Spirit itself, or [what] the Holy Spirit does in our hearts. 'For I will give my law in your gut and I will write it upon your heart' [Jer. 31.33].

The law of life is either the Spirit, or the effect of the Spirit habituating the human being. Law and the Spirit are one, as in Torah, and Spirit issues in habit. So far from an antinomian opposition to structure, the Spirit, one might say, is the Rule.[48] The Spirit writes a law on the heart, that is, provides, like Torah, a structure that liberates (Rom. 8.2). We could hardly wish for a lovelier statement. Thomas even has the good judgement to quote a passage from John naming all three persons of the Trinity, intimating that the true law, the one that succeeds in leading human beings toward the good, is already a participation in that spirited, which is to say ruled, community that is the trinitarian fellowship.

By the time the commentary arrives at the passage to which Vic referred, Thomas has emerged even farther from a discourse of grace into a discourse of the Spirit and human infirmity, in the context of impending death.[49] As in Vic's experience – had he read this passage? – the Lord's Prayer is the prayer we cannot pray.[50] The language of grace disappears because human agency has become too bare and the Spirit too present. The Spirit still does not replace or violate us. The language is of 'help' and 'prayer'. Not that we pray for help: prayer is the result of help. The language of 'help' implies that there are still two. The language of 'prayer' is that rational *dependence* upon another rational person or Person; specifically, it is still a learned, communal, linguistic prayer that the Spirit prays for us; the Spirit does not enrapture us, but it is a human thing that the Spirit does for us. It does not even particularly help us to do something, as if human beings and the Holy Spirit were two creatures on the same level, two hands pulling on one rope. Instead, the *adjuvare* of the Holy Spirit appears absolutely, that is, without qualification. The Holy Spirit simply *helps*. The help of the Spirit is global: it holds us in being; indeed, it *assumes* us.[51] In this passage of support at greatest need, the language of grace falls away, and the language of the Spirit is just as audacious as anyone could wish.

It approaches, perhaps, the audacity of glory: the Spirit, in crying 'Abba!' in sighs too deep for (this-worldly) words makes us capable of the divine Word, incorporates us into Christ's intratrinitarian address to the Father. Then indeed there is no need for the condescension of grace; we need no words if at last we possess the Word, God's own principle of intelligibility;[52] we need no room of our own to act in, when we inhabit God's infinite roominess. Then we see God no longer by a form accidental to our nature, but by a participation become intrinsic; we see God by God's essence, or 'as he is'. Just that cannot, of course, be intelligibly communicated in this life, but is a radically eschatological matter.

IV

As there is reputedly a linguistic and a mystical Wittgenstein, so there is assuredly a linguistic and a mystical Aquinas, and even a mystical Preller. If I may put his own words into his mouth, what he experienced was a '*quasi quoddam inchoativum* of a future intelligibility'.[53] The piling up of qualifications was remarkable even for Aquinas and noted by Preller with satisfaction. 'A more guarded statement would be difficult to imagine: *quasi* is "as if" language; *quoddam* is "sort-of" language; and *inchoativum* signifies a first movement or "a germ of a beginning."'[54] So Aquinas practises the way of remotion; in piling up qualifications, he takes language away. About the light of glory, he keeps volubly silent by over-specification. In the language of grace, too, Aquinas practises remotion, but now in a more positive way: the language of grace is inadequate to the Spirit, but (like 'meaning') it is not dispensable. It has its uses. 'Grace' marks a reserve – even a reticence about the Spirit – strictly appropriate to this life. The Spirit would blow our minds, or enrapture us; it must be passed over in silence.[55] But the language of grace does not silence us; rather it practises the reserve, the apophasis, that alone permits language *in via*. The 'Abba' of the Spirit is the Word *in patria*. That is why Vic could have applied to himself the words with which he closes *Divine Science*: he remained 'in a kind of shadow of ignorance (*quadam tenebra ignorantiae*), by which ignorance, insofar as it pertains to this life, we are best conjoined to God (*optime Deo coniungimur*) . . . and this is the cloud in which God is said to dwell (*habitare*)'.[56] Indeed this experienced ignorance was one by which, he said, God habituated and indwelt us, so that, well conjoined, he suspected in this life 'a kind of beginning, as it were' of beatitude.[57]

Notes

1. In April 1998 – distinct from the pneumonia that killed him.

2. See Adrienne von Speyr, 'Prayer in the Trinity', in her *World of Prayer* (San Francisco: Ignatius Press, 1985). Cf. Marcel Mauss, *The Gift: Forms and Functions of Exchange in Archaic Societies*, trans. Ian Cunnison (London: Cohen & West, 1954). That the trinitarian exchange of gift and gratitude grounds an economy different from that described in Mauss is the burden of John Milbank, 'Can a Gift be Given?' *Modern Theology* 11 (1995): 119–41.

3. *Divine Science and the Science of God: A Reformulation of Thomas Aquinas* (Princeton: Princeton University Press, 1967), p. 242, citing A. Hayen, *La communication de l'acte de l'être d'après Saint Thomas d'Aquin* (Paris: De Brouwer, 1957).

4. *Divine Science*, p. 264, in the context of the trinitarian discussions of pp. 254–61.

5. *Divine Science*, pp. 230–7, 269, citing Aquinas's commentary on that verse.

6. *Divine Science*, pp. 192–4, citing *ST* I.88.3.

7. The 'business' of the 'self-crosser' comes up for characteristically self-ironizing discussion in *Divine Science*, pp. 7–8.

8. He never mentioned the German sense of his surname, but given his psychology and his love of German it can hardly have escaped his notice. Cf. *Cassel's German and English Dictionary*, svv. *prellen* and *Preller*.

9. At best implicit in *Divine Science*. The one explicit mention appears on p. 260.

10. Rom. 8.2 appears in the first article of the tractate on grace, at I-II.106.1c, and the writing of laws on the heart is ascribed to the Spirit in a quotation from Augustine in the same place. 2 Cor. 3.3 appears in the next article at I-II.106.2 ad 3.

11. Thomas's quotation of Aristotle at *ST* I.1.5.

12. The phrase, as far as I can determine, originates with Gregory of Cyprus. For citations and commentary, see Dumitru Staniloae, 'Holy Trinity: Structure of Supreme Love,' in his *Theology and the Church*, trans. Robert Barringer (Crestwood, NY: St Vladimir's Seminary Press, 1980).

13. Rowan Williams, 'The Body's Grace', now in Eugene F. Rogers, Jr (ed.), *Theology and Sexuality: Classic and Contemporary Readings* (Oxford: Blackwell, 2002), pp. 309–21; here, p. 311.

14. I.1.10. The idea that *logos*, small 'l', might be translated in a christocentric anthropology as a form of life occurred to me while reading John Boswell, 'Introduction' to Chris Glaser, *Uncommon Calling* (Louisville: Westminster John Knox Press, 1988), now reprinted as 'Logos and Biography', in Rogers, *Theology and Sexuality*, pp. 356–61, here, pp. 359–61.

15. 'Theology and the "Plain Sense" of Scripture', in Garret Green (ed.), *Scriptural Authority and Narrative Interpretation* (Philadelphia: Fortress Press, 1987), pp. 59–77.

16. For a typical, pox-on-both-houses account of Protestant and Catholic controversies about grace from an Eastern Orthodox theologian, see Vladimir Lossky, *Mystical Theology of the Eastern Church* (Crestwood, NY: St Vladimir's Seminary Press, 1976), pp. 197–9.

17. Lossky, *Mystical Theology*, p. 198.

18. For more, see Jeffrey Stout, 'What is the Meaning of a Text?', *New Literary History* 13 (1982): 3–8.

19. It would be interesting to trace the *Wirkungsgeschichte* of that phrase or associated ideas from Luther through Dilthey to see whether Luther's thought about theological speech has in fact any historical influence on Wittgenstein, or whether they have simply an interest in common. I have often wondered, for example, whether George Lindbeck could not have replaced all the points in *The Nature of Doctrine* made by reference to Wittgenstein with points made by reference to Luther. The result would perhaps prove more persuasive to some, and less persuasive to others.

20. Augustine, *De Trinitate* 15.36, at Jenson, *Systematic Theology*, vol. 1: *The Triune God* (Oxford and New York: Oxford University Press, 1997), p. 148. Thanks to Fergus Kerr for reminding me of this discussion.

21. *De Trinitate* 15.32, very slightly modified from Jenson's translation.

22. Jenson, *The Triune God*, pp. 148–9, quotes Lombard, *Sentences* 1.d.xvii.2 and cites Luther, *WA* 1:224–8 and his own book on Edwards, *America's Theologian* (New York: Oxford University Press, 1988), pp. 65–78.

23. Jenson, *The Triune God*, p. 149, esp. n. 22.

24. Cf. *ST* II-II.23.2.

25. Jenson, *The Triune God*, p. 149.

26. '*Habitare*', *ST* I.43.3. For more, see D. Juvenal Merriell, *To the Image of the Trinity: A Study in the Development of Aquinas' Teaching* (Toronto: Pontifical Institute of Mediaeval Studies, 1990), pp. 80–94 and 226–36. For Preller's account, see *Divine Science*, pp. 255–9.

27. I.43.

28. I.106.2. Translations are my own.

29. I.106.1c.

30. III.73.1 ad 3.

31. II-II.23.2.

32. Wisdom 8.1, quoted at I-II.110.2.

33. I-II.110.1.

34. I-II.110 obj. 2, my italics.

35. Eph. 2.10 at I-II.110.2 ad 3.

36. Boswell, 'Logos and Biography', p. 359.

37. For the definitive account of deification in Thomas, see Anna Williams, *The Ground of Union: Deification in Aquinas and Palamas* (New York: Oxford University Press, 1999).

38. e.g., in the *Summa Theologiae*, I-II.110.3, 4; 112.1; 113.9; 114.3; II-II.19.7; III.2.10 ad 1; 3.4 ad 5; 62.1.2.

39. II-II.24.3 ad 2; I-II.111.3 ad 2.

40. I-II.111.3 ad 2. Cf. I-II.110.1; 114.3 ad 3; III.62 ad 3; 70.4; 72.7 ad 1.

41. I-II.112.1.

42. I-II.109.1 ad 1; 109.2, 3, 6, 8, 9, 10; 110.2–3; 111.2; 112.1; II-II.171.2 ad 3.

43. I-II.110.2 ad 1.

44. Which Thomas frequently quotes from Jer. 31, as in his commentary on Rom. 8.2 and elsewhere.

45. This is admittedly a conjecture for which my evidence is circumstantial. According to the best datings known to me, Thomas was at work on the *Summa* I-II (which ends with the tractate on grace) in 1271, and on his second *Commentary on Romans* – the one we have – between 1271 or 1272 and 1273. Cf. the appendices in Jean-Pierre Torrell, *Saint Thomas Aquinas*, vol. 1: *The Person and His Work*, trans. Robert Royal (Washington, DC: Catholic University Press, 1996).

46. So Rom. 8.4 recalls the Psalms, e.g. Ps. 1.1–3: 'Blessed is the one who walks not in the counsel of the wicked . . . ; but delights in the law of the Lord, and on that law meditates day and night. That one is like a tree planted by streams of water, that yields its fruit in due season, and its leaf does not wither. In all that he does, he prospers.'

47. For other instances in which Thomas changes his vocabulary to conform to Paul, see Otto Hermann Pesch, 'Paul as Professor of Theology: The Image of the Apostle in St. Thomas's Theology', *The Thomist* 38 (1974).

48. A theme of Adrienne von Speyr, *The Word Becomes Flesh*, trans. Lucia Wiedenhoever and Alexander Dru (San Francisco: Ignatius Press, 1994).

49. *In Rom.* 687: 'Dictum est quod per Spiritum Sanctum vivificabuntur nostra mortalia corpora, quando auferetur a nobis nostra infirmitas.'

50. *In Rom.* 690, for several paragraphs.

51. *In Rom.* 687: 'Spiritus quoque elevit me, et assumpsit me', quoting Ezek. 3.14.

52. Preller's account of how the Word is God's own principle of intelligibility, and how it differs from and undergirds ours, occupies *Divine Science*, pp. 35–107.

53. *Divine Science*, p. 269.

54. *Divine Science*, p. 239, quoting the Latin from *In Heb.* 11.1 and the definition from Deferrari's *Lexicon of St. Thomas Aquinas*.

55. *Divine Science*, pp. 193–4, citing I.88.3.

56. *Divine Science*, p. 271, quoting *In Sent.* I.vii.1.1.

57. *Divine Science*, p. 239, citing *A Lexicon of St. Thomas Aquinas*, ed. Deferrari, s.v. *inchoo*.

7. Nature's Grace

Aquinas and Wittgenstein on Natural Law and Moral Knowledge

JOHN R. BOWLIN

I went to Princeton University's Department of Religion in 1985 to write a dissertation on Wittgenstein and pragmatism's progeny, its mid-century heirs – Quine, Sellars, and Rorty. My vague hunch was that these philosophical traditions, woven together, could be used to rescue philosophy of religion from its analytic captivity. Victor was enthusiastic and right from the start treated me as one already initiated into the Prellerian mysteries. An undeserved honour, no doubt, but I was grateful for the gift. Together we read and discussed Wittgenstein often and over many years and along the way Victor suggested we read Aquinas. At first this was puzzling, as was Aquinas, but eventually Victor's motive and Thomas's texts fell into place with assistance from Wittgenstein. What Wittgenstein struggled to convey about intention, language, and representation Aquinas took for granted, or so Victor assumed. Tit for tat, Victor read Wittgenstein's remarks about grammar, meaning, and judgement with eyes tutored by Aquinas's account of nature, habit, and action.

The detour through Aquinas was a long one and I did not write the dissertation on Wittgenstein. Much later, and to my relief, I discovered that Scott Davis already had, brilliantly. By then I was fully occupied with the first half of Victor's exegetical enterprise: following Aquinas down paths that would have seemed choked with metaphysical brambles were it not for Wittgenstein's brush-clearing efforts. Now our conversations – in the lounge in 1879 Hall, in the Master's Lodge at the Graduate College, and eventually in his CD-stuffed

apartment on Stanworth Lane – were all about Aquinas, his ante-
cedents, and his interpreters. But it was Wittgenstein who got us
started, that formed the seminary of our friendship and enquiries, and
in a sense this paper returns to that beginning.

In what follows I offer an example of the kind of reading that Victor
encouraged. I argue that Wittgenstein's account of the judging and
acting that 'is the substratum of all [our] enquiring and asserting' (*On
Certainty*, §162) places him in roughly the same corner of the natural
law tradition that Aquinas occupies.[1] Tit for tat, I argue that the
relation between the natural law's primary and secondary precepts,
left artfully vague by Aquinas, can be spelled out in terms borrowed
from Wittgenstein's treatment of concept mastery and epistemic commitment. Both efforts involve what Rorty calls rational reconstruction.[2] Both figures are treated as victims of time, training, and habit, as
thinkers who might have put their remarks differently, in a new
and improved vocabulary, had they been aware of what we know
now. Rorty's examples of rational reconstruction look backward
Whiggishly: Strawson on Kant, Bennett on the British Empiricists.[3]
The views of the past are upgraded and improved by recasting them in
a more recent idiom. But there is no reason why one cannot reverse the
historical vectors as I do when I describe certain Wittgensteinian
themes in Thomistic terms. At times the more recent can be reconstructed and improved by a past it did not know but would have
benefited from knowing.

Whether rational reconstruction works forward or back, when it
succeeds, the payoff is the same. Exegetical puzzles are solved. Figures
are shuffled about and our histories of philosophy and theology are
improved. Depth is added to what we know, to what we now recognize as shallow understanding. These benefits accrue from reading
Aquinas and Wittgenstein as Victor did.

I

Pick up almost any history of moral philosophy and you will find a
story about the natural law tradition that goes something like this.
In the beginning, Aristotle offered scattered remarks about the

connections that obtain between our nature and our most basic moral obligations. Later, the Stoics tried and failed to gather together those remarks and spell out those connections. In the third century Ulpian made advances but left the task unfinished. Only in the hands of Thomas Aquinas did this project find its proper conclusion and this tradition its zenith. Soon after the death of Aquinas the tradition began to decay, and putrid it remained until the early modern period when it was revived by Suarez and Grotius and perfected by Pufendorf, Hobbes, and Locke. Despite the many differences that divide them, those who stand in this natural law tradition share a common aim. They look to nature for moral guidance. They hope that our common humanity will specify and then justify our most basic obligations. Nature, they insist, can tell us what we should do and why we should do it.[4] Indeed, it was the desire to address these kinds of doubts that precipitated the revival of natural law theory among the North American refugees of Hitler's Europe. In the words of perhaps the greatest of the mid-twentieth-century revivalists, Heinrich Rommen, 'the natural law doctrine became willy-nilly the ideological basis of the struggle against totalitarianism'.[5] One turns to the natural law in order to answer sceptics and thugs, to shame the heirs of Thrasymachus with the authoritative call of nature.

Pick up almost any recent treatment of Aquinas's account of the natural law and you will find this story reaffirmed. Most exegetes agree that the first precepts of the natural law, spelled out in *ST* I-II.94.2, provide a general outline of the human good from which specific obligations can be derived and the sceptic's challenge answered.[6] But of course, textbook histories are rarely reliable and exegetical consensus often masks complacency. In this instance, both hunches are confirmed, or so I will argue. For reasons spelled out in this section, we should not think that Aquinas offers theoretical comfort to the morally anxious, to those who can muster doubts about our most basic moral commitments. We should not think that he provides a moral theory of this sort. To say that he does tempts the charge of anachronism. Sceptical doubts about basic obligations were not in the stock of problems Aquinas needed to address, and they would not emerge as problems until Montaigne's essays and Hume's *Treatise* shaped a quite different culture, one that placed quite different burdens on its intellectuals. The burdens *Aquinas* bears are principally theological. He offers his remarks about the natural law and its first precepts in order to say how human action and its proximate causes, reason and will, are created by God and governed by providence. All things fall under divine jurisdiction, even human action, reason, and will.[7] The difficulty, the task Thomas takes on, is to say how these three do.

Once Aquinas's efforts are located in theological context, the interpretation that follows should constrain our rational reconstructions of those efforts. We can, of course, reconstruct the views of our favourite philosophers and theologians as we please, and most of us do. Most of us want our contemporary puzzles addressed by our long-dead heroes. Nevertheless, some rational reconstructions are more plausible than others, and in this instance the contextualized interpretation sets the constraints. When textbooks and Thomists insist that Aquinas's remarks on the natural law are designed to address sceptical worries, we should insist that they have confused rational reconstruction for contextual exegesis. Once those remarks are properly contextualized, we can begin to see why they are difficult to recast as a response to scepticism. Indeed, for reasons spelled out in section III below, it is better to regard Aquinas as incapable of thinking that the sceptic's doubts about obligation deserve an answer. Of course, it is an alternative reconstruction of his efforts that generates this conclusion, but it is more plausible than the reconstructions of the exegetical consensus precisely because it begins where contextual interpretation leaves off.

The most plausible contextual interpretation, in brief outline, goes something like this.[8] Agency specifies being and law governs agency. Everything is what it is and not some other thing because of the character of its agency – because of the ends it pursues and the manner in which it pursues them – and a law is nothing but a dictate of reason that governs the agency of those subject to a lawgiver (*ST* I-II.90.1). With these assumptions in hand, Aquinas treats the ends that we apprehend and will naturally as effects of God's eternal law. The fallout is an account of creation and providence as they pertain to human beings and human actions (*ST* I-II.91.1–2).

Creation regards the individuation of things, providence their governance. Both follow from God's practical judgement about the ends that a creature should pursue and the way it should pursue them (*ST* I.22.1).[9] Since a law is a dictate of practical reason (*ST* I-II.90.1.2), a summary of a ruler's judgement about the ends his subjects must pursue, Aquinas maintains that God creates and governs all things by framing laws (*ST* I-II.91.1). The eternal law is the collection of those dictates and the diversity of creation follows from the diverse ways that God's creatures participate in that law (*ST* I-II.93.1). Thus, everything is what it is because it participates in the eternal law in one way and not another, directed by God's judgement and bound by his law to act for the sake of some ends but not others (*ST* I-II.91.2; *Summa contra Gentiles* III.4–5). A swallow, for example, is the creature that it is, not an eagle, fish, or slug, precisely because it participates in God's eternal law as only swallows do. Its actions and passions are directed toward certain ends, such as nest-building, by certain means, with mud and grass, not sticks, not twine. And a swallow is a good swallow, a perfect instance of the sort of thing that it is, when it achieves the ends that it pursues naturally as a consequence of its swallow-like participation in the eternal law. Thus, we say that a good swallow has perfected its nature.

The creation and governance of human beings follows a similar course. God's practical judgement directs us to will certain ends and not others. We will them naturally, which is to say necessarily, and the pursuit of this particular collection of ends – knowledge, friendship, survival, and so on – is one of the things that distinguishes our agency, our species (*ST* I-II.10.1; 94.2). The other is the knowledge with which we act (*ST* I-II.91.2). Acting with knowledge entails knowing the ends we will naturally and necessarily in a manner that permits deliberation over the means (*ST* I-II.6.1–2). And since the ability to deliberate, to compare one course of action with another, entails a certain indeterminacy of action, we are not bound by God's eternal law to intend any one of the ends that we will naturally or to choose any particular course as a means to any particular end we come to intend (*ST* I-II.10.1; 14.1). Indeed, it is precisely because knowledge mediates our participation in the eternal law that we are able to act voluntarily and in all sorts of particular ways, while swallows have a small repertoire of actions that they must perform insofar as they are swallows. Our ability to act knowingly also explains why we are rational creatures and they are not (*ST* I-II.6.1–2; 91.6). For when pressed we can provide reasons in defence of our choices, reasons that refer to ends and means that are known to be good and pursued because of that knowledge.

Aquinas sums up this difference by saying that rational creatures, those who participate in God's eternal law by knowing its demands, act according to the natural law. 'The natural law', he insists, 'is nothing else than the rational creature's participation of the eternal law' (*ST* I-II.91.2). Other creatures participate in the eternal law, but not in a rational manner, and therefore it cannot be said that the actions characteristic of their kind, their natural actions, are actions performed in accord with law. For 'a law is something pertaining to reason', and therefore agents can be directed by law only as they know its demands (*ST* I-II.90.1; 91.2.3). Because providence makes demands upon rational creatures by giving them natural and habitual knowledge of the ends characteristic of their kind, what Aquinas calls *synderesis* (*ST* I.79.12; I-II.94.1.2), they participate in God's practical judgement – in God's eternal law – by becoming provident themselves, by making their own practical judgements as they direct their own actions. And since a law is nothing but a dictate of practical reason, our participation in God's practical judgement is called the natural law in us, whereby we become provident over the actions characteristic of our kind by sharing God's judgement about our proper ends (*ST* I-II.91.2).

Thus to say, as Aquinas does, that human beings act in accord with the natural law is to say something about human agency as such, created by God and governed by providence. It is to say, on the one hand, that it is knowledge of the ends to which we are naturally inclined that moves us to act in ways that are characteristically human. On the other, it is to say that human actions are rational precisely because of this knowledge, this judgement we share in common with God about our good. It follows that every human action, whether good or evil, participates in the eternal law and accords with the natural law in some minimal sense (*ST* I-II.91.2.1). Every human action is done knowingly and for the sake of a specific instance of one of the ends to which we are inclined naturally, one of the goods that we will simply and absolutely. It might also be done to avoid the loss of one of these goods, but no matter. In all that we do the first precept of the natural law is fulfilled, the most basic requirement of rationality in human action is satisfied. Some human good is pursued or some evil is avoided (*ST* I-II.94.2), and it is knowledge of the good to which we are naturally inclined that generates both our desire to act and the reasons we offer in defence of what we do.

Notice how little moral guidance this account of the natural law's first precepts provides. Concrete obligations receive neither specification nor justification. The content of right reason is neither outlined nor defined. Instead, Aquinas maps the boundaries of human agency, rational and voluntary, both good and evil, as he describes 'all those things to which man has a natural inclination, are naturally apprehended as good, and consequently as objects of pursuit' (*ST* I-II.94.2). An agent who falls outside of these lines cannot be said to act for the sake of one of the ends that distinguish our agency as human. What they do will be unnatural in the most basic sense. It will not be human action. It will not be rational or intelligible. For this reason Aquinas insists that, 'the precepts of the natural law are to the practical reason, what the first principles of demonstrations are to the speculative reason' (*ST* I-II.94.2). Just as the principle of non-contradiction is assumed in all human knowing, so too the first precepts of the natural law are assumed in all human action. Just as consistent failure to honour the principle of non-contradiction in belief and inference does not yield false belief, but rather nothing that can be recognized as human knowing, so too failure to act with knowledge for the sake of one of the ends specified by the natural law does not yield vicious action, but rather nothing that can be recognized as human action.

II

If this interpretation is sound, then Aquinas is hardly the sort of natural law theorist one finds in the textbooks and histories. Nor is Wittgenstein for that matter, and yet if Aquinas is a natural lawyer of some sort, so too is Wittgenstein. Like Aquinas, he has no interest in defending a moral theory that will tell us what to do and why.[10] Yet, like Aquinas, he hopes to mark the boundary between sense and nonsense, between intelligible human action and madness. He wants to describe those necessities that specify the human character of our acting in the broadest possible terms. Like Aquinas, he wants to say what's given in human life, what is natural to us in judgement, inclination, and conduct.

For the sake of argument I will assume that the principal conclusion of Part I of the *Philosophical Investigations* goes something like this. We have been held captive by a certain picture of language. We have assumed that language is a medium of expression and representation. In fact, it is not. Meaning is neither an intention expressed in language nor a state of affairs represented in language. Truth is neither accurate representation of the world, nor faithful expression of internal states. Rather, language is a tool that helps creatures like us get on in the world doing this and that. One masters a concept – one understands how to use it as the natives do – only as one comes to understand how it contributes to the success of some activity, to the pursuit of some collection of ends.

Imagine I want to teach my one-year-old son how to understand the word 'spoon'. Picking up a large wooden spoon, pointing to it dramatically, and saying 'spoon!' in my most authoritative voice will do little good. It will not help him master the concept. When I hand him the spoon he will most likely use it to swat the cat, or dig in the mud, or terrorize his older brother. 'No, no, no,' I will say, 'it's a spoon, it's a spoon, don't you see. We use it for eating, like this,' as I thrust my spoon into a bowl of oatmeal and take an exaggerated bite. 'You do it', I'll say, 'give it a try.' And of course, he will try; only he will use his spoon to lift oatmeal out of his bowl and onto the floor. Then he will try the same trick on the oatmeal in his brother's bowl. And finally, he will lift the spoon high over his head while making aeroplane noises. Oh well. The truth is, at this juncture, he does not see the point of using a spoon as I do, and it is precisely this inability that prevents him from mastering the concept. He simply does not know what a spoon is. If, however, after much training, practice, correction, and imitation he does come to see the point of acting as I do, then he will also come to understand the word as I do. Wittgenstein's insight – captured in his famous image, *Sprachspiel* – is that these are related matters (*Philosophical Investigations*, §7). One masters a concept only as one comes to see the point of certain

activities and concedes the truth of certain moral and empirical judgements. My son will acquire mastery of the concept 'spoon' only as he
acknowledges that eating in certain ways is good, presumably with
utensils and not with one's hands, and that the human community
made possible by using a spoon for eating is more desirable than the
fleeting pleasure one receives flinging oatmeal and attacking cats with
spoon-like implements. In addition to these moral judgements, he
must also assume the truth of a vast collection of empirical claims
about the world that circumscribes the activity of using spoons for
eating. Spoons do not disappear and reappear by magic. People do not
disappear when they pick up spoons. Spoons do not bite. He owns the
hand that picks up the spoon. His father, the spoon master, does not
have sawdust where his brain should be, and so on (*On Certainty*,
§§159, 207).

The conclusion we should draw regards the foundation of our
linguistic practices. At bedrock are certain ways of thinking and acting
that presuppose certain moral and ontological commitments. These
commitments are given. They are not chosen, but accepted and trusted
antecedent to all choice. We are justified in believing them, not because
good reasons warrant them, but rather because no judgements are
more certain. Our epistemic confidence in these commitments is so
high that they function more as rules of linguistic usage than as bits of
knowledge (*Philosophical Investigations*, §251; *On Certainty*, §§124,
136). Thus, for example, one cannot use the word 'spoon' as we do
without first conceding that spoons do not bite. How do we know that
they do not bite? Well, they just don't, and if you are uncertain here,
about this, it is not clear how we can respond to you. For your doubts
indicate that your mastery of the concept is insufficient for ordinary
conversation about spoons (*On Certainty*, §126). In fact, if you press
your strange doubts with sufficient sincerity, it is likely that the rest of
us will respond by doubting *your* basic rationality (*On Certainty*,
§§154-5, 219-20).

Here a distinction is needed. The moral and ontological commitments that help constitute the foundation of our linguistic practices
are of two kinds. Some are set in place by custom or convention and
are shared by the inhabitants of some linguistic communities but not
all. Thus, for example, in my linguistic community spoons are used

principally for eating food, not digging dirt, not swatting cats. Nonetheless, other linguistic communities are perfectly imaginable, communities in which the word 'spoon' or its equivalent finds its meaning in the garden, not at the breakfast table. On the other hand, some of the moral and ontological commitments that constitute our linguistic bedrock are given, not by convention, but by nature. They are judgements that form the foundation of all human linguistic practices, all human speech and conduct (*On Certainty*, §558). Judgements of this sort mark the outer boundary of what Wittgenstein calls the *Lebensform* that all human beings share by virtue of the fact they are creatures of one sort and not another, creatures that do some kinds of things but not others in a world of one sort and not another.

Consider eating. To participate in this activity, to understand its goals and make use of its concepts, one must accept certain judgements. Food stops hunger. Making hunger pangs stop is good. Food sustains life; life is good, and so on. The person who doubts the truth of these judgements could not self-consciously participate in the activity we call eating. He could not speak of food and hunger, of pain and relief. And, insofar as he could not speak sensibly about these matters, offering reasons that make his actions intelligible, we would have difficulty regarding him as one of us, as a rational human being. And since doubting is an activity pursued by rational human beings, it is not exactly clear how his 'doubts' fall under that activity. One can muster doubts about a particular account of how food stops hunger, sustains life, and ranks among other goods. About these matters disagreement abounds and nature is silent. About these matters doubt is both possible and possibly rational. But the person who 'doubts' that food stops hunger cannot speak and act and give reasons for acting as rational human beings do. This, in turn, calls into question his basic rationality, if not in general, then at least with respect to this corner of human life. And as rationality goes, so too goes the ability to sustain real doubt.

Wittgenstein puts it this way in *On Certainty*:

154. There are cases such that, if someone gives signs of doubts where we do not doubt, we cannot confidently understand his signs as signs of doubt. I.e., if we are to understand his signs of doubt as

such, he may give them in particular cases and may not give them in others.

155. In certain circumstances a man cannot make a *mistake*. ('Can' is here used logically, and the proposition does not mean that a man cannot say anything false in those circumstances.) If Moore were to pronounce the opposite of those propositions which he declares certain, we should not just not share his opinion: we should regard him as demented.[11]

The point is this: the shared linguistic competence that comes packaged with our common humanity depends on our acceptance of a collection of moral and ontological commitments, a collection of judgements about the goodness of certain ends and about the truth of certain propositions. Those judgements set us about pursuing certain activities, some of which are given with our humanity. They are the kinds of things that we do in the form of life we happen to lead. Like the first precepts of the natural law, these judgements and activities mark the outer boundary of rational speech and human conduct. That boundary is simply 'there – like our life' (*On Certainty*, §559).

Here it should be noted that most interpreters resist this conclusion, this effort to find Wittgenstein concerned with the relation between our common linguistic competence and our shared natural history. Most find Wittgenstein defending the existence of multiple human languages embedded in multiple human forms of life. By their lights, a form of life is largely equivalent to a culture or a conceptual scheme. Its boundaries are set by convention, not nature. Its consequence is a language used by some human beings but not all. This view has become a kind of orthodoxy in some quarters, and yet I think it is mistaken.[12] There is little evidence that Wittgenstein thinks in these terms. When he speaks of *Lebensformen*, his attention is fixed, not on the diversity of human cultures and conventions, but rather on the differences that divide human beings from other animals. His concern is with those features that distinguish our life from theirs, above all those features that make language possible. His remarks are designed to describe the collection of activities, powers, frailties, and judgements that specify our humanity and generate our most basic linguistic practices. Apart from that collection, we would not be human beings, we would not speak and act as we do.

Consider the following remarks, the first three from the *Philosophical Investigations*, the remainder from *On Certainty*.

19. And to imagine a language means to imagine a form of life.

25. It is sometimes said that animals do not talk because they lack the mental capacity. And this means: 'they do not think, and that is why they do not talk.' But – they simply do not talk. Or to put it better: they do not use language – if we accept the most primitive forms of language. – Commanding, questioning, recounting, chatting, are as much a part of our natural history as walking, eating, drinking, playing.

384. You learned the *concept* 'pain' when you learned language.

357. One might say: '"I know" expresses comfortable certainty, not the certainty that is still struggling.'

358. Now I would like to regard this certainty, not as something akin to hastiness or superficiality, but as a form of life.

359. But that means I want to conceive it as something that lies beyond being justified or unjustified; as it were, as something animal.

360. I know that this is my foot. I could not accept any experience as proof to the contrary. – That may be an exclamation; but what *follows* from it? At least that I shall act with a certainty that knows no doubt, in accordance with my belief.

475. I want to regard man here as an animal; as a primitive being to which one grants instinct but not ratiocination. As a creature in a primitive state. Any logic good enough for a primitive means of communication needs no apology from us. Language did not emerge from some kind of ratiocination.

The remarks from the *Investigations* highlight the connection between acting in human kinds of ways, mastering certain concepts, and speaking as human beings do. The remarks from *On Certainty* highlight the connection between acting and speaking as human beings do and conceding the truth of certain judgements. Both sets of remarks highlight the natural character of certain activities and judgements in the life human beings happen to lead. Both are designed to show how language is embedded in our nature and how our nature is distinguished by a certain collection of actions and judgements that form the bedrock of our language.

At this point, I hope I have said enough to justify my hunch that Wittgenstein's remarks about the natural history of our linguistic practices have a striking resemblance to Aquinas's account of the first precepts of the natural law. Both efforts are designed to specify the necessities that constitute our humanity, the actions and judgements that distinguish our form of life from the life that non-human creatures lead. This much seems plain enough. Still, one might wonder whether Wittgenstein offers a *natural law* account of our common humanity. Law, according to Aquinas, is a dictate of practical reason, a command that something be done. It is a dictate designed to bring about some new state of affairs, and it is promulgated by one who has authority to rule what he brings about. Aquinas can say that our nature is created and governed by law precisely because he believes in a God who creates and governs all that is. Wittgenstein, by contrast, appears to assume no equivalent God in the heavens. Nonetheless, he knows that the necessities he describes – the judgements we must maintain and the ends we must desire – give the appearance of being the effects of a lawgiver's command. Consider the following remarks from *On Certainty*.

172. Perhaps someone says 'There must be some basic principle on which we accord credence', but what can such a principle accomplish? Is it more than a natural law of 'taking for true'?

361. But I might also say: It has been revealed to me by God that it is so. God has taught me that this is my foot. And therefore if anything happened that seemed to conflict with this knowledge I should have to regard *that* as deception.

505. It is always by nature's grace that one knows something.

670. We might speak of fundamental principles of human enquiry.

I do not want to make too much of what is said here. In Wittgenstein's hands the natural law has no real theological substance. Still, a divine lawgiver who imprints certain necessities upon our intellect and will provides him with a powerful image of the fact that we must believe certain things and desire certain ends in order to speak and act as the creatures that we are. When set against Aquinas's efforts, that image acquires a certain vibrancy.

'Is it more than a natural law of "taking for true"?' In the remarks that come before and after this one, Wittgenstein cajoles us into conceding that our ability to provide justifications for what we believe comes to an end in certain activities. These activities come packaged with certain judgements that we consider true because we trust some authority (*On Certainty*, §§159–61). In this remark, the cajoled opponent resists and asks for some prior principle that we could use to assess the credibility of the authorities we trust. Wittgenstein responds with more cajoling. If language cannot be used without accepting certain judgements on authority, judgements that give our concepts substance, then we can assert no principle of credibility that escapes this dependence upon trust. At best, such a principle could do no more than point out that as language-using creatures we must take certain judgements for true (*On Certainty*, §§191, 205–6). Nature requires no less.

'God has taught me that this is my foot.' In the remarks that precede this one, noted above (p. 165), Wittgenstein speaks of the beliefs we must accept and the actions we must pursue if we are to speak and act as human beings do. Here, remarkably, he uses the image of a divine lawgiver's authority over our knowing and willing to describe the necessities that come packaged with our nature. This could be Aquinas speaking, but with credulity. God imprints certain judgements about the good upon our hearts by gentle persuasion. God constitutes our nature as he instructs the intellect and courts the will, not like a tyrant, but like a teacher who orders all things sweetly (*ST* II-II.23.2).

'It is always by nature's grace that one knows something.' This remark weds the language of natural necessity and external cause to the language of grace. We know certain things and act in certain ways because we are creatures of a certain sort. Not chosen, not earned, our human way of knowing and acting is given. It is simply 'there – like our life' (*On Certainty*, §559). The proper response is gratitude, and gratitude begins with the simple recognition that the internal sources of human action have external causes. Aquinas would put it this way: the knowing and acting that distinguish our nature and that generate the speaking and doing characteristic of our kind are unmerited gifts, real evidence of God's self-giving love for us. What we know and do by nature are the first effects of first grace (*ST* I-II.109.1–2).

And finally: 'We might speak of fundamental principles of human enquiry.' Here, Wittgenstein refers to those moral and ontological judgements that one must accept in order to speak, act, and enquire as human beings do, which is precisely how Aquinas regards the natural law's basic precepts. A principle is, for Aquinas, a law that has become a rule of action when it is known and accepted. The natural law provides rules of action, precisely because its precepts are known and accepted by us as principles that guide all our thinking and speaking about acting.

III

Suppose Wittgenstein's remarks about our natural history and Aquinas's remarks about the natural law's first precepts can be brought together in this way, shedding mutually useful light. Suppose we conclude that both attend to what is given in human life, to what is antecedent to all thinking, speaking, and acting, while refusing to look to nature for moral guidance. How might the exegetical consensus reply? Perhaps by pointing out that Aquinas appears to break ranks when he notes that we derive a small collection of *conclusiones* 'from the general principles of the natural law' (*ST* I-II.95.2). He mentions the prohibitions against harming, killing, stealing, lying, and the like (*ST* I-II.100.1). Given this observation, one might reasonably ask how can it be said, as I do, that Aquinas has no interest in answering the moral sceptic? How can it be said that he refuses to locate and justify our most basic obligations when he appears to do precisely that as he derives secondary precepts of the natural law from the first?

Well, the first thing to note is that Aquinas lived untouched by scepticism's challenge. He never had to decide whether the radical sceptic deserved to be answered or ignored. Wittgenstein did, of course, and since Aquinas and Wittgenstein are in this together, the objection can be addressed to each. Why is it that they think scepticism about fundamental moral matters is not a real option, at least not for most of us? Why do they think that worries of this kind are best bypassed, not answered? Well, imagine Wittgenstein and a moral sceptic cross paths. How might Wittgenstein reply? Perhaps by brandishing a fireplace poker and spitting insults: Hypocrite!! Deceiver!! Scoundrel!! If pressed to justify this response, he might reply roughly as he does in *On Certainty*. Pick a basic moral judgement, any one will do. Torturing children for fun is vile and cruel. Killing the innocent is unjust. When the sceptic asks for reasons that warrant these judgements, we should point out that any moral theory that we might propose in reply – whether a natural law theory or some other variety – would be far more dubious than the judgement it is designed to justify. And if no theory can address doubts about the justice of torturing children or killing the innocent, then there is little reason to muster a reply. At some point, justification comes to an end (*On Certainty*, §204).

To be sure, this conclusion leaves the sceptic's doubts unanswered, but no matter. There is little reason to think that his doubts are real, and as before it is Wittgenstein who points the way. When the sceptic asks whether it is just to torture children or kill the innocent, we should reply by asking whether he knows what 'justice' is, whether he knows what the concept entails. It is a reasonable question. If someone holds up their hand and wonders out loud whether it is *their* hand, we feel compelled to ask whether they know what a hand is. Their failure to assume the truth of certain basic judgements about hands casts doubt upon their mastery of the concept. If they doubt that the hand attached to their arm is in fact their own, then it is unlikely that they know what 'hand' means. It is unlikely that they know how to make proper use of the concept (*On Certainty*, §§369–70). Wittgenstein spells out the proper philosophical conclusion: in certain instances 'the *truth* of my statements is the test of my *understanding* of these statements' (*On Certainty*, §80). Confronted with glaring falsehoods or unimaginable doubts, we cast about for an explanation that saves the linguistic competence of our interlocutor. 'He doubts that it is his hand!! Well, he must be joking, or intoxicated, or play acting, or something, for if it turns out that he's serious, well, in that event, we will have to conclude that he does not understand what he is saying, that he does not know what a hand is. We will have to conclude that his doubts are, in fact, confusions' (cf. *On Certainty*, §81).

Returning again to our moral sceptic, he will surely reply that he knows what 'justice' means, that he has sufficient mastery of the concept to press his doubts. He is not a fool, he will insist. He simply wants to know whether torturing children and killing the innocent represent basic transgressions of justice. But this cannot be right. If he has mastered the concept, then he has also accepted a collection of basic judgements about particular instances of just and unjust conduct, judgements that he considers true, judgements he cannot doubt without losing sight of the concept he claims to know. Included in that collection we will surely find the judgement that torturing children for fun is vile or that killing the innocent is unjust. Or, if not these, then some other short list of moral banalities that give 'justice' its substance and that most of us concede. From this it follows that the sceptic is either someone who knows not what justice is, someone who needs to be taught before he can muster real doubts about concrete cases, or, as is more likely, he is someone who trades in false doubt, someone who has mastered the concept well enough to be expected to know that there can be no uncertainty in *these* particular cases. In either event, he deserves no serious reply from us, no theoretical effort.

Aquinas, I suggest, would justify his disregard for the sceptic's doubts in roughly the same terms, and it is these terms that can help us understand the notoriously obscure relation between the natural law's primary and secondary precepts. The ironies here are delicious. The exegetical consensus assumes that Thomas addresses the moral sceptic precisely because he insists that such a relation exists. In fact, this assumption is hard to maintain once his treatment of the natural law's first precepts have been spelled out in theological context and once his treatment of secondary precepts has been reconstructed in these Wittgensteinian terms.

Like Wittgenstein, Aquinas thinks that most of us understand 'justice' well enough to speak intelligently about it. If we have mastered a human language, if we live in a human community, we will know what justice is, at least in broad outline, and a good portion of what we know will be shared in common with most human beings. In addition, he agrees with Wittgenstein that concepts are mastered only as certain judgements are accepted. It follows that our ability to speak intelligently about justice makes doubt about its basic features impossible. If we know what justice is we cannot muster doubts about those basic judgements, those basic obligations, that help specify the meaning of the word.

These are empirical claims. When Aquinas looks about the moral world, he finds human beings using the languages of justice whenever and wherever they craft a life together. In addition, he finds considerable agreement among them. When asked about justice, human beings tend to say similar kinds of things. No doubt, we have always disagreed about just exchanges and relations, contracts and punishments. All that is well known and frequently noted. Less obvious, and usually ignored, is the fact that disagreements of all kinds take place against a broad background of agreement in concept and judgement, meaning and truth. Thus, for example, my neighbour and I cannot disagree about the proper location of the fence that will divide our properties without sharing a whole collection of concepts and judgements that set the terms of the dispute. If it turns out that he does not know what fences are for, then our disagreement is more apparent than real. If the set of specific judgements that give substance to his concept 'property' is vastly different from mine, then it is not disagreement that divides us, but confusion. By the same token, real disagreements about the justice of some concrete human activity presuppose broad agreement about 'justice', about the specific judgements that give it substance. To those who wonder whether this agreement actually obtains Aquinas has little to say. He can point out that the desire to render to each their due can be found in all human communities, and he can remind us that we could neither recognize this fact, nor share this desire without conceding considerable overlap between our account of justice and all others. But this is not much of a reply. It is, rather, a command to go and look.

Look around and we will notice that human beings are creatures of one sort and not another, that we act in ways characteristic of our kind precisely because we know and will a small collection of ends naturally and necessarily. We will also notice that each end marks a sphere of human conduct, an order of deliberation and choice, and that one such sphere regards our life together, our natural desire for human society (*ST* I-II.94.2). Look around again and we will find human beings in all times and places concerned with justice, with right relations among those with whom they share some sort of society (*ST* II-II.58.3). We will also find that all human beings concede the truth of a small set of precepts that regard right relations, a collection of prohibitions and prescriptions (*ST* I-II.95.2; 100.1).

These are related matters. Justice comes packaged with society and concepts come packaged with commitments. If our nature compels us to society, then it must also compel us to care about justice, and if it compels us to care about justice, to acquire basic mastery of the concept, then it must also compel assent to those commitments that give the concept substance. No doubt we will also find some diversity of opinion about the precepts that give it substance, but this should neither surprise nor worry us. Secondary precepts of the natural law are conclusions derived from primary precepts 'after very little consideration' (*ST* I-II.100.1), and in some few cases (*ut in paucioribus*) some human beings may consider things differently (*ST* I-II.94.4). Still, these differences cannot go all the way down without losing sight of the concept we share. All of us must concede the truth of some basic *conclusiones* about justice in order to make use of the concept, and we can recognize that the concept is used across our species precisely because of our substantial agreement in *conclusiones*. No doubt we will also notice considerable disagreement about what particular *conclusiones* amount to. If the prohibition against unjust killing follows at once and after very little consideration from the first precepts of the natural law, surely agreement about definitions and cases does not (*ST* II-II.64). But this kind of moral diversity is both expected and beside the point. What matters are the facts on the ground. Our agency has a certain shape and range because we are inclined to know and will a certain collection of ends, naturally and necessarily. From the fact that we know, will, and act as human beings do, certain secondary precepts follow, abstract enough to make disagreement about them unavoidable, but concrete enough to give substance to the moral terms we all employ, 'justice' above all.

IV

We can easily imagine Aquinas saying that 'justice' – the concept, the concern, not the virtue – is there, like our life, that it comes to us as nature's grace. We can also imagine him insisting that the commitments that give it substance are the rules that govern its use. Like all grammatical rules, these commitments tell us nothing about how the concept must be employed 'in order to fulfil its purpose, in order to have such-and-such an effect on human beings' (*Philosophical Investigations*, §496). That wisdom, he thinks, comes only as our use of the concept is perfected by habits, by virtues natural and supernatural whose causes are gifts from sources other than nature. Aquinas has much to say about these sources, Wittgenstein very little. It is a difference that matters, but it hardly threatens to undo what Victor assumed they share.[13]

Notes

1. I make use of the following texts and translations: L. Wittgenstein, *On Certainty*, ed. G. E. M. Anscombe and G. H. von Wright, trans. D. Paul and G. E. M. Anscombe (Oxford, 1969); L. Wittgenstein, *Philosophical Investigations*, trans. G. E. M. Anscombe (New York, 1953); Thomas Aquinas, *Summa Theologica*, trans. Fathers of the English Dominican Province, 3 vols (New York, 1947–8); Roberto Busa (ed.), *Thomae Aquinatis Opera omnia: cum hypertextibus in CD-ROM*, 2nd edn (Milan, 1996).

2. Richard Rorty, 'The Historiography of Philosophy: Four Genres', in R. Rorty, J. B. Schneewind, and Q. Skinner (eds), *Philosophy in History* (Cambridge, 1984), pp. 49–75.

3. Jonathan Bennett, *Locke, Berkeley, Hume: Central Themes* (Oxford, 1971); P. F. Strawson, *The Bounds of Sense: An Essay on Kant's Critique of Pure Reason* (London, 1966).

4. For the most recent instalment see J. B. Schneewind, *The Invention of*

Autonomy: A History of Modern Moral Philosophy (Cambridge, 1998), pp. 17–166.

5. Heinrich A. Rommen, *The Natural Law: A Study in Legal and Social History and Philosophy*, trans. Thos. R. Hanley (Indianapolis, 1998), p. 135.

6. Although divided by disagreements about other matters, in this there is exegetical consensus. For a recent sampling see, John Finnis, *Aquinas: Moral, Political, and Legal Theory* (Oxford, 1998); Anthony Lisska, *Aquinas's Theory of Natural Law: An Analytical Reconstruction* (Oxford, 1996); Ralph McInerny, *Aquinas on Human Action: A Theory of Practice* (Washington, DC, 1992); Martin Rhonheimer, *Natural Law and Practical Reason: A Thomist View of Moral Autonomy*, trans. Gerald Malsbary (New York, 2000). Notable exceptions to this consensus include Pamela Hall, *Narrative and the Natural Law: An Interpretation of Thomistic Ethics* (Notre Dame, 1994) and F. Russell Hittinger, *First Grace* (Wilmington, 2002).

7. I am grateful to Russ Hittinger for this way of putting it.

8. What follows is an abridged version of pp. 121–7 in John Bowlin, *Contingency and Fortune in Aquinas's Ethics* (Cambridge, 1999).

9. Aquinas discusses providence by referring to its analogical relation to prudential judgement. There are, of course, disanalogies. The prudent take counsel, while God has no need of 'an enquiry into matters that are doubtful'. Nevertheless, counsel concludes in 'a command as to the right ordering of things towards an end', and this is the work of providence (*ST* I.22.1.1).

10. Of course, Aquinas does make specific judgements about specific courses of action and some of those judgements are conclusions derived from the first principles of the natural law. Still, we should not think that he refers to the natural law's first precepts in order to justify those conclusions. Rather, as I shall argue in section III below, the relation between first precepts and its proper conclusions regards the grammar of certain moral concepts, not the justification of basic moral judgements.

11. See also *Philosophical Investigations*, §288.

12. Other dissenters include Joseph Incandela, 'The Appropriation of Wittgenstein's Work by Philosophers of Religion: Towards a Re-evaluation and an End', *Religious Studies* 21 (1985): 457–74 and Sabina Lovibond, *Realism and Imagination in Ethics* (Minneapolis, 1983).

13. Marin Bâlan, Dan Barbulescue, Mircea Dumitru, and Ilie Pârvu of the philosophy faculty at the Universitatea Bucuresti offered useful comments on an earlier version of this paper, as did my colleagues at the University of Tulsa – Jane Ackerman, Nicholas Capaldi, Stephen Gardner, Russell Hittinger, and Jacob Howland. The editors of this volume, Jeffrey Stout and Robert MacSwain, provided sound advice toward the end. Thanks to them all.

8. Wittgenstein and the Recovery of Virtue[1]

G. SCOTT DAVIS

In the 'Lecture on Ethics', written shortly after his return to Cambridge in 1929, Wittgenstein remarks that 'the tendency of all men who ever tried to write or talk Ethics or Religion was to run against the boundaries of language' (LE, p. 44).[2] This repeats the spirit of his remarks in the *Tractatus*, where he wrote that 'the sense of the world must lie outside the world . . . Hence also there can be no ethical propositions. Propositions cannot express anything higher' (*TLP* 6.41–6.42). The world pictured in language is one of facts and does not include values or laws, be they natural or moral. This was clearer to the ancients than to us:

> At the basis of the whole modern view of the world lies the illusion that the so-called laws of nature are the explanation of natural phenomena. So people stop short at natural laws as at something unassailable, as did the ancients at God and Fate. And they are right and wrong. But the ancients were clearer, in so far as they recognized one clear terminus, whereas the modern system makes it appear as though *everything* were explained. (*TLP* 6.371–6.372)

The ancients, when invoking God and Fate, did not deny that there were deep and puzzling aspects of human experience, involving matters 'higher' than our ordinary encounters with the facts of our world; but they insisted that those puzzles were fundamentally unanswerable. Moderns, entranced by the achievements of the sciences, assume that there is an answer for everything. Thus, in the lecture, Wittgenstein asks his audience to imagine:

> That one of you suddenly grew a lion's head and began to roar.

Certainly that would be as extraordinary a thing as I can imagine. Now whenever we should have recovered from our surprise, what I would suggest would be to fetch a doctor and have the case scientifically investigated and if it were not for hurting him I would have him vivisected. (*LE*, p. 43)

Modern, scientific, man doesn't see miracles, only odd phenomena that call out for more thorough study. Ethics, like the miraculous, doesn't defy scientific explanation; it just doesn't exist. In what follows I hope to do two things. On the one hand, I want to embrace Wittgenstein's rejection of ethics as theory, in the sense of a systematic body of knowledge about the world. On the other, I hope to suggest that this rejection opens up conceptual space for understanding ethics as a critical human enterprise.

The antinomies of liberalism

Contemporary moral and political conservatives, religious and otherwise, remain in the condition of the ancients, willing to invoke God or Tradition or Reason to justify their views. The conservative legal theorist Robert George is a prominent example. He identifies himself with the 'new natural law theory' developed by Germain Grisez and John Finnis. For them, basic human goods are 'strictly speaking "self-evident." They come to be known in non-inferential acts of understanding' (George 1999: 231). Like 'the walls of our cage', the basic goods are simply there for reasonable people to see. People who don't see them are either self-deluded or depraved (cf. George 1999: 300–14).[3]

Liberal theorists, however, are in a more difficult situation. Not only must they face the objections of their conservative critics, they often find themselves trapped in what I'll call the antinomies of liberalism.[4] By this I mean the sort of situation where what appears to be one fundamental commitment of liberalism runs up against another, *prima facie* equal, commitment. For example, liberals have learned from the pogroms of the last 200 years that it is important to protect group rights, particularly those of minorities, but then those minorities use that privilege to perpetuate an exclusive and intolerant tradition (cf. Okin 1999: 9–24). Freedom of conscience would appear to be one of the great rights secured by the Enlightenment from the authoritarianism of the *ancien régime*, but as often as not that freedom is invoked against some individual or unfavoured group (cf. Nussbaum 1999: 81–6).

Consider the following case. An earnest couple intent on having children seek fertility treatments. As a result they conceive and remove from their remote island residence to the capital of the commonwealth, where the mother can receive advanced prenatal care. In the course of this care doctors determine that the mother is carrying Siamese twins, who unequally share a single heart and respiratory system. Both will die unless surgery is performed to detach the more viable from its less viable sibling. The doctors insist that they *must* sever the two at birth so that one may live.

Even if the couple were not, as I will assume, earnest and devout Roman Catholics, this would be a tragic situation. They want children. They are overjoyed at the thought of twins. And now, whatever they do, there will be tragic consequences. Their Catholicism leads them to one tragic choice – do not intervene to bring about directly the death of an innocent – even though they know that both will die. The alternative looks, to them, a lot like murder, or at least the sacrifice of one individual for another. The liberal public, on the other hand, finds it unthinkable that the parents should sacrifice a baby for their private religious feelings.

The dilemma is exacerbated by the fact that the parents don't see the matter as one of 'private religious feelings'. If the doctors act as they see fit, they violate the deeply held moral and religious views of the parents themselves. The parents are willing to allow their children to die because they love both equally and they believe their God does so as well. As parents, the couple wants nothing more than to embrace their children, protect them and bring them up in a world of love and devotion. But, finally, they are willing, despite a congeries of conflicting feelings, to let the children both die because they revere the moral law promulgated by God. On the level of what Rawls calls 'comprehensive doctrine', the conservative Catholic vision of the parents is as rich and complexly developed as the liberal individualism that would protect the viable newborn against its parents.[5] The parents have a story to tell about the origins and order of the universe, genuine, as opposed to merely apparent, goods, and the ultimate hopes they have for the highest good of themselves and their children. Such comprehensive teachings may, as Rawls admits, be true (Rawls 2001: 183). He merely denies that this story can have any standing in public discourse.

Suppose, in order to avoid state interference, the couple decides to check the mother out of the hospital and remove to a conservative Roman Catholic country where hospitals follow rather different guidelines, which prohibit a direct attack on the innocent. Can the liberal state justly prohibit their going? On one hand, the answer would seem to be no. Rawls distinguishes early on in the most recent statement of his theory between a 'person', who has moral and intellectual powers, and 'a member of the species homo sapiens' (2001: 24). The parents are clearly persons; the status of the foetuses is unclear. What right does a state have to compel otherwise free adults to stay within its borders?

On the other hand, the answer would seem to be yes. Rawls claims that the 'basic rights' of 'children as future citizens are inalienable and protect them wherever they are' (Rawls 2001: 166). If children are future citizens, why not viable foetuses? If one can be saved, perhaps the state does have a duty to do so. Then again, is it just to save the one at the expense of even five minutes of the life of the other? Does the lack of viability in the one reduce its value even though, presumably, it becomes a citizen at birth?

I don't think there is an answer, 'in principle', to these questions, at least not within the parameters of rights-based liberal theories. Cosmopolitan political theorists such as Martha Nussbaum and Brian Barry may insist on 'the familiar list of basic human rights', and go on to insist that 'anybody whose human rights are violated – say, by being denied freedom of speech or freedom of religious worship – has a legitimate complaint' (Barry 1998: 156–7). But it is precisely how these purported rights get established, and who gets to establish them, that remains unclear. If we usually tolerate state intervention, particularly in cases where the parents would deny life-saving medical care for reasons of religion, it is because the majority feels that the commitments of such religious minorities are ill-conceived and pernicious. That, however, seems very much like the tyranny of the majority.[6]

Unless they can maintain a credible argument for the self-evidence of 'the familiar list of basic human rights', contract theorists like Rawls have, as Gilbert Harman points out, 'no reason to expect agreement to be reached under the stated conditions, or at least no reason to think a unique agreement would be reached under those conditions' (Harman 2000: 67). It doesn't help for Rawls to shift his claims from the 'metaphysical' to the 'political'. In the absence of a 'metaphysical' justification, 'justice as fairness' has the status of any other convention a given group might choose to embrace. But in that case, as Harman sees it, we have a straightforward instance of moral relativism.

The spectre of relativism

Rather than a nightmare of moral chaos, Harman sees his relativism as

> a soberly logical thesis – a thesis about logical form, if you like. Just as the judgement that something is large is true or false only in relation to one or another comparison class, so too, I will argue, the judgement that it is wrong of someone to do something is true or false only in relation to an agreement or understanding. (Harman 2000: 3)

If we use the language of 'right' as the basic language of ethics, then there has to be some stipulation of what moves are allowed within the system. This requires that certain cases constitute the norm against which other moves or outcomes are to be judged. Once we accept, for example, a convention that only legitimate agents of the state, in accordance with the rule of law, can execute a convicted criminal or use deadly force against the agents of aggression, then we can hold each other accountable for the injuries we do. But until he has accepted the convention, the mafioso has no overriding reason to abide by its demands (cf. Harman 2000: 33). We don't have to tolerate him, but not because he has made some philosophical mistake.

If reasons are relative to sets of principles, and if there is nothing in the nature of things to dispose people to choose one set of principles over another, then we should conclude, Harman thinks, 'that our current principles of justice are the result of ongoing implicit bargaining and adjustment' (2000: 73). There seems to be something right about this. Even if we were persuaded by Rawls's account of justice, for example, our present practice would be the result of some actual historical give-and-take. Harman wants, obviously, to say something stronger. In particular, he argues that the 'absolutism' of what he calls the 'naive view of morality' – the view, for example, that such institutions as slavery are always and everywhere evil – is untenable. 'Those who are attracted to that conception', he writes, 'find themselves in the position of those who think morality is the law of God and then decide there is no God. Relativism implies that morality so understood is a delusion, a vain and chimerical notion' (2000: 46). Morality as universal law, Harman thinks, should be replaced by 'morality as politics', for which 'the principles that give you moral reasons to do things are the moral principles that you actually accept' (2000: 56).

Harman's sober relativism appears to follow the lead of the later Wittgenstein, who writes that 'logical inference is part of a language-game. And someone who carries out logical inferences in the language-game follows certain instructions which were given him in the actual learning of the language-game' (RFM V-23). On this account logic is one game among many, and the way it is played depends on how it is learned. Furthermore, 'rules of inference cannot be right or wrong' (RFM V-23), since right and wrong only function in the context of obeying rules. Ways of proceeding depend upon the paradigm or picture that has been adopted, and 'inference is a transition that is justified if it follows a particular paradigm, and whose rightness is not dependent on anything else' (RFM V-45). There is, it would seem, no compelling necessity which forces us to adopt one picture over another. 'When someone sets up the law of excluded middle,' Wittgenstein suggests, 'he is as it were putting two pictures before us to choose from, and saying that one must correspond to the fact' (RFM IV-10).

This correspondence, however, is an illusion. So is the appearance of necessity in following the steps of logical inference. 'The reason', he writes, 'why they are not brought in question is not that they "certainly correspond to the truth" – or something of the sort, – no, it is just that that is called "thinking", "speaking", "inferring", "arguing"' (RFM I-155). Logic is no more stable than the language-games in which it is found; there is no deeper justification for it than for any game. That, Wittgenstein seems to be saying, is just the way we do things here, and this seems to put Wittgenstein at one with Harman.

But this isn't the whole story. Wittgenstein considers the case of a student learning the natural numbers:

> First of all series of numbers will be written down for him and he will be required to copy them ... At first perhaps we guide his hand in writing out the series 0 to 9; but then the *possibility of getting him to understand* will depend on his going on to write it down independently. (*PI* §143)

This needn't preclude mistakes, so long as it is possible to correct them. But suppose, Wittgenstein goes on, 'we get the pupil to continue a series (say +2) beyond 1000 – and he writes 1000, 1004, 1008, 1012'. It looks as though he takes the rule to require doubling the step after 1000, or something like that:

> We say to him: 'Look what you've done!' – He doesn't understand. We say: 'You were meant to add *two*: look how you began the series!' – He answers: 'Yes, isn't it right? I thought that was how I was *meant* to do it.' – Or suppose he pointed to the series and said: 'But I went on in the same way.' – It would now be of no use to say: 'But can't you see ... ?' – and repeat the old examples and explanations. – In such a case we might say, perhaps: It comes natural to this person to understand our order with our explanations as *we* should understand the order 'Add 2 up to 1000, 4 up to 2000, 6 up to 3000 and so on'. (*PI* §185)

There is nothing in the command itself that rules out the pupil taking it as he does. The steps are not, so to speak, concealed within the rule, so that to *mean* something is to mean the constituent steps. Nor is there a tiny voice, whispering the next step; going on doesn't require feeling 'that one has always got to wait upon the nod (the whisper) of the rule' (*PI* §223). If it proves impossible to wean the pupil away from his natural inclination there is nothing left to do. As Wittgenstein puts it, 'our pupil's capacity to learn may come to an end' (*PI* §143). It is futile to appeal to self-evidence, since that's the point at issue.[7]

But that someone cannot learn our technique need not lead to calling our activities into question, or even to thinking them conventional or arbitrary. This comes out in the much discussed wood-sellers of the *Remarks on the Foundations of Mathematics*. We suppose, generally, that no philosophical justification is needed for forms of exchange; that's just how they organize their economy. 'Very well,' Wittgenstein grants:

> but what if they piled the timber in heaps of arbitrary, varying heights and then sold it at a price proportionate to the area covered by the piles? And what if they even justified this with the words: 'Of course, if you buy more timber, you must pay more'? (*RFM* I-148)

If followed to what we would imagine its natural conclusion, this would violate not only 'common sense' but the central laws of logic. Nonetheless, Wittgenstein continues:

> How could I shew them that – as I should say – you don't really buy more wood if you buy a pile covering a bigger area? – I should, for instance, take a pile which was small by their ideas and, by laying the logs around, change it into a 'big' one. This *might* convince them – but perhaps they would say: 'Yes, now it's a *lot* of wood and costs more' – and that would be the end of the matter. – We should presumably say in this case: they simply do not mean the same by 'a lot of wood' and 'a little wood' as we do; and they have a different system of payment from us. (*RFM* I-149)

If this were the end of the matter, we would have an example of 'Wittgensteinian relativism'. Here it is not simply a matter of one pupil unable to get the hang of a particular mathematical rule. Now we seem to have an entire society whose means of thought and livelihood are bound up with approaches that seem absurd. Not only this, but Wittgenstein suggests in his concluding remark that the most that can be said is that these people have a different system from us.

Intelligibility and argument

But is this the end of the matter? I have already suggested one peculiar consequence of taking the wood-sellers at their word and Wittgenstein himself suggests another in the passage above. Barry Stroud argues that the wood-sellers represent an apparent alternative 'only because the wider reaching consequences of counting, calculating, and so forth, in these deviant ways are not brought out explicitly' (Stroud 1965: 488). Suppose that we expand the example by saying that among these people wood piles are often exchanged for goods and services. Taking a 1' × 6' × 2" board, consider the customer who enters the general store where he recently bought the board, measured along the 1' × 2" side, for $2.40. He slaps it on the counter, 6' × 2", to pay for $14.40 worth of groceries. The clerk cheerfully complies, delivering the goods and laying the board 'flat' with the rest of his daily take. At the end of the week he pays the delivery boy $86.40 by means of this 'same' board.

And so it goes, with fortunes lost and won. How are we to take this? We cannot consider the first person a crafty entrepreneur, since this would require his recognizing the peculiarity, or whatever we want to call it, of the system. But, *ex hypothesi*, he cannot do this without acknowledging the greater intelligibility of ours. The vendor cannot be called simple-minded, for that would be to invoke our own standards; as far as he is concerned he has only given the delivery boy his due. Nor does the delivery boy have any grounds for thinking that he has received a handsome bonus. Given the rules of this game, how much he now has depends on the way he pays his next bill. It is not even predictable what the value of his fortune will be tomorrow. And this is the central point, for a system that 'worked' like this could not be a form of exchange, since there would be no possibility of predicting at any moment what there was to be exchanged. A community for whom this might be possible would have to be indifferent to the amount of food it consumed. Extend it to glasses of water. People for whom a 1 litre glass with a 2" base held slightly less than an ordinary wine glass could not be people in any recognizable sense. The more we try to make sense of their way of life, the less we're able to keep hold of our own. As Stroud puts it:

to live in their world inevitably leads us to abandon more and more of our own familiar world and the ways of thinking about it upon which our understanding rests. The more successful we are in

projecting ourselves into such a world, the less we will have left in
terms of which we can find it intelligible. (1965: 489)

If the activity of the wood-sellers is confined to a narrow and circum-
scribed portion of their social world then it will not impinge on
recognizably human behaviour. Perhaps it is a relic from the past, or
from some particular cultic practice. But attempting to imagine it as
an integral part of a system of exchange leads to intolerable consequences. Nonetheless, as Stroud points out, the lack of intelligibility
does not rest in the 'logical' impossibility of anything being imagined.
It is a simple fact that nothing even remotely analogous to a human
community could work this way and this, Stroud concludes, is
precisely Wittgenstein's point.

Placed in context, the example of the wood-sellers is not intended as
an alternative logic or mathematics. Its point, rather, is to bring
out the impossibility of providing a 'philosophical' foundation for
mathematics in the sense, say, of Carnap (see Carnap et al. 1931).
Thus it is closely related to Wittgenstein's general discussion of philosophical theories and, as in the case of the unteachable pupil, the
example of the wood-sellers displays the limits of argument and
justification. An appeal to logical necessity or the self-evidence of a
particular rule or procedure fails in both cases because that necessity
only presents itself to us if we have already learned the technique for
going on. In fact, the *Remarks* make common cause here with the
Investigations, not in presenting a philosophical theory but in
exposing the inclinations that impel us towards theory. The idea that
meaningful language requires a foundation which possesses the 'crystalline purity' of logic (*PI* §107) is itself a symptom of deep confusion,
which an older tradition attempted to overcome through theories, but
which can only be seen for what it is by working through cases and
examples, unearthing the picture that tempts us.

Confusion ensues when I am 'seduced into using a super-expression.
(It might be called a philosophical superlative)' (*PI* §192). Requiring
justification for every statement leads to demanding justification for
language in general and to the fear that without this super-justification
my ability to make true, or even intelligible, statements collapses.
But this quest for the super-picture is fruitless. The very possibility of

learning a language depends upon agreeing how to go on. In the case of the pupil, his inability to see what was wanted marked the end of his ability to learn. In the case of the wood-sellers, more widespread disagreement, if it can be called that on such a scale, brought into doubt our ability to think of them as persons. They are too different and, as Wittgenstein notes, the 'common behaviour of mankind is the system of reference by means of which we interpret an unknown language' (*PI* §206).

Isn't this, nonetheless, a species of conventionalism? In one sense Wittgenstein acknowledges this. It is, presumably, a contingent fact that we exist in the form we do. If we had been substantially different from the way we are, we would operate with different concepts, or no concepts at all. But for Wittgenstein, as opposed to Harman, this doesn't lead to 'relativism'. What underlies our mathematical practices is not an ideal, Platonic, realm which models our mathematical ideas and provides a norm against which we measure the abilities of our students and ourselves. It is, rather, a set of practices that have emerged out of the problem-solving imaginations of our predecessors. Continuity with those predecessors is assured, to the extent that it is assured, by the training we receive, with its combination of memorization, correction, testing, and application overseen by professionals whose own training goes back to those esteemed elders.

Historical accounts of how we came to do things the ways we do are not derailed when someone points out, correctly, that they might have been done differently. They only look rickety when she goes on to exclaim that, since they are not necessary, they must be arbitrary, or unjustified, or, worst of all, irrational. But this is nonsense. The standards of reasonable action are keyed to the activity in question, a point made famously by Aristotle at *Ethics* 1098a, where he remarks that 'we do not look for the same degree of exactness in all areas, but the degree that fits the subject-matter'. Wittgenstein generalizes this when he insists that 'if language is to be a means of communication there must be agreement not only in definitions but also (queer as this may sound) in judgments' (*PI* §242).

Part of the modern worry about relativism stems from the illusion that there is something paradigmatically 'rational' about the procedures of the natural sciences. Wittgenstein attempts to dispel this illusion, in its positivist form, when he remarks that 'asking whether and how a proposition can be verified, is only a particular way of asking "How d'you mean?" The answer is a contribution to the grammar of the proposition' (*PI* §354). A scientific formula, or string of formulae, used to articulate a particular theory or theoretical finding, is shorthand for an account of how a particular investigator or group of investigators thinks, on the basis of their work in the field, that the part of the world they're interested in will be found to hang together. But once you put it this way, 'scientists' differ from the rest of us in nothing but the objects that interest them, the apparatus available for investigating those objects, and the preferred notation for writing up what they've learned. The certainty of their claims, and the ways in which they are qualified, will differ among the various investigators and their communities, but this isn't surprising.

More to the point, nothing about this licenses stigmatizing one sort of investigation as 'subjective'. If the subjective/objective distinction has any usefulness it is, I suppose, for signalling that in some investigations we commit ourselves to considering the responses of subjects other than a uniformly trained group of expert investigators. But there are almost no enterprises, particularly if they involve commitments of money, time, and resources, where we think that just anybody's response is worth considering. So, unless there are special circumstances, we discount the views of astrologers on the policy choices of Ariel Sharon, the views of Kansans on sushi, and the views of serial rapists on justice (cf. Stout 1988: 37–45). More generally, societies have typically looked to their elders for moral guidance because the elders have encountered similar problems, have seen, made and learned from their mistakes, and are, as likely as not, best positioned to guide the community successfully through its problems.

The recovery of virtue

Suppose we admit that, when seen from a Wittgensteinian perspective, Harman's relativism doesn't have the worrisome connotations the term often calls to mind. How does any of this lead us to an ethics of the virtues? Part of the problem, of course, is that it is unclear what 'virtue ethics' amounts to. Rather than attempt to survey the different things that 'virtue' has meant since MacIntyre reanimated the term in mainstream Anglo-American ethics, I'll simply lay out how I intend the term.[8] In a nutshell, my view is that human beings are animals capable of overlaying their first, animal, nature with a second nature that disposes them to act not on instinct but on the basis of reasons. These reasons are formulated in a complex language which may vary from group to group, and in the process of learning that language humans typically acquire a variety of habits, some of which are applauded by members of their immediate communities and others looked at more critically.

In this conceptual environment, what distinguishes actions from products of art is that judging acts depends on knowing the character of the agent, who, according to Aristotle,

> must be in a certain condition when he does them; in the first place he must have knowledge, secondly he must choose the acts, and choose them for their own sakes, and thirdly his action must proceed from a firm and unchangeable character. (*EN* 1105a–b)

For these conditions to obtain it is essential that both the agent and the members of his community agree on what makes actions choice-worthy. To choose something is to recognize in it a good to be pursued now. This means that standards of goodness are built into the learning processes. Thus Aristotle rejects the Platonic account, which takes 'good' to be a univocal term for a single property, only partially instantiated in particular things, in favour of the pragmatic observation that the good

> seems different in different actions and arts . . . What is the good of each? Surely that for whose sake everything is done. In medicine this is health, in strategy victory, in architecture a house, in any other sphere something else, and in every action and choice the end. (*EN* 1097a)[9]

If the good is the end of a practical action, and if the actions for which we are held accountable are either endorsed or blamed by a community by which our character has been shaped, then the good must be, *pace* Rawls, prior to the right.

For Aristotle, the virtues make possible not only the pursuit, but the perception, of the good. This sounds, perhaps, paradoxical, but it reflects our ordinary experience of learning. Early on, Aristotle wonders

> what we mean by saying that we must become just by doing just acts, and temperate by doing temperate acts; for if men do just and temperate acts, they are already just and temperate, exactly as, if they do what is grammatical or musical they are proficient in grammar and music. (*EN* 1105a)

Consider the case of grammar. The human infant responds to sounds in its immediate environment in a variety of ways, but usually, sometime around eight months, it begins to mimic the sounds made by adults. Within the next six months, exposed to the give and take of mimicry, response and reward familiar to most parents, the toddler develops a basic vocabulary and rudimentary grammar, though it wouldn't understand those particular terms. As Aristotle remarks, 'it is possible to do something grammatical either by chance or under the guidance of another' (*EN* 1105a). In fact, it is the combination of chance and guidance that coaxes the infant from pre-reflective instinct and response to incipient language-use, with the emerging panoply of desires and intentions that language makes possible. And for the next 17 or so years, as it matures from toddler to adolescent to young adult, the human language-user will perfect its linguistic skills. But 'a man will be proficient in grammar, then, only when he has both done something grammatical and done it grammatically; and this means doing it in accordance with the grammatical knowledge in himself' (*EN* 1105a). As with grammar, so with the other arts and excellences that we expect members of our community to practise and exemplify. We perform and perceive well-done acts by being trained into shared practices.

Aristotle distinguishes, of course, between arts and excellences, or virtues, but not on the grounds of their being learned through regular training and practice. The product of an art, say painting, is good solely because of the qualities of the product. It's the painting that we prize, not the abusive jerk who created it. But when we attribute virtue, the acts are only part of the story. 'The agent', as noted above, 'must have knowledge . . . must choose the acts, and choose them for their own sakes' (*EN* 1105a–b). Failure of knowledge or choice makes the act accidental or involuntary, a matter of good luck to the beneficiary, but not an instance of excellent, or virtuous, activity. Not only that, but we are all familiar with acts for which we have been praised that, if our real intentions were known, would be a matter of shame and embarrassment. And sometimes, if we're lucky, praise for some thoughtless, spur-of-the-moment act leads us to rethink and reorient our behaviour in ways that are genuinely praiseworthy, even if the process began indifferently. Imagine the ten-year-old who stoops for the dropped wallet only to be thanked, unexpectedly, by the old man just turning to see what has happened.

Of course, there is no guarantee that anyone will be perfect in the virtues, or even develop all the virtues equally. It is possible for an individual to be notably just and upright in public dealings, but to be deficient, say, in temperance. Aristotle's discussion of temperance is particularly interesting, for here he illustrates an intermediate stage where a person knows how he *should* see the world, but has not been able to mould his perceptions accordingly. In Book III of the *Ethics*, Aristotle describes temperance as the mean with regard to the pleasures specifically of 'touch and taste' (*EN* 1118a). It is perfectly reasonable to enjoy wine, but the temperate person knows when enough is enough and it is second nature to see the fourth glass, say, as too much and to decline it as a matter of course. The self-indulgent person, on the other hand, is so taken by the pleasures of the vine that he sees every option to consume as desirable and choiceworthy. His specific vice is drunkenness. But somewhere between these two, as we discover in Book VII, is the incontinent person, who knows that he has had enough but still indulges, to his later regret. 'Incontinence', writes Aristotle, 'is not a vice . . . for incontinence is contrary to choice while vice is in accordance with choice; not but what they are similar in respect of the objects they lead to' (*EN* 1151a). The incontinent person does what he knows he shouldn't, swayed in the instance by the expectation of pleasure. Aristotle compares incontinence to a disease like epilepsy, which comes and goes (*EN* 1150b). The continent person is just the flip-side of the incontinent. He restrains himself, but the need for restraint shows that to experience and to anticipate pleasure in accord with the mean is not yet second nature. Because human beings are always subject to new experiences, pleasures, and interests, we should expect most people, on occasion, to act in ways they regret. Attributions of virtue are about the way individuals can typically be expected to see and react to the world.

The cardinal virtues in particular – prudence, justice, courage, and temperance – allow us to explain how we organize the propriety of our choices, distinguishing, for instance, pursuits of sex which are just and reasonable from those that would be defective, through a failure of knowledge or choice, or wicked due to a breach of virtue. Thus rape, to take a particularly heinous act, is a violation of justice because it takes from the victim something to which the assailant has no right, namely sexual favours.[10] This is why it remains rape, and vicious, even if there is no physical injury, or if the assailant showers the victim with money and presents.[11] Not only that, but our training in the virtues, which allows us to see injustice for what it is, does not need the further addition of law to identify the evil of rape.

Law has an intermediate status in Aristotle's moral world. On the one hand, any complex society will generate a body of law, whether common or statutory, to simplify and clarify the mutual relations among its institutions and practices. Well-formed law plays an important role in moulding individuals into the sorts of persons who recognize and appreciate the goods embraced by the community. In this sense, the law is a teacher.

On the other hand, while law 'is universal', there are a great many things about which 'it is not possible to make a universal statement which will be correct . . . And this is the nature of the equitable, a correction of law where it is defective owing to its universality' (*EN* 1137b). It is the nature of the legal paradigm that an indefinite number of particular situations will not be resolvable within the context of the law itself. This is the origin of what I earlier called the antinomies of liberalism. Virtuous agents, not content to allow injustices to persist, recognize the need for equity, which corrects legal justice by bringing the situation in line, as much as that is possible, with our shared judgements about the good.

In this sense ethics is traditional and conservative, beginning with the phenomena. But it is also critical, recognizing various rival accounts of the good life and admitting up-front that the goal of ethics is to sort through the options, rejecting some and revising others where needed. There is no state of nature. Early in the *Politics* Aristotle reflects on the development of the *polis* out of the family (*Pol.* 1252a ff.), but ethics, like everything else human, takes place *in medias res*, with the nature of the various goods and activities constantly a matter of negotiation. It is here, however, that Harman's model of ethics as politics is accurate only when qualified by reflection on Wittgenstein's wood-sellers. The possibility for variation in local practice is great, but to the extent that the ramifications involve more and more departures from the cardinal virtues, the more that form of life is unintelligible.

There are certain goods it is unthinkable to live without, not because they are deduced from our 'nature' or delivered by some intellectual intuition, but because it is hard to recognize ourselves in a world wholly devoid of them. And the cardinal virtues persist, even where two competing moral paradigms seem wholly incommensurable. Hume, for example, thought that 'celibacy, fasting, penance, mortification, self-denial, humility, silence, solitude, and the whole train of monkish virtues' (1902: 219) were absurd, but this only means that he ostentatiously refused even to consider the sort of story that would make these plausible virtues.[12] We know people who believe such a story and in the best of them recognize the courage and temperance necessary for rendering what they believe they owe to their god. Their presence in the world, and their success in negotiating its demands, shows them to be closer to us, for the most part, than Wittgenstein's wood-sellers or the victims of some science fiction nightmare.

Von Wright remarks of Wittgenstein that 'I do not think that he could have enjoyed Aristotle or Leibniz, two great logicians before him' (Malcolm 1984: 19). I suppose that Aristotle, read as a systematic and comprehensive theorist, would have appealed to Wittgenstein as little as Descartes (see Monk 1990: 322, 496). But Aristotle the critic of his predecessors, using the poets to expose their one-sided theories, is another matter altogether. Ethics, for Aristotle and for Wittgenstein, does not stand in need of a superhuman foundation or justification, and worries about relativism result from a misplaced 'scientism'. What the philosopher attempts to do is display various pictures of the good as more or less compelling. What counts as compelling will depend on the various competing views of the way the world is and this means that conceptually the good will always take priority over the right. That we learn the good as part of being educated into our institutions means that doing ethics will always be about where excellence lies.

Notes

1. The occasion calls for reminiscence and recognition. For the last two decades I have worked almost exclusively in various areas of ethics. My original interest, however, was in Wittgenstein and the rationality of belief. I first read Wittgenstein in Anthony Kenny's 1972 course at Stanford, in the summer after my freshman year. This initial taste inspired me to work on Wittgenstein with Douglas Magee at Bowdoin and George Pitcher at Princeton. But it was only in discussion, mostly subterranean, with Victor Preller, from about 1978 to 1980, that I was able to formulate an account of Wittgenstein on these issues that both made sense to me and made sense of the text. The end result was a Princeton dissertation, for which Preller was the advisor, that I defended in the autumn of 1983. In the meantime I had been teaching Aristotle's ethics to freshmen at Stanford and then at Columbia and came to realize that I was reading the newspaper through eyes that were both Aristotelian and Wittgensteinian. For this essay I revisited my dissertation to see if I could explain how the reading of Wittgenstein I learned in Princeton has, through all these years, reinforced my thought that Aristotle's account of ethics captures what being human is all about.

2. The works of Aristotle, Aquinas, and Wittgenstein, which exist in various editions, I cite by abbreviated title and the accepted form: Bekker numbers for Aristotle, though without the line number; part, question and article for Aquinas; and the paragraph or page number for Wittgenstein. For all other works the citation is by author, date, and page number. See 'References and abbreviations' below.

3. For recent critical comments on Finnis and George see Davis (2001).

4. By 'liberal theorists' I intend pretty much the usual suspects who rile conservatives like George. Pre-eminent in this group are Ackerman, Dworkin, Feinberg, and Rawls. I intend blithely to ignore the differences in detail and let Rawls stand in for the varieties of rights-based, procedural, liberalisms, acknowledging all the while the important differences. Nussbaum and Okin, mentioned below, are deeply dependent on Rawls, even when Okin, for example, criticizes him for being inadequately sensitive to injustices in the family.

5. In most cases the attack on Rawls for asserting an unargued individualism

seems to be unjustified. In this case, however, individualism of some sort does seem to be at work. When Rawls asserts that the future goods of the infant as citizen are what is being protected, it can't be that the state has an interest in protecting every potential individual. It can't know anything about that newborn's contribution to the pursuit of freedom and equality. Not only that, but Rawls seems to suggest that, in justice as fairness, women would have to be granted a right of abortion, so if, in our case, the mother had changed her mind and decided to terminate the pregnancy, her choice would take precedence over any state interest in creating citizens. Furthermore, the explicitly stated good of changing residence would seem to allow parents who conceive in a democratic regime to emigrate to a theocracy in order to make sure that their children are brought up in a society ordered contrary to justice as fairness: the antinomies of liberalism.

6. It's worth mentioning at this point, if only to stave off a certain kind of criticism, that while I find the language of human rights unpersuasive, I have no objection to the notion of rights generally. I just think that what 'rights' people enjoy are sometimes the result of custom, sometimes of positive legislation. Sometimes custom and legislation clarify the demands of justice and in other cases they establish entitlements and protections that go beyond what justice would require. Sometimes they are defective with regard to virtue, in which case being a right may be contrary, typically, to justice. Once this point is granted, it is possible to tell the story of 'rights talk', as part of the emerging vocabulary of modern democracies, in a way that is consistent with the language of virtues. Jeffrey Stout does this in Stout 2004. The difference between us then becomes whether or not, and in what contexts, the language of rights is helpful in resolving our current moral concerns. I remain sceptical, not because I dispute Stout's just-so story, but because in most instances where I have encountered proponents of 'human rights', the language plays much the same role as 'scientific method' in earlier disputes about religion and rationality, with the same sanctimonious air of western self-righteousness that Conrad excoriates in *Heart of Darkness*.

7. It won't help to appeal to nature or mental events; his way of going on is as much in accord with those as ours. The failure of agreement between us is so great that he simply cannot learn this technique. It would be pointless to say, however, that he gives the rule a different meaning. Such talk obscures the depth of the gulf between us. By way of analogy, people occasionally say of an abusing parent that love means something different for that person, and violence is its natural expression. But this distorts language and fact, potentially blinding us to the depth of the evil.

8. While I think it is close to Aristotle's understanding, nothing much turns here on the adequacy of my reading of the Philosopher. It is substantially the same as I developed in Davis 1992 and connected to Aquinas, in opposition to the 'new natural law theorists', in Davis 2001. Of recent interpreters, my reading is most similar to the now neglected account of J. H. Randall (cf. Randall 1960: 267ff.)

9. That Aristotle is rejecting Plato's theory of Forms is explicit in 1096a–b. There Aristotle marshals a very compressed version of the 'third man' argument

of Plato's *Parmenides* against the very idea of 'a thing itself'. On the argument in Plato see Vlastos 1973: 342–65.

10. 'Spousal rape' and 'spousal rights' are notions where it strikes me that the language of human rights is particularly inept. Mary Douglas instances the Walbiri, among whom 'the least complaint or neglect' may result in being 'beaten or speared. No blood compensation can be claimed for a wife killed by her husband, and no one has the right to intervene between husband and wife' (Douglas 1966: 141). At the same time, sexual roles among the Walbiri are part of a social order which 'accepts as one of its objectives that all members of the community shall work and be cared for according to their ability and needs' (Douglas 1966: 141). To inveigh against Walbiri men for their gross violations of their women's human rights would be: (1) unintelligible to the Walbiri themselves; and (2) pointless as an exercise in moral judgement among us. What we find horrifying, I assume, is that societies have developed along such lines. But that's rather different from the question of what, if anything, should be done, by whom, with what justification. For some reflections on humanitarian intervention along Aristotelian lines see Davis 2002.

11. While Aristotle's own discussions of the cardinal virtues are very rich, the most illuminating discussion of the workings of the virtues, how they succeed and how they fail, is that of Thomas Aquinas in the *Summa Theologiae*. In I-II, particularly questions 18–21, Aquinas goes well beyond Aristotle in analysing the relations of the internal act of will to the completed action. The discussion of the cardinal virtues in *ST* II-II, particularly the ways in which the virtues are realized in our social environment, are unparalleled in their subtlety. *ST* II-II.154.5, on whether wet dreams are sinful (they're not), is a model of moral analysis. Although perhaps regrettable, it is not surprising that the Second Part of the Second Part circulated more widely, and in more diverse contexts, than the rest of the *Summa* during the later Middle Ages and early modern period. For this see Boyle 1982: 23–30. This important essay is now happily reprinted in Pope 2002: 1–16.

12. This may be unfair to Hume, though his own intemperate language invites it. A more sympathetic recent account of these matters is Herdt 1997: ch. 5.

References and abbreviations

Aquinas, Thomas:
ST   *Summa Theologiae*, ed. Thomas Gilby, 60 vols (London: Blackfriars, 1964–81)
Aristotle:
EN   *Nicomachean Ethics*, trans. Ross, rev. Urmson, in *Works*, vol. 2
Meta.   *Metaphysics*, trans. Ross, in *Works*, vol. 2
Pol.   *Politics*, trans. Jowett, in *Works*, vol. 2
Works   *The Complete Works of Aristotle: The Revised Oxford*

Translation, ed. Jonathan Barnes, 2 vols (Princeton: Princeton University Press, 1984)

Wittgenstein:

LE 'Lecture on Ethics', ed. and trans. Rush Rhees, reprinted in *Philosophical Occasions, 1912–1951*, ed. James Klagge and Alfred Nordman (Indianapolis: Hackett, 1993), pp. 36–44

PI *Philosophical Investigations*, 3rd edn, ed. Anscombe and Rhees, trans. Anscombe (Oxford: Basil Blackwell & Mott, 1958)

RFM *Remarks on the Foundations of Mathematics*, 2nd edn, ed. von Wright, Rhees, and Anscombe, trans. Anscombe (Oxford: Basil Blackwell, 1967)

TLP *Tractatus Logico-Philosophicus*, trans. Ogden (London: Routledge & Kegan Paul, 1922)

Barry, Brian, 1998. 'International Society from a Cosmopolitan Perspective', in David R. Mapel and Terry Nardin (eds), *International Society: Diverse Perspectives* (Princeton, NJ: Princeton University Press), pp. 144–63

Benacerraf, Paul, and Hilary Putnam (eds), 1964. *Philosophy of Mathematics: Selected Readings* (Englewood Cliffs, NJ: Prentice-Hall)

Boyle, Leonard, 1982. *The Setting of the Summa Theologiae of St. Thomas* (Toronto: Pontifical Institute of Mediaeval Studies)

Carnap, Rudolf, Arend Heyting, and Johann von Neumann, 1931. 'Symposium on the Foundations of Mathematics', reprinted in Paul Benacerraf and Hilary Putnam (eds), *Philosophy of Mathematics: Selected Readings* (Englewood Cliffs, NJ: Prentice-Hall, 1964), pp. 31–54

Davis, G. Scott, 1992. *Warcraft and the Fragility of Virtue: An Essay in Aristotelian Ethics* (Moscow, Ida.: University of Idaho Press)

Davis, G. Scott, 2001. 'Doing What Comes Naturally: Recent Work on Thomas Aquinas and the New Natural Law Theory', *Religion* 31: 407–33

Davis, G. Scott, 2002. 'Humanitarian Intervention and Just War Criteria', *Journal of Peace and Justice Studies* 12/1: 63–94

Douglas, Mary, 1966. *Purity and Danger* (London: Routledge & Kegan Paul)

George, Robert, 1999. *In Defense of Natural Law* (Oxford: Oxford University Press)

Harman, Gilbert, 2000. *Explaining Value and Other Essays in Moral Philosophy* (Oxford: Oxford University Press)

Herdt, Jennifer, 1997. *Religion and Faction in Hume's Moral Philosophy* (Cambridge: Cambridge University Press)

Hume, David, 1902. *Enquiries concerning the Human Understanding and concerning the Principles of Morals*, 2nd edn, ed. Selby-Bigge (Oxford: Oxford University Press)

Malcolm, Norman, 1984. *Ludwig Wittgenstein: A Memoir and a Biographical Sketch by G. H. von Wright*, 2nd edn (Oxford: Oxford University Press)

Mapel, David R., and Terry Nardin (eds), 1998. *International Society: Diverse Perspectives* (Princeton, NJ: Princeton University Press)

Monk, Ray, 1990. *Ludwig Wittgenstein: The Duty of Genius* (New York: Free Press)

Nussbaum, Martha, 1999. *Sex and Social Justice* (Oxford: Oxford University Press)

Okin, Susan Moller, 1999. *Is Multiculturalism Bad for Women? With Respondents*, ed. J. Cohen, M. Howard, and M. Nussbaum (Princeton, NJ: Princeton University Press)

Pitcher, George (ed.), 1966. *Wittgenstein: The Philosophical Investigations* (Garden City, NY: Doubleday)

Pope, Stephen (ed.), 2002. *The Ethics of Aquinas* (Washington, DC: Georgetown University Press)

Randall, John Herman, 1960. *Aristotle* (New York: Columbia University Press)

Rawls, John, 2001. *Justice as Fairness: A Restatement*, ed. Erin Kelly (Cambridge, Mass.: Harvard University Press)

Stout, Jeffrey, 1988. *Ethics After Babel: The Languages of Morals and Their Discontents* (Boston: Beacon Press; 2nd edn Princeton, NJ: Princeton University Press, 2001)

Stout, Jeffrey, 2004. *Democracy and Tradition* (Princeton, NJ: Princeton University Press)

Stroud, Barry, 1965. 'Wittgenstein and Logical Necessity', reprinted in George Pitcher (ed.), *Wittgenstein: The Philosophical Investigations* (Garden City, NY: Doubleday, 1966), pp. 477–96

Vlastos, Gregory, 1981. *Platonic Studies*, 2nd printing (Princeton, NJ: Princeton University Press)

9. The Stoical Aquinas

Stoic Influences on Aquinas's Understanding of Charity

DOUGLAS LANGSTON

Introduction

In his intriguing *Divine Science and the Science of God*, Victor Preller presents an account of Thomas Aquinas's theology that casts Aquinas in a very Kantian light.[1] The mind does not passively receive reality as impressions imposed upon it from an external world. Rather, the mind constructs and interprets the world it perceives through its own innate structures, common to all human beings.[2] Intelligible experience comes from the mind and its modes of constructing and interpreting reality.

According to Preller, Aquinas thinks that human beings are successful in describing the world and can connect meaningfully with the items of the ordinary world of experience. Human beings have intelligible concepts of various objects and actions, and these concepts match the world of objects and actions that human beings experience. This is not the case with our knowledge of God, however. God is a being transcending all finite modes, and human beings cannot meaningfully refer to God. The meaningful concepts human beings do have are derived from the world perceived through the senses, and these concepts give no understanding of God. Lacking understanding of God, human beings can form no meaningful intentions about God, and, lacking meaningful intentions about God, human beings cannot meaningfully discuss God.

Preller sees intentionality – how the mind is related to the objects it treats – as crucial to Aquinas's theology. In fact, he argues that Aquinas believes that *fides infusa* (infused faith) from God gives a type of intentionality to theological discourse that renders it meaningful.[3] While one cannot understand these intentions as comprehensive in the way our intentions of sticks and stones are comprehensive of the sticks and stones we encounter, they are the best we can do relative to the unknowable God Aquinas places at the centre of his theology.[4]

The issue of intentionality is very important for other aspects of Aquinas's thought. In ethics, intentionality is key to Aquinas's understanding of weakness of will, i.e. why it is that a person may know what is to be done in a circumstance but fail to will it. In his discussion of the issue in *Commentary on the Nicomachean Ethics*, Aquinas claims that the incontinent man (one suffering from weakness of will) lacks in *synesis*. This Greek term can mean 'a coming together, union' or 'quick comprehension or sagacity' and Aquinas uses it with the sense of 'good judgment about the things treated by prudence'.[5] According to Aquinas, the incontinent man has failed to develop the virtues and consequently understands a particular situation in an inappropriate way; he lacks *synesis*.

Following Aristotle, Aquinas thinks that our practical reasoning consists in applying universal principles of behaviour to particular situations. For example, a person might have a general principle that 'he should avoid inordinate tasting of sweets'. In accordance with this principle, when encountering a box of chocolates, the person refrains from eating any of the chocolates because he sees such indulgence as a violation of the principle. Yet, many people do so indulge even when they know that they should not. Rather than hold that such people have directly in mind the general principle, see the situation as a violation of this principle, and act in direct violation of the principle, Aquinas proposes a different account. The person who has the principle 'he should avoid inordinate tasting of sweets' probably also has some other rule like 'pleasant objects should be enjoyed'. When confronted with a box of chocolates, the incontinent person, influenced by his appetites, sees the box as an example of a pleasant object, and, subsuming it under the rule, he indulges in the chocolates even though he also has the principle 'he should avoid inordinate tasting of sweets'. He acts contrary to his principle (and with weakness of will) because he perceives the box of chocolates as a pleasant thing (thus falling under the rule) rather than as a forbidden sweet (falling under the principle). The incontinent person perceives particular objects and situations in the way he does because his perception of the particular has been moulded by the life he has led, and his failure to pursue the virtues results in his misperception of the situation. To put it succinctly, the perception of particulars is a product of the moral character one has given to oneself.[6]

While one might assume that Aquinas's discussion of weakness of will is derived exclusively from his reading of Aristotle's writings, such a view misses a very important influence on Aquinas's thought. Aquinas was greatly influenced by thinkers in the Stoic tradition, and this is true of his discussion of weakness of will. Aquinas ties weakness of will to issues surrounding the virtue of prudence. In his discussion of prudence in the Second Part of the Second Part of the *Summa Theologiae*, we see that Aquinas uses Cicero's division of prudence into parts, and Cicero, influenced by the doctrines of the Stoic Chrysippus, plays an important role in his discussion of the components of prudence.[7] In discussing the aspect of prudence that involves seeing how a general principle is embedded in a particular situation, Aquinas employs Cicero's notion of intelligence (*intelligentia*), which Aquinas takes to be the correct appreciation of an ultimate principle.[8] It is the ability or inability of a person to see a particular as a case of a general rule that is key to Aquinas's understanding of weakness of will. Therefore, it appears that Aquinas's familiarity with Cicero's work, and through him Chrysippus's work, is an important component of his discussion of weakness of will.[9]

The presence of Stoic influence on Aquinas's analysis of weakness of will introduces the possibility that there may be Stoic influences in other aspects of Aquinas's discussion of the virtues. In fact, I wish to show that there is a strong Stoic influence on Aquinas's analysis of the theological virtue of charity, and that this link supports Preller's claim that an intentional relationship to an unknown God is key to understanding Aquinas's thought. I must admit at the outset, however, that my argument will only presume to show the plausibility of the influence of Stoic thought on Aquinas's views about charity. In part, this is a result of the facts about the writings of the Stoics and their influence on the development of medieval thought. I will also confess that Preller himself might not have agreed about Stoic influence in this area of Aquinas's theology. He offers no discussion of Stoicism in *Divine Science and the Science of God*, which was directed mainly against traditional interpreters of Aquinas like Garrigou-Lagrange and Maritain, and we never discussed the issue in person or through correspondence.

An overview of Stoic thought

Hellenistic philosophy has been a relatively neglected area of study, perhaps even more neglected than the study of medieval philosophy. Since the 1960s, however, there has been increased attention paid to the Hellenistic philosophers, especially the Stoics, and several important books and articles have been published about Stoicism. There are various reasons for the past neglect. In the first place, the enormous influence of Plato and Aristotle seemed to leave little desire to investigate lesser lights. More importantly, there are only isolated fragments of the writings of the founders of Early Stoicism: Zeno of Citium (333/2–262 BCE), Cleanthes of Assos (342–232 BCE), and Chrysippus of Soli (277–*c*.204 BCE). As the principal source for their doctrines, we have reports of their views from the writings of later thinkers, some of whom were disciples and others critics.[10] Given the difficulties of reconstructing the thought of thinkers through the writings of others, many scholars have turned their efforts to other thinkers (e.g. Aristotle, Plato, Plotinus) whose writings can be identified. Moreover, Stoicism itself went through three stages – Early (Ancient), Middle, and Late (Roman) – and there are apparent differences among the three stages. Nevertheless, a general picture of Stoicism has been widely accepted.[11]

Stoics divide philosophy into physics, logic, and ethics. All stages of the school accept that ethics is the most important division and the other two are of interest mainly for the light they shed on it. One of their most fundamental doctrines is that matter and spirit are the same. This extreme monism causes the Stoics to understand everything that exists as a body of some type. Like many other schools, the Stoics regard the physical body of a human being as a body, but they also consider the mind to be a body. According to their doctrine of *krasis*, two bodies can share the same space at the same time and this doctrine helps to explain how a human being can have a physical body as well as a mind. The mind was also seen as composed of *pneuma*, a very fine substance that permeates the universe. In fact, the mind perceives objects by way of the *pneuma* it sends out that interacts with objects and returns to the mind to form impressions. The mind is thus active in its perception of other bodies. Moreover, the mind and the universe display *logos*, which can be understood as both a rationality and an ordering. Physical bodies have *tonos*, which is a type of tension that constitutes the shape of physical objects. *Tonos*, *logos*, and *pneuma* are not really three different types of substance; rather, they are degrees of one another and are all to be understood as bodies.

The universe, which undergoes cyclical processes of destruction (*ekpyrosis*) and re-creation (*diakosmesis*), displays a geocentric order as well as a rational order. The planets and stars revolve around the earth in an order and unity produced by the *logos* of the universe. This *logos* is thought of as a type of personal divinity by many of the Stoics, who also maintain that the divinity and human beings are composed of the same substance. As identical to the divinity, the universe is both rational and completely organized so that there is no notion of chance or accident. Such a strict ordering suggests that all events, even human actions, occur necessarily. This deterministic outlook, however, seems in conflict with human freedom. Since the Stoics base their ethics on moral choice, they wish to preserve a notion of human freedom, and various Stoic thinkers propose ways to reconcile the apparent conflict.

While bodies exist, four categories of objects subsist: the void, space, time, and the *lekta*. The void is used by the Stoics to explain the expansion of the universe during the process of *ekpyrosis*. *Lekta* are perhaps best understood as extra-mental meanings of propositions that correlate with aspects of minds.[12] They play a critical role in the logic and philosophy of language developed by Chrysippus and his students. The correlates of the *lekta* in the minds of human beings are important for both epistemological and ethical issues.[13]

The Stoics divide the human *psyche* (mind or soul) into eight parts or faculties: the five senses, speech, procreation, and the *hegemonikon*. The key part is the *hegemonikon*, which directs the others. John Rist argues that this aspect of the *psyche* is best understood as one's personality.[14] The Stoics often talk about the person as the *hegemonikon* and go so far as to say that a person's body does not move but the *hegemonikon* moves through the body.[15] The *hegemonikon* is clearly something that changes in an individual over time, based on the experiences an individual has and his reaction to them. While it directs the other parts of the *psyche*, information through the five senses affects it and its development.[16] It plays an important role in the development of the virtues for the Stoics, and it is important for comprehending their ethics.

In line with much of Greek thought, the Stoics hold that human beings naturally seek the good. For them, the good consists in living in accordance with Nature (equivalently, given their monism, reason). Since each person's *hegemonikon* consists of the same *logos* as everyone else's, human beings form both a natural and a moral community, where all human beings, regardless of gender, are equal. As members of this moral community, human beings are obligated to serve their fellow human beings as well as marry and raise a family. Each person tries to live in accordance with Nature by eliminating all passions. Since the passions are seen as misperceptions of the true nature of reality, Stoics understand intellectual development as key to transforming the moral individual.

One of the key ethical doctrines of the Stoics is *oikeiosis*. The term derives from the Greek term '*oikeioo*' which means 'making something one's own' and is obviously connected to the word '*oikos*' which means 'house' or 'family'. The Stoics believe that each human being at birth has a natural instinct to preserve himself. This instinct, shared by animals, becomes an attachment to and love of self and what benefits the self, and these qualities direct all the agent's actions. The orientation to self, however, is expanded to other members of one's immediate family so that one's orientation becomes a preservation of self and other members of the family. Eventually this orientation extends beyond the family, and one becomes concerned about the preservation of other human beings and what benefits them. Essentially, the ties that bind one's immediate family, which are extensions of instincts about one's own self, are extended to others, making them part of a larger family.[17]

Many scholars believe that the Stoics offer *oikeiosis* as an explanation for human behaviour, particularly as it pertains to groups. One behaves, for instance, justly towards other human beings and their possessions because they possess an extension of the same instinct for self-preservation that one naturally possesses at birth. *Oikeiosis* is also seen by some scholars as the mechanism by which human beings pursue the good, which is living in accordance with Nature.[18] The order of Nature is such that, unlike plants and animals, human beings have reason (*logos*). Through this reason, they are able to reflect on their self-preserving actions and see that they are self-preserving. They can also see that their own acts of self-preservation are part of a rational system of self-preserving actions ordered by Nature. Finally, they are able to grasp that one can engage in such reflections because one is rational. Effectively, this is to see oneself as an individual under some general law-like description; that is, one is able to objectify oneself. Once this has been done, one can grasp that one does not matter as an individual; whatever one reasons to from one's own case will be just as valid when applied to anyone else.[19] One discovers that one's individuality is unimportant for the order of Nature. This intentional stance towards Nature is required to live in accordance with Nature. So one must develop *oikeiosis* to achieve the Stoic good.[20]

The objective stance one achieves through *oikeiosis* is absolutely critical for understanding Stoic views about the passions and even freedom. The Stoics are well known for their desire to eliminate passions and reach a state of *apatheia*, which the truly wise man (the sage) possesses.[21] Passions are regarded as disturbances and thus stand in the way between a human being and the natural order. As mentioned above, the Stoics do not regard passions as affective phenomena. Rather, they understand passions as intentional states resulting from an inconsistency in one's set of beliefs.[22] In particular, passions come from a disharmony between one's subjective point of view (I fear my death) and the objective view of the order of Nature (all beings cease to exist at some time), which is arrived at through *oikeiosis* . The elimination of passions, then, is not a matter of changing habits or changing one's affections so much as a matter of correctly understanding and perceiving the order of Nature through the development of *oikeiosis*.[23] Once one sees oneself as part of Nature, one can accept with equanimity what has been the source of discontent.[24] Similarly, some Stoics urge that seeing oneself as part of the order of Nature that unfolds in a necessary fashion allows one to embrace the actions one performs out of necessity.[25] For them, this point is best expressed in the famous simile: Man is like a dog that is tied to a cart; if the dog is willing to follow the cart, he will both follow and be drawn by it, thus acting in accordance with his own will while also acting in accordance with fate; if, however, he is not willing to follow, he will be forced to do so nevertheless.[26]

At the centre of *oikeiosis*, then, is the seeing of oneself and Nature in a certain way. With the proper perception of oneself as a part of the order of Nature, one can live in accord with Nature and be virtuous. The Stoic stress on the intentional relationship between the agent and the world is key to much of their system.

Cicero's interpretation of Stoicism

Although the stress on the intentional relationship between human agents and Nature is found throughout the early Stoics,[27] the strongest proponent of so interpreting Stoic thought was Marcus Tullius Cicero. He himself was not a Stoic; however, he studied with important Stoics – Diodotus and Posidonius – and was well versed in Stoic thought.[28] In fact, his recounting of Stoic theories in *De finibus*, *De officiis*, *Tusculanarum disputationum*, *Academica*, and *Paradoxa Stoicorum* constitutes the greatest source for Stoic thought available in the Middle Ages.[29] His understanding of Stoic doctrines was thus formative for the medieval schoolmen.

In his *De finibus*, he outlines the key elements of *oikeiosis* and links it to issues of intentionality.[30] Following this reading of *oikeiosis*, Cicero emphasizes that passions are essentially intellectual misperceptions and are eliminated through the development of the correct understanding of the nature of things. Moreover, achievement of the goal of Stoic thought – living in harmony with Nature – is possible only through the correct understanding of Nature and one's place in it. While these doctrines and Cicero's understanding of them are clearly embedded in the Stoic tradition, Cicero offers several surprising interpretations of Stoic doctrines. Perhaps the most interesting is his insistence that there is no fundamental disagreement between the

Stoics and Aristotle's followers, the Peripatetics. Apparently, he inherited this view from his teacher, Antiochus of Ascalon, who argued that the Peripatetic, Epicurean, Stoic, and Platonic schools are in basic agreement on key doctrines and differed only terminologically.[31] Cicero seems to have modified this view somewhat, since in his *De finibus* he rejects Epicureanism but sees the Stoics and Peripatetics as endorsing the same doctrines, differing only in terminology.[32]

Needless to say, Cicero's interpretation that the Stoics and Peripatetics are in basic agreement is hard to square with the textual evidence. Many scholars see strong differences in the doctrines of the two schools. In particular, they stress that Aristotle has a much more teleological view of the development of the goal of one's life, *eudaemonia*, than do the Stoics.[33] By developing the virtues through a trial and error path of gaining practical wisdom, a human being may arrive at *eudaemonia*, which is living well and faring well, by practising the virtues. In contrast, the Stoics think that the end of life is to live in harmony with Nature, and this can only be achieved through a proper understanding of the nature of things. This intentional relationship to Nature is not the culmination of the practice of the various virtues, however, but rather constitutes Virtue itself.[34] Yet, it is difficult to deny that Cicero's view that there was basic agreement between Stoics and Peripatetics deeply influences much of the interpretation of Greek thought one finds in the Middle Ages, if only because his writings are such an important source for Stoic thought.

The Stoical Augustine

Among those most influenced by Cicero and his understanding of the Stoics was Augustine of Hippo. While many scholars have argued that Neoplatonism was the strongest influence on Augustine, there is little doubt that he was deeply influenced by Stoicism.[35] He embraces the Stoic notion of a divine order to the world and uses this notion in his discussion of natural evil. He adapts the Stoic view that the mind employs *pneuma* to relate externally to objects of perception.[36] Moreover, he uses the Stoic notion of *lekta* to explain the meaning of 'nothing' and employed the notion of *krasis* to help explain the nature of Christ's hypostatic union of divine and human natures.[37] He also follows the Stoic view that the passions are false intellectual judgements and offers Stoic-like definitions of the virtues in several works.[38] Augustine's use of Stoicism places him as one of the key disseminators of Stoic doctrines in the Middle Ages.[39] Behind Augustine's knowledge of Stoicism is his reading of Cicero.

In his *Confessions*, Augustine indicates how he was led to study philosophy through his reading of Cicero's *Hortensius*, and Cicero is referred to many times in his writings.[40] In the *City of God*, for example, Augustine discusses Cicero's work *De finibus* and explicitly embraces Cicero's view that the Stoics agree with the Platonists and Peripatetics in doctrine and differ only in terminology about the role of external goods in pursuit of the final good.[41] He clearly follows Cicero's understanding of the role intentionality plays in the Stoic pursuit of the final good, but offers an extremely important modification of the Stoic position.

As we have seen, the Stoics through their doctrine of *oikeiosis* hold that the correct grasp of the true nature of things gives to the sage an intentional ordering that is part of the final good of living in accordance with Nature. Without this universal understanding, a person cannot eliminate the passions and live in accord with Nature. Augustine also accepts the notion that one needs a universal understanding to reach one's ultimate good. But Augustine thinks that the final good for all human beings is God, and in order to reach God one must orient all of one's actions towards God. The clearest presentation of this point of view is in his work *On the Morals of the Catholic Church*. In Chapter XV of this work, Augustine writes:

> As to virtue leading us to a happy life, I hold virtue to be nothing else than perfect love of God. For the fourfold division of virtue I regard as taken from the four forms of love. For these four virtues . . . I should have no hesitation in defining them: that temperance is love giving itself entirely to that which is loved; fortitude is love readily bearing all things for the sake of the loved object; justice is love serving only the loved object, and therefore ruling rightly; prudence is love distinguishing with sagacity between what hinders it and what helps it. The object of this love is not anything, but only God,

the chief good, the highest wisdom, the perfect harmony. So we may express the definition thus: that temperance is love keeping itself entire and incorrupt for God; fortitude is love bearing everything readily for the sake of God; justice is love serving God only, and therefore ruling well all else, as subject to man; prudence is love making a right distinction between what helps it towards God and what might hinder it.[42]

While some read Augustine here as advocating that Christians must add a level of orientation towards God to a basic Aristotelian account of the virtues, this does not really capture Augustine's point.[43]

In Book XIX, Chapter 25, of *The City of God* Augustine says that 'the virtues on which the mind preens itself as giving control over the body and its urges, and which aim at any other purpose or possession than God, are in point of fact vices rather than virtues'.[44] His point here is that any action other than one performed with the universal intention of love of God is not a virtue. Such an action is not an incomplete virtue; it fails to be a virtue because it lacks the correct general intention of moving towards the final good, God. It is quite similar in spirit to the Stoic notion that what is not a virtue is in fact a vice because, lacking the general understanding of the true nature of things and the intention of living in accord with Nature, a person cannot be virtuous and perform virtuous actions. With the correct intention of living in accord with Nature, all actions are virtuous for the Stoic sage; without this intention, all actions are vices. It is similar for Augustine. If a person comprehends that God is the final good and acts with the intention of loving God, the person performs a virtuous action. If a person lacks the comprehension or the intention, the actions performed are vices. The influence of the Stoics on Augustine here is unmistakable.

Stoic influences on Aquinas's discussion of charity

Augustine's influence on the thinkers of the Middle Ages has been detailed by many. Perhaps due to the difficulties enumerated above about the writings of the Stoics, little attention has been paid to the specific Stoic influences Augustine passed on to the Schoolmen. An obvious place where Augustine's stoicism influenced Aquinas is in his discussion of the theological virtue of charity.

Aquinas holds that there are two levels of the virtues: natural and supernatural. The natural virtues are divided into the intellectual and moral, while the theological virtues are three: faith, hope, and charity. Prudence is the principal moral virtue. Through it one is able to achieve the natural goods of finite happiness. As we have seen, Aquinas's discussion of prudence draws upon various classical sources, and it appears that, on one level, he is content with the analysis of many non-Christian philosophers like Cicero and Aristotle about the moral virtues. Unlike Augustine, he thinks of these natural virtues as virtues even if they are not placed in a Christian context. Despite his disagreement with Augustine on this point, Aquinas draws heavily from Augustine in his discussion of the theological virtues.

Aquinas claims that the three theological virtues are infused by God and cannot be acquired through moral training. Charity is the greatest (*excellentissima*) of the three and is the greatest of all virtues.[45] In elaborating on this point, Aquinas talks about how charity is the form of all the virtues and explains this by saying that charity 'impresses its form' on all the other virtues.[46] The form Aquinas has in mind when he says this is 'love of God', and he explicitly endorses Augustine's notion that virtues performed without love of God are not true virtues in an unqualified sense.[47] They are not unqualifiedly true because they lack the proper ordering (*ordinatio*) to God.[48] Aquinas is thus arguing that only virtues performed with the intention of loving God are unqualifiedly true virtues, because only these virtues are directed in the correct way to the truly ultimate object, God. Virtues not so directed are true virtues but only in a qualified sense. They are natural virtues, and they are directed at the finite and non-ultimate good that the non-Christian Greeks, for example, pursued. Aquinas has thus adapted Augustine's modification of the key Stoic notion of *oikeiosis*. For the Stoics, intending correctly by being correctly related to the true nature of things is necessary for the cultivation of virtue and attainment of sagehood. Augustine substitutes 'love of God' for the correct intentional element required for development of the virtues. Aquinas follows Augustine in seeing love of God as necessary for possessing unqualifiedly good virtues, but allows the existence of the natural virtues discussed by many non-Christian thinkers.

In a manner similar to the Stoics' comments about the difficulty of becoming a sage in this life, Aquinas acknowledges that, on his understanding of charity and unqualifiedly true virtues, it is difficult to possess charity in the best way possible:

> On the lover's side, we talk of charity being perfect when a person loves to his utmost, which can happen in three ways. First, when his whole heart is always actually intent on God, which is the perfection that charity has in heaven, but cannot have in this life where the weakness of the human condition makes it impossible to be always actually thinking about God and loving him. Second, when he devotes all his zeal to the consideration of God and divine things, leaving aside everything else except what the demands of this present life impose. This perfection is possible for a wayfarer, though not all those who possess charity attain to it. Third, when someone habitually directs his whole heart to God, so that he neither thinks nor wills anything contrary to and incompatible with divine love. And this perfection is something which all those who possess charity hold in common.[49]

This passage suggests that it is only in heaven that we will be able to have the full intentional relationship to God that will make us virtuous. In this present life, some few may reach the second level of putting their zeal for the intentional relationship to God above everything but the essential demands of life. Presumably, this is seen by Aquinas as a less perfect expression of love than what is found in the first level because even these extraordinary people in the second level do not have the direct contact with God found in the next life. Those in the second level surely are virtuous people but imperfectly so in comparison to those in the next life. For most of us, who at best inhabit the third level, our intentional relationship to God comes down to directing ourselves to God by not acting contrary to divine love.

Aquinas does not elaborate on this surprising observation, but it becomes clearer if we recall Preller's comments about the intentions we can have in this life about the unknown God: we cannot direct our intentions to the unknown God through our own capacities; God must give to us, through infused grace, such intentions, which we do not fully understand. With infused charity, we do not form full intentions of the ultimate object, God. We can only form a general, vague intention towards the ultimate object and act in accordance with what we think are the manifestations of the love that the unknown being gives us. The intentional relationship that is essential for becoming virtuous, according to Aquinas, is more like a set of instructions for behaving that we have been taught than a direct intending of the ultimate end. Yet, there is no other way to form intentions towards the unknown God, even given God's infusion of charity.

Conclusion

I hope I have shown that Aquinas was influenced by Stoic thought in one crucial aspect of his theology. But my present discussion leads me to talk briefly about the broader issue of Stoic influence on Aquinas's thought. Unfortunately, I can only assert my view without defending it, and the reader is invited to regard this as a promissory note on future research.

If my present essay has been successful to any degree, it establishes what one might call a direct influence of Stoic thought on Aquinas. Through an examination of Aquinas's texts and the influences he himself cites, we can trace solid connections between Stoic doctrines and Aquinas's views. Yet, there is undoubtedly an even more important, indirect Stoic influence on Aquinas. If one examines, for example, what Aristotle claims about the Prime Mover in Book XII of the *Metaphysics*, the mechanistic, highly impersonal nature Aristotle attributes to it fits poorly with the personal, uncaused creator Aquinas elaborates on in various writings. How could Aquinas move so readily from the one to the other? The answer, I believe, lies in how Aristotle was interpreted by Aquinas and the medieval thinkers he drew upon, particularly Augustine.

Influenced by Cicero, Augustine embraced a number of Stoic views, which he equated with Peripatetic views. The blurring of the Stoic with the Peripatetic undoubtedly yielded interpretations of Greek thought that, to our eyes, are less than faithful. Once such interpretations entered the intellectual milieu of the Middle Ages, they created a tradition of interpretation that was brought to the newly rediscovered texts of Aristotle. With this long tradition of interpretation, Aquinas, a very careful student and interpreter of Aristotle, read the texts through a lens not entirely produced by what today we might call genuine Peripatetic thought. Given the undeniable presence of Stoic thought in the production of that interpretive lens Aquinas used, it should come as little surprise that Stoicism affected Aquinas's understanding of Aristotle and thus influenced Aquinas's metaphysical and theological works. It seems to me that those who are engaged in the contemporary articulation and reappropriation of Aquinas's thought would be wise to look to Stoic influences on it.

Notes

1. *Divine Science and the Science of God* (Princeton: Princeton University Press, 1967). Vic described his book to me as 'the green and yellow monster' in a typical downplay of it. He acknowledges the Kantian element throughout the work, e.g. pp. 75 and 78.

2. Preller, *Divine Science*, p. 54.

3. On p. 267 he mentions with approval Sellars's discussion of the dance that scout bees perform to inform other bees about a clover field in the distance. The unconscious intentions the bees form from viewing this dance give some insight into the type of intentions human beings receive in *fides infusa*. Vic once told me that this mention of the dance of the bees was his favourite part of the book.

4. Preller, *Divine Science*, pp. 270–1.

5. *Commentary on Aristotle's Nicomachean Ethics* (Notre Dame, Ind.: Dumb Ox Books, 1993), p. 391 (para. 1237).

6. A fuller explanation of these points can be found in my *Conscience and Other Virtues* (University Park, Pa.: Pennsylvania State University Press, 2001), ch. 3.

7. *ST* II-II.48 is entitled 'Parts of Prudence' and *ST* II-II.49 is entitled 'Components of Prudence'.

8. *ST* II-II.49.2 *sed contra* (Blackfriars edn, vol. 36, p. 65).

9. Diogenes Laertius ascribes to Chrysippus, Apollodorus, and Hekaton the view that *synesis* is a part of prudence in Hans von Arnim, *Stoicorum veterum fragmenta*, 4 vols (Leipzig, 1903–24), vol. 3, pp. 72–3, para. 295: 'And likewise (they say) these others turn around their concerns. Good deliberation and judgement follow prudence' (my translation).

10. Collections of fragments and of other authors' comments on the Stoics are: von Arnim, *Stoicorum veterum fragmenta*, and A. A. Long and D. N. Sedley (eds), *The Hellenistic Philosophers* (Cambridge: Cambridge University Press, 1987).

11. I rely on Marcia Colish's description of this general view in her *The Stoic Tradition from Antiquity to the Early Middle Ages*, vols 1 and 2 (Leiden: Brill, 1985). Another valuable introductory source is Gerard Verbeke's *The Presence of Stoicism in Medieval Thought* (Washington, DC: Catholic University of America Press, 1983). It is often held that the Middle Stoic, Posidonius of Apamea, rejected key doctrines of Early Stoicism like the indivisibility of the soul/psychic monism. Recent essays by John Cooper and others in *The Emotions in Hellenistic Philosophy*, New Synthese Historical Library 46, ed. Juha Sihvola and Troels Engberg-Pedersen (Dordrecht and Boston: Kluwer Academic, 1998) question this claim.

12. See, for example, Benson Mates's description of *lekta* in his *Stoic Logic* (Berkeley and Los Angeles: University of California Press, 1961).

13. Colish, *Stoic Tradition*, vol. 1, p. 26. Also A. A. Long, 'Representation and the Self in Stoicism', in A. A. Long (ed.), *Stoic Studies* (Cambridge: Cambridge University Press, 1996), pp. 283–5.

14. J. M. Rist, *Stoic Philosophy* (Cambridge: Cambridge University Press, 1969), p. 24.

15. Rist, *Stoic Philosophy*, p. 34.

16. See Long, 'Representation and the Self in Stoicism', op. cit., esp. pp. 277 and 283.

17. See Troels Engberg-Pedersen, *The Stoic Theory of Oikeiosis: Moral Development and Social Interaction in Early Stoic Philosophy* (Aarhus: Aarhus University Press, 1990), pp. 123–4.

18. See Brad Inwood, *Ethics and Human Action in Early Stoicism* (Oxford: Clarendon Press, 1985), p. 185.

19. Engberg-Pedersen, *Stoic Theory of Oikeiosis*, pp. 84–90.

20. Engberg-Pedersen, *Stoic Theory of Oikeiosis*, p. 135. For another account of the importance of the intentional stance towards Nature for Stoic ethics, see Michael Frede's essay 'On the Stoic Conception of the Good', in Katerina Ierodiakonou (ed.), *Topics in Stoic Philosophy* (Oxford: Clarendon Press, 1999).

21. Engberg-Pedersen, *Stoic Theory of Oikeiosis*, pp. 170–206.

22. Engberg-Pedersen, *Stoic Theory of Oikeiosis*, pp. 191–2; see also Simo Knuuttila and Juha Sihvola, 'How the Philosophical Analysis of the Emotions was Introduced', in Sihvola and Engberg-Pedersen, *Emotions in Hellenistic Philosophy*, p. 1.

23. Sihvola and Engberg-Pedersen, *Emotions in Hellenistic Philosophy*, p. 4.

24. Sihvola and Engberg-Pedersen, *Emotions in Hellenistic Philosophy*, p. 17.

25. Engberg-Pedersen, *Stoic Theory of Oikeiosis*, pp. 207–34.

26. Engberg-Pedersen, *Stoic Theory of Oikeiosis*, p. 233.

27. See, for example, Diogenes Laeritus's presentation of *oikeiosis* in Engberg-Pedersen, *Stoic Theory of Oikeiosis*, p. 36 and following.

28. Cicero, *De finibus Bonorum et Malorum*, trans. H. Rackham, Loeb Classical Library (Cambridge, Mass.: Harvard University Press, 1914), p. ix.

29. Colish, *Stoic Tradition*, vol. 1, p. 158.

30. Much of Engberg-Pedersen's book *Stoic Theory of Oikeiosis* is concerned with linking *oikeiosis* to issues of intentionality.

31. Colish, *Stoic Tradition*, vol. 1, p. 70.

32. *De finibus*, pp. 301–3.

33. Engberg-Pedersen, *Stoic Theory of Oikeiosis*, ch. 1, but especially pp. 19–25.

34. Colish, *Stoic Tradition*, vol. 1, p. 130.

35. Colish, *Stoic Tradition*, vol. 2, summarizes this influence on pp. 234–8, and discusses it more completely on pp. 144–234.

36. Colish, *Stoic Tradition*, pp. 170–1.

37. Colish, *Stoic Tradition*, pp. 184 and 202.

38. Colish, *Stoic Tradition*, pp. 207 and 215.

39. Colish, *Stoic Tradition*, p. 142. Colish claims that Augustine is the single most important figure in the Stoic tradition between the third and sixth centuries.

40. *Confessions*, Book III, Chapter 4, and Book VIII, Chapter 7.

41. *City of God*, Book IX, Chapter 4.

42. Whitney J. Oates (ed.), *Basic Writings of St. Augustine*, vol. 1 (New York: Random House, 1948), pp. 331–2.

43. An interesting treatment of Augustine's views is found in Scott Davis's article, 'The Structure and Function of the Virtues in the Moral Theology of St. Augustine', in *Acta Congressa Augustiana, 1986* (Rome: Institutum Patristicum Augustinianum, 1987), pp. 9–18.

44. Augustine, *The City of God* (New York: Image Books, 1958), p. 479.

45. *ST* II-II.23.6 resp. (Blackfriars edn, vol. 34, p. 25).

46. *ST* II-II.23.8 ad 1 (Blackfriars edn, vol. 34, p. 33).

47. *ST* II-II.23.7 resp. (Blackfriars edn, vol. 34, p. 29).

48. *ST* II-II.23.7 ad 1 (Blackfriars edn, vol. 34, p. 28). I translate '. . . quia deest debita ordinatio ad ultimum finem' by rendering 'ordinatio' as 'ordering' (' . . . because it lacks the due ordering to the final end') rather than follow the Blackfriars translation, 'because it lacks due reference to man's ultimate end'. The stronger notion of ordering is clearly meant here.

49. *ST* II-II.24.9 *responsio* (Blackfriars edn, vol. 34, pp. 59–61).

10. Vision and Love

A Wittgensteinian Ethic in *Culture and Value*

M. JAMIE FERREIRA

It is generally acknowledged that Wittgenstein wrote very little about ethics. Indeed, commentators have claimed that he 'barely mentions' it after the lectures of 1930–2,[1] as well as that the 'most striking difference' between his earlier and later work is 'the absence of an explicit ethical intention' or 'overtly ethical considerations after 1930'.[2] Nevertheless, there has been a continued effort over the years to derive an ethic informing, implied by, or at least consonant with, Wittgenstein's later thought. For example, Stanley Cavell has elaborated an ethic implicit in the *Philosophical Investigations*, namely, an ethic of 'acknowledgement' of the other.[3] James Edwards has suggestively placed Wittgenstein's work within a 'long tradition' of a 'sort of Greek–Judaeo-Christian ethic of love and character', contrasting it with a Kantian ethic of duty.[4] I want to look again at the question of the character of a later Wittgensteinian ethic (and indirectly at the question of continuity), and I want to do this by focusing on the collection of remarks published as *Culture and Value*.[5] This eclectic collection, I suggest, reveals a striking preoccupation on Wittgenstein's part with a number of related themes that mark an ethic of truthfulness and courage, as well as with Wittgenstein's sense of the ethical importance of clarity of vision. In addition, I suggest that the particular formulations of some ethical themes in *Culture and Value* reveal a foundational role for love of self in this ethic. In both these ways I try to show that sections of *Culture and Value* add a unique dimension to the proposals of an ethics of acknowledgement or an ethics of love, highlighting the importance of vision as well as the relevance of love of self to both proposals. Finally, I suggest that a transformative, hence normative, ethic is compatible with his later view of the task of philosophy.

1. *The debate about continuity*

There is no question that Wittgenstein's remarks in the *Tractatus* offer some insight into his early view of ethics, a view that is reinforced by his well-known 'Lecture on Ethics' from 1929.[6] We can find expression of that early view of ethics as unconditional, a parallel with the mystical and the religious, in *Culture and Value* as well; for example, in a remark from 1929, Wittgenstein writes that his view of ethics involves the equation between the good and the unconditional: 'What is good is also the divine. Queer as it sounds, that sums up my ethics. Only something supernatural can express the Supernatural.'[7]

There is, however, a lot of debate about whether this early view of the status of the ethical is maintained in or even compatible with Wittgenstein's later thought. I deliberately speak about the status of the ethical, because there is no question of any later ethical 'theory'. The debate, then, is about whether there is a continuation of the early ethic, whether there is a new ethic, or whether there is no ethic at all to be found in the later writing.

The debate focuses on two key issues – context and description. It has been argued that incommensurability or irreconcilable disagreement between contextualized grammars is an inevitable implication of Wittgenstein's later account, precluding any notion of an unconditional right or wrong. It has also been argued that Wittgenstein's account of the task of philosophy, as limited to dealing with philosophical problems as linguistic confusions that need to be clarified, precludes either a substantive or a normative moral philosophy.[8] Both arguments imply that the earlier account of ethics cannot be retained.

Other commentators, however, have argued for a significant continuity between Wittgenstein's early and late thought on the status of ethics. Drury was one of the earliest to do so, claiming that 'all the subsequent writings . . . point to an ethical dimension'.[9] B. R. Tilghman suggests that it is precisely Wittgenstein's later thought that allows him to carry out 'the ethical intention' of the *Tractatus*, insofar as the *Investigations* facilitates an appreciation of our 'understanding and concern for other people'.[10]

James Edwards offers two perspectives on the question of continuity. On the one hand, he claims that 'the philosophical-ethical vision adumbrated in the *Notebooks* and the *Tractatus*' was 'dislodged' by 'a revolution in his thinking'.[11] On the other hand, he offers a provocative account of continuity, concluding that Wittgenstein's later ethic is an ethic of love in continuity with his earlier mystical ethic.[12]

Culture and Value provides support for the continuity of Wittgenstein's interest in the ethical in the period between 1939 and 1950. In 1939, Wittgenstein compares 'having oneself psychoanalysed' with 'eating from the tree of knowledge', explaining that in both cases 'the knowledge acquired sets us (new) ethical problems' (p. 34). In 1949 he discusses the doctrine of predestination, claiming that 'teaching it [to someone] could not constitute an ethical upbringing' and would, moreover, be prejudicial to such an upbringing unless it were taught '*after* having educated him ethically', and even then it could only be assigned to the realm of 'incomprehensible mystery' (p. 81). The 'ethical' idea of punishment was incommensurable with the notion of a good God's arbitrary choice (p. 81). In addition, in 1950 he considers the incompatibility between the ethical and coercion: 'How *could* a man, the ethical in a man, be coerced by his environment?' (p. 84).

These remarks explicitly (and others implicitly[13]) affirm the continuing importance of the ethical to Wittgenstein, even in his later years, but they do not illuminate its status. To see the character of his later view of ethics, we need to look closely at other elements that he repeatedly emphasized during this later time period. Fortunately, despite the paucity of explicit references to 'ethics', *Culture and Value* contains important resources for reconstructing an account of the ethical held by Wittgenstein after 1932.[14]

2. *The goal of clarity of vision*

Culture and Value reveals a striking preoccupation with several themes that bear heavily on what Wittgenstein considered 'the ethical in a man' (p. 84). First, warnings against self-deception abound. The stridency of his 1938 recognition that 'Nothing is so difficult as not deceiving yourself' (p. 34) is matched by the poignant realism of his acknowledgement eight years later: 'Understanding oneself properly is difficult, because an action to which one *might* be prompted by good, generous motives is something one may also be doing out of cowardice or indifference. Certainly, one may be acting in such and such a way out of genuine love, but equally well out of deceitfulness, or a cold heart' (p. 48).

The concern with deception is also found in Wittgenstein's repeated references to lying (*lügen*), which he repeatedly contrasted with the 'true' or 'truth' (*wahr* or *Wahrheit*). It was the ethical dimension of truth that fascinated him; lying, rather than error or incorrectness, was the alternative to truth.[15] Wittgenstein emphasizes the temptation to lie: he admits to a 'strong inclination to lie', even in cases where it is only 'very slightly more disagreeable to tell the truth than to lie' (p. 37, 1940) and reports, as if sadly, that 'Someone who knows too much finds it hard not to lie' (p. 64, 1947). These warnings against lying in favour of truth, however, are clearly addressing love of truth, rather than mere truth-telling. He insists that it is not enough for truthfulness that we do not *in fact* lie, for 'You can't be reluctant to give up your lie, and still tell the truth' (p. 39, 1940). Wittgenstein's intriguing formulation here calls to mind Zarathustra's conviction that 'the inability to lie is far from the love of truth'.[16] And it should be remembered that Nietzsche describes Zarathustra as 'more truthful than any other thinker', asserting that 'his doctrine, and his alone, posits truthfulness as the highest virtue'.[17]

Moreover, Wittgenstein echoes Kierkegaard's view of truth as something one is 'in' rather than something one 'has': 'The truth can only be spoken by someone who is already *at home* (*ruhe*) in it; not by someone who still lives in falsehood and reaches out from falsehood towards truth on just one occasion' (p. 35, 1939–40). Being 'at home' means that one has to 'rest' in the truth; Wittgenstein is effectively insisting that what is meant by telling the truth is not an accidental or episodic matter. It is the virtue of truthfulness or love of truth that is contrasted with 'falsehood'.

In still another reference to truth, Wittgenstein implicitly distinguished truth from the notion of objective accuracy. He writes: 'A poet too has constantly to ask himself: "but is what I am writing really true?" – and this does not necessarily mean: "is this how it happens in reality?"' (p. 40, 1941). This is particularly intriguing in the light of his earlier claim that he 'summed up [his] attitude to philosophy when [he] said: philosophy ought really to be written only as a *poetic composition* (*dichten*)' (p. 24, 1933–4). In poetic compositions the requirement of accurate representation is replaced by the requirement of revelation – truth as revelatory. Such compositions are intended to prompt self-understanding as well as insights about human relationships; the poet is called upon to bring us into the truth. In sum, in all but one case,[18] Wittgenstein's references to truth express a concern with 'truthfulness', or what is more precisely called love of truth.

Culture and Value is especially useful in reminding us that, for Wittgenstein, the primary locus of truth-telling and lying is in relation to ourselves. This is revealed by the rather unexpected way in which Wittgenstein contrasts not only lying with truth, but also with 'originality' (*Originalität*): 'Someone who does not lie is already original enough' (p. 60, 1947). He points to the ethical dimension of 'originality' when he goes on to explain that 'the beginnings of good originality are already there if you do not want to be something you are not'. Wanting to be something one is not, or conversely, not wanting to be something one is: these are ways of lying. Telling the truth to oneself about oneself requires an affirmation of what one is.

Wittgenstein adds another ethical dimension to the task of originality (the task of affirming what one is) when he writes that 'Courage is always original' (p. 36, 1939–40). Courage is always expressed in the endeavour to be what one is, to affirm oneself. It is revealing that the sections which most deal with lying, deception, and truthfulness (the years between 1939 and 1946) also contain the most numerous references to virtues like 'courage' (pp. 35–6, 38, 38–9, 52).

Moreover, Wittgenstein explicitly connects courage with the task of clarification. In an early description of his work, he explains: 'my contribution once again was really clarification. What I do think essential is carrying out the work of clarification with COURAGE, otherwise it becomes just a clever game' (p. 19, 1931, emphasis is Wittgenstein's own). This confirms his general emphasis on clarity: 'For me ... clarity, perspicuity are valuable in themselves' (p. 7, 1930).

A decade later Wittgenstein is still insisting on clarity or clear vision: 'How hard I find it to see what is *right in front of my eyes*!' (p. 39, 1940), and again, 'God grant the philosopher insight into what lies in front of everyone's eyes' (p. 63, 1947). From early to late, the philosophical task is to clarify, which means to see clearly, to make perspicuous what is obscure because too familiar.

The task of philosophy as clarification is the generalized task of being ethical, of seeing clearly, and clear vision takes courage because 'looking intently is difficult. And it's possible to look intently without seeing anything, or to keep thinking you see something without being able to see clearly' (p. 74, 1948). More specifically, the focus is on seeing ourselves: 'A man can see what he has, but not what he is. What he is can be compared to his height above sea level, which you cannot for the most part judge.without more ado' (p. 49, 1946). To be ethical one must judge oneself rightly, and to do so implies resistance to putting hindrances in the way of our seeing: 'a man will never be great if he misjudges himself: if he throws dust in his own eyes' (p. 49, 1946).

This latter formulation, warning against throwing dust in our own eyes, allows us to determine how this ethic is an ethic of vision, in contrast to an ethic of action, decision, choice, obedience to rules. The will is, no doubt, involved – the emphasis on courage is appropriate because, he explains, 'what has to be overcome is a difficulty having to do with the will, rather than with the intellect' (p. 17, 1931). But the notion of will is always problematized by Wittgenstein in his sensitive musings about ability and inability: for example, he asks, 'Where is the line between will and ability? Is it that I *will* not open my heart to anyone any more, or that I *cannot*?' (p. 54, 1946).[19] Moreover, when he warns us against the temptation to put hindrances in the way of our seeing, he alludes to the role of free activity, but this role of the will is in the service of our vision; we cannot simply choose to see, and it is the seeing that is crucial.

That we have here an ethic of vision is supported even by those who would describe Wittgenstein's later ethic in different terms. When Stanley Cavell, for example, proposes an ethic of 'acknowledgement', on the basis of the *Investigations*, he invokes the Wittgensteinian notion of 'seeing-as'; the ethical is construed in terms of seeing the other 'as human'.[20] Moreover, Cavell's descriptions of the hindrances to acknowledgement support my suggestion of an ethic of vision; he writes: 'The block to my vision of the other is not the other's body but my incapacity or unwillingness to interpret or to judge it accurately, to draw the right connections. The suggestion is: I suffer a kind of blindness, but I avoid the issue by projecting this darkness upon the other.'[21]

Even those who emphasize Wittgenstein's challenge to an ocular model of knowing allow for the importance of vision. For example, James Edwards is keenly sensitive to the later Wittgenstein's rejection of the 'metaphysical gaze' and the 'metaphysical seeing eye', issuing from his rejection of a model of rationality-as-representation.[22] 'In philosophy,' Edwards writes, 'and in the forms of life constituted by it, the paradigmatic mode of relationship to reality is vision: it lies out there to be viewed, understood, *known*,' whereas on Wittgenstein's view, 'understanding no longer appropriates reality solely in the mode of vision'.[23] Edwards, however, effectively qualifies Wittgenstein's challenge to vision, for in proposing that Wittgenstein's later ethic is an ethic of love, Edwards relies heavily on notions of vision: not merely 'seeing', but 'seeing through'. It is worth considering how Edwards indirectly supports the notion of an ethic of vision even while rejecting the notion of the 'metaphysical gaze'.

Although Edwards does not refer to Wittgenstein's suggestion, which I cited earlier, that all philosophy should be written like a poetic composition, he construes Wittgenstein's later thought as paralleling the way in which a poet 'wants us to see ourselves in all our seeing, to break the grip of the self-forgetfulness of representation'.[24] For Edwards, Wittgenstein's attack on the rationality-as-representation model respects 'the integrity of the image' by refusing to take it literally: namely, respects an image by using it 'as a way of seeing' so that 'the image becomes a way to *see through* the object to which it is applied'.[25] If one appreciates the way in which 'every new image reveals a new world, but every revealing is at the same time a concealing', one will conclude that 'poetry is never over with'.[26] In this deliteralization of our seeing is 'a corresponding expansion', in which the mind is 'free to move among the realities that nourish it'.[27] For Edwards, then, 'seeing is accomplished only by seeing through; literalness is replaced with depth, with oblique reflection'.[28]

Edwards's account of Wittgenstein's ethic replaces the 'metaphysical gaze' with the 'loving gaze' – he draws on Iris Murdoch's ethic of loving attention in which '"a just and loving gaze directed upon an individual reality" supplants will as the focus of ethical life'.[29] Love's attentiveness is an integral part of love, for, says Edwards, 'it is a feature of love that it never literalizes any perception; love is always ready to go deeper, to see through whatever has already been seen. From the perspective of loving attention, no story is ever over.'[30] 'Love is the central concept in morals because it names that capacity to go ever deeper in attention', because it is 'constantly seeing through, not just seeing'.[31] Edwards finds Wittgenstein's 'ethical vision'[32] in an ethic of love, and I have wanted to show how this ethic of love is first and foremost an ethic of vision.

It is worth noting that Wittgenstein's continuing emphasis on clarity of vision is not necessarily tied to the kind of clarity sought by the author of the *Tractatus* – namely, the crystalline purity of the ideal language. In the later work, the search for clarity amounts to an affirmation of a 'deliteralizing vision', a vision that *sees through* images and sees ourselves in all our seeing.

3. Transparency and the courage to love the self

Edwards's notion of 'seeing through' easily calls to mind the category of transparency, and I want to consider one way in which transparency plays a role in Wittgenstein's conception of the ethical. Consider again Wittgenstein's claim that genuine originality (truthfulness) consists in not wanting to be something one is not. This claim is significant to Wittgenstein, for he feels the need to add that 'all this has been said before *much* better by other people' (p. 60, 1947). One person who famously said it was Nietzsche, who tells us in the *Gay Science*: 'You must become who you are' and later repeats that message in *Ecce Homo*.[33] Nietzsche also put in the mouth of Zarathustra, whom he called 'the most honest philosopher', the injunction to 'Become who you are'.[34]

However, a more likely candidate for Wittgenstein's admiration is Kierkegaard, whose pseudonymous representative of ethical subjectivity, Judge William, claimed that ethical 'greatness is not to be this or that but to be oneself'.[35] Judge William clarifies this when he writes that 'the esthetic in a person is that by which he spontaneously and immediately is what he is', whereas 'the ethical is that by which he becomes what he becomes'.[36] When the ethical person 'chooses, or more correctly, receives' himself, 'he does not become someone other than he was before, but he becomes himself'.

Given Wittgenstein's repeated references to Kierkegaard within *Culture and Value*,[37] as well as the documented appreciation of him[38] (M. O'C. Drury tells us that Wittgenstein saw Kierkegaard as 'by far the most profound thinker of the last century'[39]), it may be instructive to look more closely at Kierkegaard's view of this ethical task of becoming oneself. Kierkegaard's pseudonym Anti-Climacus offers an interesting way to understand Wittgenstein's ethical warning against wanting to be something one is not, a way that makes a connection to transparency. Anti-Climacus claims, in *The Sickness Unto Death*, that the 'formula for all despair' is 'in despair to will to be rid of oneself'.[40] There are two kinds of despair – 'in despair not to will to be oneself' and 'in despair to will to be oneself'. The first is exhibited by a person when 'the self that he wants to be is a self that he is not'.[41] Not willing to be oneself is equivalent to willing to be something other than one is; it is the 'torment' of being forced 'to be the self he does not want to be'. It is to despair of what we are; it is to hate what we are.

The second kind of despair ('in despair to will to be oneself') seems counter-intuitive in this light. If 'wanting to be a self that one is not' is despair, then we might expect the alternative to be to 'will to be oneself', but Anti-Climacus alerts us to the way in which that too can be a despairing move when he refers to someone who 'despairingly wills to be himself'. The only way to make sense of this is to construe it as a description of how one can defiantly fixate oneself in one's present self, refusing to be open to growing, to developing, to becoming oneself. Like a child who obstinately says 'I will stay the way I am – you can't make me change,' so the self at any given moment can choose to stand in a stagnating pool, refusing the challenge implied in the call to grow, to become more. This too can be an expression of hating what we are.

The alternative to despair, for Anti-Climacus, lies in transparency – he represents a religious tradition according to which one is called to ground oneself transparently in the ground of one's being. Faith, the alternative to despair, says Anti-Climacus, is the state in which 'in relating itself to itself and in willing to be itself, the self rests transparently in the power that established it'.[42] To rest transparently in the power that established it is a variation on resting in the truth. Transparency means seeing through to the ground – one sees oneself truly by seeing what one can become. Throwing dust in one's eyes is the defiant refusal to take up the challenge to be what one is – a self called to a continuing creation of self, a continuing becoming. Transparency to the ground of one's being is the opposite of wanting to be rid of oneself as well as of wanting to stiflingly fixate oneself. If despair is the obscuring of that transparency, we could say that transparency is the medium through which one affirms createdness and a call to continuing creation rather than a denial of it. In other words, we could say that transparency is the medium through which one can love oneself.

The connection between transparency and love is made explicitly by Kierkegaard's pseudonym Judge William. Judge William insists that people who live aesthetically 'lack transparency'.[43] 'In every person there is something that up to a point hinders him from becoming completely transparent to himself, and this can be the case to such a higher degree . . . that he cannot open himself'; and he concludes that 'the person who can scarcely open himself cannot love, and the person who cannot love is the unhappiest of all'.[44] In other words, one who is not transparent to himself cannot love. This is intended to refer to the ethical transparency of being grounded in the universal, the publicly observable ethical; it is, moreover, intended to refer to the ability to love others. But it is equally true on a Kierkegaardian ethic that one who is not transparent cannot love oneself. Kierkegaard stands in the tradition of those who claim that without proper love of self one cannot love others properly.

Kierkegaard has argued that the 'as yourself' of the love commandment implies the legitimacy of 'proper self-love': 'if the commandment is properly understood it also says the opposite: *You shall love yourself in the right way.* Therefore if anyone is unwilling to learn from Christianity to love himself in the right way, he cannot love the neighbor either.'[45] Do people need such a reminder? Kierkegaard notes that

'Whoever has any knowledge of people will certainly admit that just as he has often wished to be able to move them to relinquish self-love, he has also had to wish that it were possible to teach them to love themselves.'[46] The importance of affirming the self lies in the way an independent whole self is a *sine qua non* of love, for 'without a *you* and an *I*, there is no love'.[47]

For Anti-Climacus, that one is tempted to despair shows that it is hard to be transparent, to see through oneself in a sense – to see that one is created and called to continuing affirmation (i.e. that one is lovable). Love of self parallels vision of self. One cannot love or affirm what one does not see. The difficulty of not deceiving oneself can point to the difficulty of loving oneself, seeing oneself clearly enough to see that one is lovable. Seeing clearly means seeing through whatever seems to suggest we are not lovable, seeing that we are more than our particular failings.

Consider again Wittgenstein's warnings against deception and misjudging oneself: it's hard not to deceive oneself, not to lie; it's hard to rest in the truth, to see oneself clearly, not to misjudge oneself, not to throw dust in one's eyes. These seem at first glance like warnings against being too lenient or indulgent with oneself, and it is true that Wittgenstein refers to a fear of having someone 'look inside us, since it's not a pretty sight in there' (p. 46, 1944). As late as 1951 he writes: 'God may say to me: "I am judging you out of your own mouth. Your own actions have made you shudder with disgust when you have seen other people do them"' (p. 87). Wittgenstein was hard on himself. But someone who appreciates Kierkegaard (as Wittgenstein did) could construe such warnings as reminders not to despair, as reminders to love oneself. Whether or not Wittgenstein himself intended it, we can reconstruct a foundational role of love of self in Wittgenstein's ethic, insofar as Wittgenstein (1) claims that clarity is first of all required with respect to ourselves, and (2) calls attention to the danger of putting hindrances in the way of seeing ourselves clearly.

Although there may be theological traditions that preclude any role for love of self, Wittgenstein would be in this respect perfectly in line with one strong ethico-religious tradition which sees love of self as both valuable and necessary. The rationale for an affirmation of proper self-love is both formal and substantive. Formally, it is a matter of simple consistency – if no-one is to be excluded from our love, we cannot arbitrarily exclude our own self. Substantively, one could argue that it is part of our duty to others that we maintain our self, in order to be able to support others, to have something to give. A variation of this theme is (as Kant suggests) that proper concern for the self prevents the temptation to transgress our duties to others.[48] In a different vein, one could argue that if love's proper object is 'the good' (as Aristotle and Aquinas think), then one must love the good in oneself as much as the good in others.[49] A version of this theme is that if one has reverence for God's creation or God's gifts, one must have reverence for one's self.

The importance of love of self is not limited to a traditional religious foundation. Paul Ricoeur offers a contemporary philosophical account of how love of self is implied in the 'reflexive structure' of self-esteem; he describes his own work as a 'phenomenology of the "you too" and of "as myself"'.[50] The 'as myself' of the love commandment expresses how self-esteem is 'understood as a reflexive moment of the wish for the "good life"'; for Ricoeur, in the ethical relation I must hold you in esteem 'as I hold myself in esteem'.[51] The importance of love of self is grounded in the fact that, for Ricoeur, we would be 'unable to hear the injunction coming from the other' if we detested ourselves.[52] One could argue that Wittgenstein too would have appreciated this.

Cavell's proposal of a Wittgensteinian ethic of 'acknowledgement' of others leaves room for such a reading, for one could argue that acknowledgement of self is necessary for acknowledgement of others. Adding the notion of acknowledgement of self can deepen Cavell's proposal of an ethic of acknowledgement of others and by others. Even Edwards's proposal of a Wittgensteinian ethic of love gains an important underpinning with the notion of love of self, because Edwards himself notes in passing that 'To love oneself – to give to oneself a truly profound and just attention – is no easier than to love any other part of the world.'[53]

The importance of love to the truly human life is summarized pithily by Wittgenstein: 'Man's greatest happiness is love' (p. 77, 1948). Six years earlier he had poignantly pointed both to its value and its grace: 'If you already *have* a person's love no sacrifice can be too much to give for it; but any sacrifice is too great to *buy* it for you' (p. 42, 1942).

225

He acknowledged, however, both the vulnerability of loving and its difficulty: 'The linings of my heart keep sticking together and to open it I should each time have to tear them apart' (p. 57, 1947). The difficulty of determining how much is 'in [our] power' troubles his forthright affirmation that 'Man's greatest happiness is love'; he writes: 'he does not love, he cannot love, he refuses to love – what is the difference?!' (p. 77, 1948). And when he goes on immediately to consider the statement that 'God has commanded it, therefore it must be possible to do it,' it is not too far a stretch to assume that the command in question is the command to love, contextualized by the anguished ambiguity of the ability to fulfil it.

4. The achievement of transforming vision

The suggestion that Wittgenstein proposes an ethic of vision might seem to substantiate the charge that his later thought, claiming that philosophy 'leaves everything as it is',[54] precludes a substantive and normative ethic. Can an ethic of vision be an ethic of transformation? Is the recommendation of clear vision merely a recommendation of careful description – a recommendation that leaves everything as it is?

I have argued elsewhere that Wittgenstein's construal of the task of philosophy contains within it the challenge to transform oneself.[55] In particular, I argued that although his understanding of the task of philosophy precludes attempts to revise notions of religion, it does not preclude a call to revisioning that leads to transformation, and I suggest that the same can be said for his view of ethics. Wittgenstein never saw philosophy as an exercise in quietism. The philosopher, he tells us, intends to transform because a philosopher says, '"Look at things like this!" . . . [although] that doesn't ensure that people will look at things like that' (p. 61, 1947). 'Getting hold of the difficulty *deep down* is what is hard' because it involves 'beginning to think about these things in a new way', and at times 'the change is as decisive as, for example, that from the alchemical to the chemical way of thinking' (p. 48, 1946). In this respect the task of philosophy has not changed for Wittgenstein: doing philosophy was always meant to be a way of 'working on oneself', and ultimately working on oneself is a matter of changing 'one's way of seeing things' (p. 16, 1931).

Further support for the ethical importance of vision is suggested by Wittgenstein's references to 'trained' eyes and 'practised' observation (p. 29, 1937), as well as to a 'particular kind of lens' (p. 35, 1939–40). He affirms a deliberate effort to enlarge our horizon, to obtain a different vantage-point. But again, that a deliberate effort to look may be required does not mean that we can simply choose to see – the deliberate effort is in the service of the non-deliberate achievement of clear vision.

The importance of a transforming vision, found in *Culture and Value*, is found just as clearly in other accounts of his goal; for example, he insists: 'I wanted to put this picture before your eyes, and your *acceptance* of this picture consists in your being inclined to regard a given case differently . . . I have changed your *way of seeing*.'[56] This theme is an elaboration of Wittgenstein's concern in the *Investigations* with the notion of the 'dawning of an aspect' or 'noticing an aspect'; what is achieved is a new way of seeing, for 'I *see* that it has not changed; and yet I see it differently.'[57]

The metaphor of vision covers both looking and seeing. This carries on the line of thought in his early work: a deliberate attempt to get a different 'point of view' (p. 4, 1930), a 'perspicuous view of the foundations of possible buildings' (p. 7, 1930), can issue in what Wittgenstein calls a 'fertile new point of view' (p. 18, 1931). Such imaginative revisioning can transform us, so that we no longer act in the same ways.

Wittgenstein's understanding of the ethical can be summarized in the phrase, 'Let us be human' (p. 30, 1937). To 'be human' means both not wanting to be other than we are and wanting to be what we are. Both of these involve ethical transformation; indeed, his suggestion that 'That man will be revolutionary who can revolutionize himself' (p. 45, 1944) implies the possibility of radical change. The general goal of the ethical life – to see oneself clearly, not to misjudge oneself – is to understand oneself in such a way that one changes oneself; that is, it is the goal of transforming oneself (what Kierkegaard calls 'upbuilding').

Wittgenstein sees the task of philosophy as transformative because it is meant to dispel illusions; Kierkegaard saw his own task similarly, and this could well explain Wittgenstein's praise for him. Wittgenstein wants to cause the kind of change that happens when one sees that one was under an illusion and no longer needs to hold on to a particular idea or perspective. His call for description is a call to 'look and say what it's really like – but you must see something that throws new light on the facts' (p. 39, 1941). Seeing what is there may require a change in us; it may also initiate a change in us.

Wittgenstein's early ethical view was obviously normative, and I have argued that his later thought supports a transforming, hence normative, ethic. But Wittgenstein's early ethical view, it has been said, also implied a kind of unconditionality that is not possible to any later ethic emphasizing contextual grammars. Does his later thought preclude continuity in this respect? Let me respond by simply noting two things. First, Wittgenstein makes the following judgement on the limits of ethical justification:

> Nothing we do can be defended absolutely and finally. But only by reference to something else that is not questioned. I.e. no reason can be given why you should act (or should have acted) *like this*, except that by doing so you bring about such and such a situation, which again has to be an aim you *accept*. (p. 16)

This sounds like precisely the view of ethics appropriate to the later thought on language-games and diverse grammars. But this passage comes from 1931 – it is held alongside a view of the ethical as unconditional, not a rejection of it. It is coherently held alongside such a view of the ethical so long as we do not confuse the unconditionality of the ethical with ethical dogmatism. We can avoid that confusion by remembering that it is a mistake to demand that a response to the unconditioned be itself unconditioned. Moreover, an appeal to absoluteness does not imply that there is unconditioned or immediate revelation; we always receive, as Aquinas noted, according to the mode of the receiver.

Second, Wittgenstein's later thought continues a theme found in his early thought that may well suggest some kind of unconditionality or ultimacy – namely, the notion of an ultimate 'light'. In 1937, Wittgenstein made the following remark: 'The light work sheds is a beautiful light, which, however, only shines with real beauty if it is illuminated by yet another light' (p. 26). A decade later he echoes that reference: 'Is what I am doing really worth the effort? Yes, but only if a light shines on it from above. . . . And if the light from above is lacking, I can't in any case be more than clever' (pp. 57–8). It is hard, I think, not to see these as references to a transcendent dimension of value, perhaps the light of love or grace. The same notion of a gracious light is found again in his suggestion that 'It may be that what gives my thoughts their lustre on these occasions is a light shining on them from behind' (p. 66, 1948).

There are, admittedly, some dark sayings attributed to Wittgenstein, but perhaps one could say that Wittgenstein's dying words – 'Tell them I've had a wonderful life'[58] – are an evaluation of himself informed by a 'light from above' that illuminated a lovable self.[59]

Notes

1. Colin Radford, 'Wittgenstein on Ethics', in Brian McGuinness and Rudolf Haller (eds), *Wittgenstein in Focus*, Grazer Philosophische Studien 33/34 (Amsterdam and Atlanta, 1987), p. 85.

2. James Edwards, *Ethics Without Philosophy: Wittgenstein and the Moral Life* (Tampa, 1982), p. 207.

3. Stanley Cavell, *The Claim of Reason* (Oxford, 1979), Part IV.

4. Edwards, *Ethics Without Philosophy*, p. 240.

5. *Culture and Value*, ed. G. H. Von Wright, trans. Peter Winch (Oxford, 1980).

6. *Philosophical Review* 74 (1965).

7. *Culture and Value*, p. 3 (hereafter references to CV will be in parentheses within the text).

8. These issues are brought up by Radford, 'Wittgenstein on Ethics', pp. 107, 113, and by Paul Johnston, *Wittgenstein and Moral Philosophy* (London, 1989), pp. 21, 25.

9. 'Some Notes on Conversations with Wittgenstein', in Rush Rhees (ed.), *Recollections of Wittgenstein* (Oxford, 1984), p. 81.

10. *Wittgenstein, Ethics and Aesthetics* (Albany, 1991), p. 91.

11. Edwards, *Ethics Without Philosophy*, p. 206.

12. Edwards, *Ethics Without Philosophy*, pp. 230–46; Johnston, on the contrary, rejects both 'mystical and metaphysical theses' (*Wittgenstein and Moral Philosophy*, p. 75).

13. e.g., Wittgenstein refers in *Culture and Value* to concepts of pride (p. 26), resentfulness (p. 61), responsibility (p. 63), humility and suffering (p. 71).

14. I am not attributing an ethical *theory* or a moral philosophy to Wittgenstein.

15. This section elaborates an earlier, less-developed suggestion I made in my 'Between Ontology and Ethics: Wittgenstein on Religious Imagination', *Biblioteca dell' 'Archivio di Filosofia'* (Rome, 1995), pp. 717–18.

16. *Zarathustra*, Book IV, 'Of Higher Men', section 9.

17. *Ecce Homo*, 'Why I am a Destiny', 3.

18. He contrasts the truth of Christianity with falsehood (*Culture and Value*, p. 83).

19. He questions the difference between saying of someone: 'he does not love, he cannot love, he refuses to love' (p. 77).

20. Although Tilghman agrees that the issue of discerning 'the humanity in a man' is central to all of Wittgenstein's ethical thought, he qualifies the relevance of 'seeing-as' to our understanding of people (*Wittgenstein, Ethics and Aesthetics*, pp. 91, 110–12).

21. Cavell, *The Claim of Reason*, p. 368.

22. Edwards, *Ethics Without Philosophy*, p. 215.

23. Edwards, *Ethics Without Philosophy*, p. 216.

24. Edwards, *Ethics Without Philosophy*, p. 214.

25. Edwards, *Ethics Without Philosophy*, p. 212.

26. Edwards, *Ethics Without Philosophy*, p. 214.

27. Edwards, *Ethics Without Philosophy*, pp. 215–16.

28. Edwards, *Ethics Without Philosophy*, p. 215.

29. Edwards, *Ethics Without Philosophy*, p. 238.

30. Edwards, *Ethics Without Philosophy*, p. 236.

31. Edwards, *Ethics Without Philosophy*, p. 238.

32. Edwards, *Ethics Without Philosophy*, p. 237.

33. *Gay Science*, §270; see also *Ecce Homo*, II.9, III; *Untimely Meditations*, 3, §1. Of course, Pindar said it long before Nietzsche.

34. *Zarathustra*, Book IV, 1.

35. *Either/Or*, Part II, in *Kierkegaard's Writings*, vol. 3, ed. Howard V. Hong and Edna H. Hong (Princeton, 1987), p. 177.

36. *Either/Or,* Part II, p. 178.

37. *Culture and Value*, pp. 31, 32, 38, 53.

38. Waismann, Russell, Drury, Malcolm, and Von Wright all attest to Wittgenstein's familiarity with and/or esteem of Kierkegaard.

39. 'Some Notes on Conversations with Wittgenstein', p. 87.

40. *Sickness Unto Death*, in *Kierkegaard's Writings*, vol. 19, ed. Howard V. Hong and Edna H. Hong (Princeton, 1980), p. 20.

41. Kierkegaard does not distinguish here between 'willing' and 'wanting'.

42. *Sickness Unto Death*, p. 241.

43. *Either/Or*, Part II, p. 179.

44. *Either/Or*, Part II, p. 160.

45. *Works of Love* (1847), in *Kierkegaard's Writings*, vol. 16, ed. Howard V. Hong and Edna H. Hong (Princeton, 1995), pp. 18, 22. For more on this, see

Ferreira, *Love's Grateful Striving: A Commentary on Kierkegaard's 'Works of Love'* (New York, 2001), pp. 31–5.

46. *Works of Love*, p. 23.

47. *Works of Love*, p. 266.

48. Kant suggests that 'To secure one's own happiness is at least indirectly a duty, for discontent with one's condition under pressure from many cares and amid unsatisfied wants could easily become a great temptation to transgress duties' (*Foundations of the Metaphysic of Morals*, trans. Lewis White Beck (Indianapolis, 1959), p. 15).

49. For example, Aristotle brings out the ambiguity in the phrase 'lover of self' and explains the 'nature of true self-love', affirming that 'the good man should be a lover of self' (*Nicomachean Ethics*, IX.8).

50. Ricoeur, *Oneself as Another*, trans. Kathleen Blamey (Chicago, 1992), p. 193.

51. Ricoeur, *Oneself as Another*, p. 192, 193.

52. Ricoeur, *Oneself as Another*, p. 189.

53. Edwards, *Ethics Without Philosophy*, p. 237.

54. *Philosophical Investigations*, §124.

55. See my 'Normativity and Reference in a Wittgensteinian Philosophy of Religion', *Faith and Philosophy* (2002).

56. *Zettel*, ed. G. E. M. Anscombe and G. H. von Wright, trans. Anscombe (Berkeley, 1967), §461.

57. *Philosophical Investigations*, pp. 193–212.

58. Ray Monk, *Ludwig Wittgenstein: The Duty of Genius* (New York, 1990), p. 579.

59. I dedicate this essay to Victor Preller, who first introduced me to Wittgenstein's thought in graduate school at Princeton University; Victor's own life and teaching have enriched my life in countless ways.

11. Justification's End

Aquinas and Wittgenstein on Creation and Wonder[1]

JENNIFER A. HERDT

1. Wittgensteinian Christian ethics

One of the primary areas in which a Wittgensteinian influence on recent Christian thought is visible is in the notion that ethical concepts are meaningful only within the context of particular communities and practices that embody them. This Wittgensteinian notion, along with broadly historicist and pragmatist trends, has been seized upon as a way of recovering an emphasis on the distinctively Christian. Such trends are evident in the writings of George Lindbeck, Hans Frei, and their students, but Stanley Hauerwas is the most noteworthy example of this Wittgensteinian influence within Christian ethics.[2] Christian ethics first emerged in the modern period out of an attempt to salvage from Protestant theology something valid in a context in which many doctrinal claims were seen as problematic. As Hauerwas characterizes its origins, 'the recovery of the ethical significance of theological discourse was part of a theological movement within Protestantism that in large measure sought to avoid the more traditional particularistic claims of Christianity. Ironically, just to the extent that the development of Christian ethics as a field was a success, it reinforced the assumption that more positive theological convictions had little purchase on the way things are or should be.'[3] A Wittgensteinian vision of the particularity of language-games, in contrast, gave Christian ethics a way of denigrating abstract philosophical ethics and an impetus for reclaiming a thicker theological language.

But there is also an irony that surrounds approaches, like Hauerwas's own, that draw on Wittgensteinian insights to justify an emphasis on 'traditional particularistic claims' of Christianity. The dependence of Christian ethics on the community and practices of the Church is not insisted upon on distinctively Christian grounds, but on the basis of a methodology that is general in scope. Acknowledging this problem, Hauerwas has over the course of the past several decades moved from speaking of character, narrative, and community in general to speaking of the Church in particular. It is still the case, though, that his grounds for renouncing universalistic pretensions and embracing the particularistically Christian remain general, not distinctively Christian.

A theological justification for this methodological move begins by noting that we may unproblematically acknowledge that we have learned something of the true character of the Church from a thinker who does not speak from within the Church, as long as we also acknowledge that God's realm extends beyond the Church, just as we may speak theologically while speaking of the human as such if we claim, with Barth and Rahner, that Christ's humanity reveals to us the truly human. This much Hauerwas grants, at least at times: 'what allows us to look expectantly for agreement among those who do not worship God is not that we have a common morality based on autonomous knowledge of autonomous nature, but that God's kingdom is wider than the church'.[4] But we must say more: it is also the case that the particular location from which Christians speak is not always explicitly that of the Church, that we move dialectically from one location to another, and that we often cannot sharply distinguish between one community or tradition and another. This fluidity means, finally, that no radical contrast between universal and particular can be maintained; it is an illusion to think that we can finally define the location from which we speak or the precise scope of our address. This admission has the effect of chastening radically particularist claims. It does so, though, without denaturing theological discourse.

More worrisome than the apparent incongruity involved in relying on a non-Christian methodology to ground commitment to the distinctively Christian is the fact that Wittgensteinian Christian ethics seems to foster a mode in which the Church sees its task as talking about itself, rather than as responding to God. So while a Wittgensteinian approach sanctions a return from generic discussions of ethical concepts and norms to traditional theological understandings of life in Christ, it still gives would-be theologians today something to talk about *other* than God – character, virtue, narrative, community, tradition, church. Hauerwas strives to deflect such criticisms by suggesting that we think of God as the central character in a story told by the Church: 'there is no way, if we are to be faithful to God's gift at Pentecost, that the church can avoid calling attention to itself. To be sure, like Israel, the church has a story to tell in which God is the main character. But the church cannot tell that story without becoming part of the tale.'[5] However, it is not just that the Church becomes part of the tale, but that whenever Hauerwas sounds the methodological note, which turns out to be almost all of the time, we find the Church talking about the Church, and thus, it seems, the Church as central character rather than God. Claims that 'the story is not self-referential' therefore appear disingenuous.[6] Insofar as this is true, Wittgensteinian Christian ethics thus appears to continue, rather than break from, the liberal approach in which theology's starting-point is anthropology. Moreoever, in its preoccupation with sustaining itself as community and tradition, the Church deviates from pre-modern tradition, which did not in this way thematize the historical mediation of its own identity.

In what follows, this problem of self-absorption and self-referentiality is approached in a somewhat roundabout way, through a discussion of language-games in light of Thomas Aquinas's reflections on the virtues. We set out by exploring analogies between training in a language-game and habituation into the virtues, analogies which allow us to begin to assimilate Aquinas's approach to that of Wittgenstein. Differences become evident when we raise questions of justification – not epistemological justification of our beliefs, but justification in the realm of practice. What are our reasons for acting and, pressing farther, the reasons for our practices? For Wittgenstein, justification comes to an end in a form of life as a whole, which we can only describe. Aquinas, in contrast, speaks of a last end and specifically of God as our true last end. Thus, Wittgenstein appears to embrace a horizontal account of justification and meaning, while Aquinas embraces a vertical account.

Some followers of Wittgenstein seek to resolve this conflict by translating vertical in terms of horizontal: speaking of God is a way of expressing certain existential attitudes. This amounts to a reductionist move. There is, though, an alternative way to proceed, which avoids reductionism and can at the same time help Wittgensteinian Christian ethics respond to the charge of self-referentiality. It requires that we take our bearings from certain comments Wittgenstein makes about wonder. It is not simply that justification comes to an end in description of a form of life. Rather, Wittgenstein's hope is that awareness of the limits to our capacity to give reasons will open us up to wonder at the existence of forms of life and all that which is. To wonder at the existence of contingent things is, at least potentially, to grasp how all that which exists points beyond itself. Although we can comprehend only finite, contingent things, and in this sense remain always occupied with ourselves and our communities and traditions, we can do so in a way that refers them always to that which renders the existence of all finite things intelligible. That is, we can relate to all things as created by God.

2. *Language-games and training*

Wittgenstein spoke of 'language-games' in order to highlight the variety of ways we use language and to draw attention to the fact that these uses reside within human practices that are equally diversified. Focusing in this way on the uses of language allows us to see that meaning is not something we grasp theoretically, but rather something we experience practically, in the course of using language in specific ways. 'The children', writes Wittgenstein, 'are brought up to perform *these* actions, to use *these* words as they do so, and to react in *this* way to the words of others.'[7] Entrance into a new language-game happens through a process of training.

In *Philosophical Investigations*, Wittgenstein denies that there is anything common to all language-games apart from the expression used to refer to them: 'Instead of producing something common to all that we call language, I am saying that these phenomena have no one thing in common which makes us use the same word for all, – but that they are related to one another in many different ways' (*Philosophical*

Investigations §65). Helpful as the notion of family resemblances can be in allowing us to appreciate that a class of objects need not share a distinct 'essence', we can after all, with the help of Wittgenstein's work, say something significant about what language-games share: they are all forms of intentional action, despite the fact that clearly not all language-games are 'about' intentions. Intentional actions are those done 'on purpose', i.e. for reasons. Consider these examples, taken from Wittgenstein's extended list in *Philosophical Investigations* §23:

> Giving orders, and obeying them –
> Describing the appearance of an object, or giving its measurements –
> Constructing an object from a description (a drawing) –
> Reporting an event –
>
> . . .
> Singing catches –
> Guessing riddles –
>
> . . .
> Asking, thanking, cursing, greeting, praying.

All of these, unlike sneezing or digesting, are meaningful actions, not simply natural events, even if they are not directed toward the achievement of any goal external to the practice itself. To become a player of a new language-game is thus to acquire new reasons for acting. Only if I am a chess-player can I checkmate my opponent. Only then can my response to 'Why did you move that piece there?' be 'I'm about to capture his queen.' Someone who did not understand the game of chess would not be able to give such a reason, although she might make the same move with the same piece. She might offer a different reason, indicating that her move was a move in the context of a different 'game': 'I liked the look of this diagonal pattern on the board.'

Training in a language-game cannot take place through the provision of lists of words and corresponding objects or definitions, for no such list can capture the implicit rules or logic governing the language-game. This is linked to the realization that 'picturing' or describing states of affairs is not the primary form of a proposition, but is a specialized use of language, which requires that others already be in place. In the primitive language-game described by Wittgenstein at the outset of the *Philosophical Investigations*, children do not learn how to participate simply through the ostensive teaching of 'slab', 'block', and 'pillar', even if ostensive teaching plays some role. The same ostensive teaching could have taken place, i.e. uttering 'slab' and pointing to a certain object, but within the context of a different language-game, and the child would have learned something quite different – i.e. not that one brings a slab to the person who calls out 'slab', but that the proper response is to bury a slab in the ground, point to other grey-brown objects and say 'slab', or perhaps to applaud in appreciation.

If ostensive definition fails to initiate others into a language-game because it cannot capture the rules of the game, could we perhaps make the rules explicit? We can formulate some rules, but no list of rules could ever be complete. This is so because rules must always be interpreted and applied. Is this a thin 'slab' or a fat 'pillar'? If the person who calls out 'slab' walks away from the building site, do I leave the slab at the site or follow the person? ' "Do the same." But in saying this I must point to the rule. So its *application* must already have been learnt. For otherwise what meaning will its expression have for him?'[8] To seek to specify rules for interpreting the rules would lead only to an infinite regress.

Participating in a language-game is an active process, a matter of judging and acting in certain ways and not others. But there is something passive about entering into a language-game. It is fundamentally something I undergo, something that happens to me, not something I perform. Thus, I cannot enter into a language-game by act of will. I cannot simply decide that I will become a chess player; I must be taught how to play. Moreover, I cannot simply decide that I will learn chess, though I can decide to try to learn. There is something about entering a language-game that is akin to experiencing a change of aspect. Once I am capable of seeing Jastrow's duck–rabbit as either a duck or a rabbit, I may of course switch at will from one to the other, but if, when I first encounter the figure, I see it as a rabbit, I cannot simply decide to see it as a duck, even if I am told that it can be seen as a duck.

Related to the passive element in entering a language-game is an indeterminacy always present within the process of training. If, looking at the drawing of the duck–rabbit for the first time, I see a rabbit, the most you can do to help me out is to say 'Look, that curve there is the duck's bill,' or 'You need to turn the picture on its side to see the duck.' You can strive to put me in a situation where I will see it your way, but that is all. Wittgenstein recognized this in his discussion of following a rule. Most people will become able to see the duck, but there may be some who never can, who never 'get it', just as there are some who never 'get' a joke (*Philosophical Investigations*, §143). They may say things like 'that curve there is supposed to be the duck's bill, but I just don't see it'. To teach someone the rules of a particular language-game is, says Wittgenstein, to change his or her 'way of looking at things' (*Philosophical Investigations*, §144), and there is no surefire method for doing so. I can try to learn a language-game through mimicry, doing what you do and saying what you say. But whether I have really learned the game will depend on whether I can 'go on', whether I can make the next move, on my own. Otherwise you will conclude that I just don't get it, that I haven't yet come to see things your way, that the aspect has not dawned on me. Training can dispose us to become a participant in a language-game, but it does not guarantee that this will take place.

3. Habituation and the acquisition of ends

Habituation into the life of the virtues may be seen as a special case of training in a language-game. We can consider ethics a language-game insofar as it is not just a matter of acting in certain ways, but of acting in certain ways for certain reasons, i.e. of acting intentionally, and of being ready to offer to others the reasons for our actions. Moreover, we must be trained so to act and reason, and this training must be practical, not purely theoretical. Aquinas, following Aristotle, tells us that we require habits because we are affective and not purely rational creatures. Repeated action can bring about a habit by disposing the appetitive powers so that they accord with reason.[9] This formulation, though, implies that we have a prior grasp, through reason, of the proper ends of human action, and need only become more unified in our pursuit of them, as if weakness of will were the sole obstacle to virtue. It would be as if I did know how to 'go on' within a certain language-game, but had a tendency now and again to falsely assimilate a newer use to a more familiar older use. Or, in terms of change of aspect and Jastrow's familiar duck–rabbit, as if I knew how to see the duck, but was so used to seeing the rabbit that I always saw the rabbit first. In such a case, repeated employment of the new use, repeated 'seeing' of the figure as a duck, would allow us to render our participation in the language-game more fluid, more natural.

In fact, though, Aquinas does not think that habituation is simply a matter of the appetitive powers being disciplined by reason. Since intellect is always moved by will, reason's proper grasp of the end requires rectitude of the will. So Aquinas writes that it is a condition of prudence 'that man be rightly disposed in regard to the principles of this reason of things to be done, that is in regard to their ends, to which man is rightly disposed by the rectitude of the will' (ST I-II.56.3). We do not normally first grasp the point of a virtue and then begin to exemplify it, but rather we grasp the point only in living this way. Reason and the appetitive powers are formed in tandem through habituation, which centrally involves teaching by others more fully formed in virtue than ourselves. Similarly, Wittgenstein wants to deny that we first understand a language-game and then play it; rather, our understanding of it emerges and is displayed in the course of our playing. (He is equally concerned to show how misleading it is to think of understanding as arriving, as though it were some sort of light-bulb turning on in the brain.)

Both training in a language-game as envisioned by Wittgenstein and habituation in the virtues as understood by Aquinas, then, suggest that our way of seeing things can change insofar as we begin to act in ways we do not at first understand, and that we are capable of grasping the point of acting this way and of learning how to 'go on'. They are concerned, though, to stress different aspects of training or habituation. Wittgenstein sought to avoid thinking of meaning or understanding as mental events or mental processes. He therefore focused on how meaning is displayed in use, how understanding is displayed in 'going on', and how much these vary from one context to another. Aquinas, in contrast, was more concerned to illuminate the ways in which we learn to overcome our tendency to act in a disordered way and integrate our action in virtuous character. These different emphases do not to my mind, though, reflect a fundamental incompatibility between their two enterprises.

Can we learn more from Aquinas about what it means to acquire new reasons for action? This is not simply a matter of habituating the appetitive powers to move in accord with reason as discussed above, but neither is it merely a matter of theoretical persuasion. It has to do with our apprehension of something as good, with 'seeing' something 'as' good and therefore as attractive, as an end to be pursued in our action. This emerges more fully when we consider the question of how we come by our ends.

The end of our action is that for which we act, the object of the will. The will inclines naturally toward that which is apprehended as good, so ends serve as such only in being perceived as good. Importantly, then, we do not acquire ends by choosing them; when we choose, we choose means to ends we already possess (ST I-II.13.3). Of course, what in one context is an end and therefore not in question may in another context be seen as a means to some other end, and therefore subject to choice (ST I-II.14.2 resp. 1). If Mike's end is to eat well, he may deliberate about whether eating a Big Mac and a Cinnabon for lunch will allow him to achieve this end. But he does not deliberate about whether to eat well. This is his aim, and is not currently in question. If his end is to be healthy, on the other hand, he may deliberate about whether or not eating well conduces to the end of health. 'Shall I eat well?' is a question that makes no sense in the context of the first deliberation, but perfectly good sense in the context of the second.

So we may say that one way in which people come by the ends they have (i.e. the end of eating well) is as a result of deliberation about – and perhaps empirical investigation into – how to achieve more comprehensive ends (i.e. being healthy). Before, Patty did not perceive eating well as a good and did not desire it, but now she does, because she has come across a copy of Nutrition Action Healthletter, and has learned that eating well does indeed contribute to good health, something she already desired. She did not, of course, choose to make eating well an end of her action, although she can choose to act for that end now that it exists for her. She was also able to choose to investigate what sorts of activities might conduce to good health. It would be nonsensical to say that the acquisition of eating well as an end somehow undermined her freedom or that it was imposed on her against her will. Still, its becoming an end for her is something that happened to her, not something that she did.

We are not self-movers. Rather, we always act in response to what attracts us, that which presents itself to us as an end. Here it is the Augustinian rather than the Aristotelian heritage of Aquinas that is more in evidence. Insofar as we come to recognize that different goods are interrelated, our commitment to one will easily bring along with it a commitment to another – particularly if we can grasp one as ordered to another. Repeated experiences can create associations between something we already desire and something related which we do not yet desire. So we can acquire many sorts of new ends by learning about things that conduce to ends we already have. But this only takes us so far in our attempts to understand the acquisition of ends. How do we acquire the comprehensive end(s) toward which we can understand other ends as leading or which we can understand them as constituting?

Aquinas explores this issue in terms of the 'last end'. If we ask Mike why he desires to eat well, he can say, 'because it conduces to my end of being healthy'. If we ask him why he desires to be healthy, he can say, 'because it conduces to (or, better, is constitutive of), my end of living well'. But if we ask him why he desires to live well, we are unlikely to get much of an answer. He might try to redescribe the end for us – 'because living well is essential to happiness', 'because that's the whole point' – but the fact that this is simply redescription or persuasive rhetoric indicates that the chain of reason-giving has given out.[10] Thus, if we ask how Mike acquired the end of living well, we cannot show that he discovered that living well conduces to some more comprehensive end that he previously possessed – there is no such end toward which this one is ordained.

According to Aquinas, though, there ought to be, for our true last end, that which perfects and completes us, is God. We love God as our last end when we possess the virtue of charity. To be infused with, in-formed by, charity, is to love God, and to love everything else, including ourselves, for God's sake. To love everything for God's sake is to desire that everything else (insofar as it is capable of doing so) partake of the fellowship of charity, which is the everlasting happiness of friendship with God. God becomes the final cause – our reason – for loving all that exists.

When it comes to the fundamental conversion of the will from resting in finite goods to taking God as our last end, we have no account to give other than to appeal to grace. Charity is spoken of as a new habitual form infused by grace (ST II-II.23.2). To say that charity is infused is, for Aquinas, to say that it cannot be acquired through habituation because it disposes us in a higher manner toward a higher end than that toward which we are naturally directed (ST I-II.110.43). Like the acquisition of any new end, it is something that comes to us, that happens to us, not something we do or choose. Any reason we can give for loving God counts as a reason from within the state of grace. Again, like the acquisition of any new end, it is not something that happens against our will. We have not acted but have been transformed, and something so all-pervasive has changed that we may speak of having been given a new will (ST I-II.109.6; 111.2). Not all gratuitous moral change is grace, of course; Satan's fall was also gratuitous, in the sense that we can give no coherent account of Satan's reasons for turning away from God. But while I cannot explore here the distinctions among different forms that such changes of the will may take, it is, I think, helpful to place grace within a broader context of gratuitous transformations of character.

Wittgenstein might say at this point that one need not have a last end, that such thinking is symptomatic of our confusion about meaning. Rather than focusing on how one language-game or human practice might be ordered to or encompassed within another, Wittgenstein was, as we have already noted, interested primarily in loose 'family resemblances' among such games. This suggests that he thought in terms of horizontal rather than vertical connections among language-games. In order to say more about this issue, it will be helpful to consider the question of the last end in light of what Wittgenstein had to say about the justification of language-games. For Aquinas, the chain of reasons terminates in the last end. Where does it terminate for Wittgenstein? We begin by considering Wittgenstein's early account of absolute value, certain features of which are preserved in his later remarks about the limits of justification.

4. *Wittgenstein and the end of justification*

When Wittgenstein, in the *Tractatus*, insisted that value was necessarily transcendental, since what ought to be the case cannot be reduced to what is the case, he found that this seemingly clear distinction between is and ought required the introduction of a further distinction between absolute value and relative value.[11] Some evaluative statements, he thought, could be analysed without loss into statements of facts. These were therefore just judgements of relative value. He insisted, though, that not all evaluative statements could be so analysed, just as hypothetical imperatives in Kant are relative to my desires, but categorical imperatives are not. So, if told 'You ought to serve the ball this way', I can reply, 'Not if I don't care to become a good tennis player.' But if I torture small children and am told that I am behaving horribly, and I say, 'Well, I know, but I just don't care to behave better', that reply will not be accepted; I will be told that I ought to care.[12] Of such statements of absolute value, Wittgenstein said, 'not only [would] no description that I can think of . . . do to describe what I mean by absolute value, but . . . I would reject every significant description that anybody could possibly suggest, *ab initio*, on the ground of its significance. . . . Ethics so far as it springs from the desire to say something about the ultimate meaning of life, the absolute good, the absolute valuable, can be no science. What it says does not add to our knowledge in any sense.'[13] Any description would be simply of what is the case and would thus not capture the value of the experience. If I desire to become a good tennis player, that desire and its corresponding hypothetical imperatives are aspects of what is the case and may thus be described, but that I ought to care, irrespective of any desires that I or anyone else has, about not being a torturer of small children, is not – according to the early Wittgenstein – a state of affairs capable of description.

W. D. Hudson argues that Wittgenstein's distinction between absolute and relative value cannot hold, because even statements of relative value are not mere statements of fact. 'Implicit within the statements of fact into which a judgement of relative value can be put are criteria or principles of evaluation which determine what facts constitute relative value as distinct from what facts do not.'[14] That is, 'This knife is sharp' implies 'This is a good knife' only given the criterion 'Knives that are sharp are good knives.' Hudson is quite right: statements of relative value are not mere statements of fact. We might also note that 'thick' ethical concepts, such as the virtues of courage and generosity, seem more descriptive (though no less evaluative) than thin ethical concepts such as 'good' and 'right'.

This difficulty in sustaining a clear distinction between descriptive and normative statements points us in the direction of Wittgenstein's later thought. When we understand meaning as use, a distinction between is and ought remains, in the sense that evaluative statements cannot be reduced to or translated into neutral statements, yet we now see that any account of human action as such will be normative – that is, as opposed to an account of unintentional pieces of human behaviour, such as twitching or sneezing (unless, of course, I take snuff), or any scientific account of processes going on within the human as a biological organism or physical body. Rather than saying (as on Wittgenstein's earlier picture theory of meaning) that any account of value must be rejected as capturing only what is and never what ought to be the case, one might now almost turn this on its head: no description of what is the case in the realm of human action can exclude what ought to be the case; to understand a description of a human action, one must understand what was being done, i.e. the agent's intention and reasons for action, and this means that we are always already within the ethical realm. To be within the sphere of reason-giving is to ask questions of justification and evaluation. 'Why are you carrying an umbrella on such a nice day?' 'Because the weather forecast calls for rain' will call forth a very different response from 'It's a weapon – I'm planning to take revenge on the professor who failed me in French' – but we move seamlessly from one to the other, from reasons for action which may not seem significant enough to merit the title 'ethical', to those which raise serious moral concern. Any account of human action as such will be normative.

It follows that there are no sharp boundaries to 'the ethical'; as on any broadly Aristotelian account, ethics is a matter of doing the right things for the right reasons, where the right reasons may sometimes be prudential, sometimes altruistic, etc., and where they vary as well with social, cultural, and historical context. 'Moral acts are the same as human acts,' writes Aquinas (ST I-II.1.3). Thus, Wittgenstein's early analogy between logic and value retains some usefulness in the context of his later thought. Logic has to do with the (usually implicit) rules according to which language-games are conducted. Ethics is a particular logic, regulative of the particular language-game of giving reasons for human actions. But the language-game of reason-giving is constitutive of the human world. It is a contingent game, but one we cannot stop playing without ceasing to be recognizably human. In this sense, logic and ethics continue to be transcendental – conditions of the possibility of being human. This is not to deny that we are capable of isolating certain sub-realms of discourse from these rules, abstracting an arena of 'pure description', for instance. But such sub-realms of discourse will always be secondary and derivative in character. Physicists are human beings before they are physicists, and physics is a form of intentional human activity for which reasons may be required.

Even if no primary contrast between descriptive and normative can be sustained, there remains some point to Wittgenstein's earlier distinction between absolute and relative value. While ethics has to do with the practice of giving reasons, that is, of justification, the possibility of justification gives out at some point. We are not able to offer a justification for entering into the game of reason-giving in the first place.[15] If the practice of reason-giving is constitutive of a particular language-game, then insofar as we offer a reason, we are already within that language-game, not outside talking about the possibility of moving inside. This helps to illuminate the absolute character of a categorical ought. We may say, 'it is good to be courageous because it allows one to defend the innocent', but going beyond that becomes less informative and eventually tautologous: so, 'it is good to defend the innocent because it is good', and 'it is good to be good because it is good'. Our various moral judgements are interrelated with one another such that reasons we give for pursuing one course of action may be intelligibly related to reasons for pursuing another, but the danger of trying to give reasons for developing virtue as such is that we end up in another sphere altogether – i.e. that we attempt to offer a self-interested justification for conforming to 'ethical' norms, or a sociological, psychological, or neuroscientific explanation of patterns of human action.

Wittgenstein suggests that we turn at this point from justification to description:

> the difficulty – I might say – is not that of finding the solution but rather that of recognizing as the solution something that looks as if it were only a preliminary to it. 'We have already said everything. –
> Not anything that follows from this, no, this itself is the solution!' This is connected, I believe, with our wrongly expecting an explanation, whereas the solution of the difficulty is a description, if we give it the right place in our considerations. If we dwell upon it, and do not try to get beyond it.
> The difficulty here is: to stop. (*Zettel*, §314)

The 'solution of the difficulty' is to be found finally in description of an entire form of life, in which its panoply of rules, its grammar, shows itself. Justification comes to an end in a form of life in the sense that we ultimately act in certain ways just because the rules of the game dictate so acting. We play the game of ethics because that is constitutive of what it is to be human. If we were to act in another way, we would not be who we are.

5. *Wonder and creation*

Wittgenstein and Aquinas agree that the chain of reasons gives out at some point, and further that we gain nothing by leaving the realm of reasons, i.e. by turning at this point from reasons to causes. But does the chain of reasons come to an end in a form of life as a whole, or does it stop at a last end? Should we seek a horizontal or a vertical account of meaning?

One way to seek to eliminate the divergence between Wittgenstein's horizontal and Aquinas's vertical accounts of meaning is to say that for Aquinas, too, the chain of reasons comes to an end in a form of life. After all, it is only within the Church, formed by Scripture, shared traditions, and communal liturgy, that the language of God as last end has meaning. Only within the Church can one's chain of reasons end with the God who created the world and came to us in Jesus. Beyond the Church, to say 'I love all things in God' will invite a probing for further reasons, rather than being recognized as the end to all reason-giving.

Up to a certain point, such a Wittgensteinian translation of Aquinas is unobjectionable. Christian commitment to loving all things in God ought to be firmer than anything to which we might appeal to justify that commitment.[16] But many Wittgensteinian thinkers seem willing to take a further step, and make the reductionist or radically imma-nentist claim that, in fact, to spell out what it means for God to be our last end just is to describe the Church's form of life, that statements about God are grammatical in that they are the rules that define a par-ticular form of life. Religious discourse becomes self-referential in just the way Hauerwas sought to avoid. So D. Z. Phillips writes that belief in the Last Judgement 'is not a conjecture about the future, but, as it were, the framework, the religious framework within which [the believer] meets fortune, misfortune, and the evil that he finds in his own life and in life about him'.[17] He sees religious statements simply as pictures that regulate our thinking and acting. Or, as William Brenner writes, 'For example, the sentence "We're safe in the hands of God," as [Wittgenstein] understands it, is the expression of a particular attitude towards the normal human preoccupation with keeping safe and secure,' even if Brenner adds that this attitude is a categorical rule and not simply a contingent trust.[18]

Many of Wittgenstein's explicit references to religion can be inter-preted along these lines. They can also, however, be interpreted in a different direction, one which might allow us to reconcile Wittgenstein and Aquinas without offering a reductionist interpretation of theology as grammar. One of the most sustained, if never fully explicated, themes in Wittgenstein's thought, both early and late, was that of wonder at the existence of the world, or seeing the world as a miracle. In his 'Lecture on Ethics', Wittgenstein offered this as a personal example of the experience of absolute value, noting that:

> I believe the best way of describing it is to say that when I have it I wonder at the existence of the world. And I am then inclined to use such phrases as 'how extraordinary that anything should exist' or 'how extraordinary that the world should exist'.[19]

Elsewhere, he wrote that 'When someone who believes in God looks around him and asks, "Where did everything that I see come from?" "Where did everything come from?" he is not asking for a (causal) explanation.'[20] On Brenner's interpretation, what this means is that 'believing in a Creator requires, not accepting a causal hypothesis . . ., but prescinding at a certain point from the causal point of view . . . ; it is connected, essentially, with a particular way of acting and reacting . . . ; it requires relativizing the everyday practice of judging ourselves and others'.[21]

Now, it is true that believing in God as creator is not a matter of accepting a causal hypothesis and that it is a matter of prescinding at a certain point from the causal point of view. But affirming God as creator prescinds from the causal point of view just because causality, which has to do with relationships between events in the world, cannot be applied to the whence of this world as such. We can speak of God as causing the world to be only if we note that in doing so, we are speaking analogically.[22] We are naming 'God' that which would, if we could know it, render intelligible the finite, contingent existence of everything that is.[23] So while it is true that believing in a creator is connected essentially with a particular way of acting and reacting, this is not all it is, nor does it somehow amount to suspending our everyday practice of judging one another, as Brenner's interpretation easily leads us to conclude.

James Edwards suggests that this theme in Wittgenstein is central to understanding the underlying ethical thrust of his thought. Wittgenstein abhorred scientific, technocratic, instrumentalizing modes of life and sought instead to engender 'a stance which treats the world as a miracle, as an object of love, not of will'.[24] Edwards characterizes this as an ethic of love, contrasting it with Kantian and utilitarian ethics and suggesting that it shares much in common with Iris Murdoch's elevation of 'attention' as the heart of the moral life. Wittgenstein's later philosophy, he writes, 'is at its core a return to an important moment of the Western religious vision, namely, that moment which exalts the essential sacredness and mystery of all things, which demands an astonished worship as the proper response to that mystery, and which identifies worship of God with an infinitely patient, detailed, and self-surpassing attention to the individual realities facing one, which is love'.[25]

Edwards manages, I think, to avoid the reductionist move, and points us in the direction of a mediation between Wittgenstein's horizontal and Aquinas's vertical accounts of meaning. For Aquinas, God is not in the usual sense a new good to be pursued, since God is not among the objects in the world. To think of God as such an object is to render God finite, to lose sight of God's radical transcendence.[26] But neither is God an object external to the world, for the world is everything that exists. One way to think of this is in terms of the transcendentals of beauty, truth, and goodness.[27] Whenever we will, we will what appears to us good. But God is the universal good, goodness itself. Any particular good thing is good by virtue of participation in God (ST I-II.2.8). What we can say, then, is that when God is our last end we love everything within the world in a new way – we love these things as participating in God. To have charity is to be related to all of reality in a particular way, by loving it as directed to the fellowship of goodness. It is thus to live in a different world, even though the world contains just the same objects as before.

For Wittgenstein, meanwhile, as for Aquinas, justification does not simply come to an end in the web of practices that make up a form of life. It is not, as one standard reading of Wittgenstein assumes, that justification comes to an end because, recognizing that we are extending the application of this language-game beyond its proper scope, we simply lose interest. Rather, justification ought to come to an end not simply with the contingency of forms of life, but in wonder at the mystery of the world's existence, including the existence of our own forms of life (and note: not simply that form of life which we call the Church). It is not that talk about God is really just talk about human attitudes and forms of life. And it is true but trivial that, for example, talk of the Trinity is meaningful only in the context of a Christian form of life. Meanwhile, from the other direction, for Aquinas as for Wittgenstein, mystery always remains just that; to have God as our last end is not to comprehend God, nor to comprehend the how of creation. But this is not to say that it means nothing to have God as our last end; when we love all things in God, we love all things as created; we love them as sharing in the wonder of existence that we name as coming from God.

Is it 'training' that allows us to treat the world as a miracle?

Wittgenstein certainly hoped that his writings could serve as an occasion for undergoing this change of aspect. That his later writings, in contrast to the *Tractatus* and other early writings, have nearly nothing to say about ethics suggests how indirect he thought this occasioning would need to be. He hoped to disrupt our normal 'ways of seeing' the world to allow room for another way – not simply to allow us to see our many and varied uses of language, but to open space for awe at the existence of these myriad language-games. To suggest that justification and explanation come to an end in description of forms of life is to invite us to be attentive to the contingency of finite existence and thus to pose the question of its intelligibility. It is thus to invite us to ask for the 'reason' for reason-giving, the 'cause' of causes, even while recognizing that the quotation marks must always remain in place.

This proposed mediation between Aquinas and Wittgenstein requires, I suspect, that we allow our theological convictions to govern our interpretation of Wittgenstein. When we do so, what we stand to gain from Wittgenstein is not just a general methodology that applies to all forms of life, all language-games, but a particular way of seeing that can be the occasion for us to 'see' our own theological convictions better. This approach does not, though, go so far as to 'baptize' Wittgenstein; it does not see in him something distinctively Christian. To wonder at the existence of all things opens the door to affirming creation, i.e. to affirming that there is something which renders fully intelligible the existence of all finite entities, but it is not yet an affirmation of creation, nor do all who affirm creation affirm that the 'Reason' of reasons and 'Cause' of causes was revealed to us in Jesus.

Here, then, is a starting-point for a Wittgensteinian theology. Does it give theologians something to talk about other than God? Does it render Christian ethics ultimately self-referential? No. It is not just a way of talking about our own form of life and the rules by which it is governed. It is, though, a reminder that we direct our attention to God through attending to – through loving – finite existing particulars.[28]

Notes

1. These reflections are rooted in my experience as a student of Victor S. Preller from 1989 to 1994. I had the great good fortune of studying both Aquinas and Wittgenstein with Victor Preller, and my readings of both are deeply indebted to his lectures and tea-time conversations. I am glad to own myself a Prelline disciple, but cannot claim to know that he would have agreed with what I have written here; I only wish we could have discussed it over one last cup of tea.

2. Many of Hauerwas's central writings have been collected together in *The Hauerwas Reader*, ed. John Berkman and Michael Cartwright (Durham, NC: Duke University Press, 2001). Lindbeck's most important work is *The Nature of Doctrine* (Philadelphia: Westminster Press, 1984). By Frei, see *The Eclipse of Biblical Narrative* (New Haven: Yale University Press, 1974).

3. 'On Keeping Theological Ethics Theological' (1982), in *Reader*, p. 69.

4. 'Why the "Sectarian Temptation" is a Misrepresentation: A Response to James Gustafson' (1998), in *Reader*, p. 108.

5. 'The Church as God's New Language' (1986), in *Reader*, p. 149.

6. 'The Church as God's New Language', p. 160.

7. Ludwig Wittgenstein, *Philosophical Investigations*, 3rd edn, trans. G. E. M. Ansombe (New York: Macmillan, 1958), §4. (References are to numbered remarks, except where a page number is indicated by 'p.'.)

8. Ludwig Wittgenstein, *Zettel*, ed. G. E. M. Anscombe and G. H. von Wright (Berkeley: University of California Press, 1967), §305.

9. St Thomas Aquinas, *Summa Theologica* I-II, trans. Fathers of the English Dominican Province (New York: Benziger Brothers, 1908), 51.2. Further references will be given parenthetically in the text.

10. Jeffrey Stout rightly pointed out, in comments on an earlier draft of this essay, that this does not necessarily mean that conversation comes to an end at this point; to say that we 'hit bedrock' does not exclude the possibility of 'doubling back to other considerations'. His comments help to clarify that my claim is not that we experience a breakdown in the social practice of reason-giving, but just that we do now and then 'hit bedrock' in that process, regardless of where the conversation moves on from that point.

11. Ludwig Wittgenstein, *Tractatus Logico-Philosophicus*, trans. C. K. Ogden (London: Routledge & Kegan Paul, 1922), 6.41.

12. 'A Lecture on Ethics', *Philosophical Review* 74 (1965): 4.

13. 'Lecture on Ethics', p. 10.

14. W. D. Hudson, *Wittgenstein and Religious Belief* (London: Macmillan, 1975), p. 84.

15. To be more precise, the only justification possible would be a reflexive justification, grounding the practice of reason-giving from within. Such a reflexive justification must proceed by uncovering the performative contradiction that emerges in the attempt to argue (i.e. to give reasons) for ceasing to participate in the practice of reason-giving. See Jennifer Herdt, 'Alasdair MacIntyre's "Rationality of Traditions" and Tradition-Transcendental Standards of

Justification', *Journal of Religion* 78/4 (1998): 524–46, and Vittorio Hösle, *Die Krise der Gegenwart und die Verantwortung der Philosophie* (Munich: C.H. Beck, 1990), 143–78.

16. As Fergus Kerr writes, commenting on the analogy between the colour system and the grammar of God-talk, 'There is no position from which the existence of the colour system might have been a discussable hypothesis. We could not answer the question "What difference does the existence of colour make?" by pointing to an item in the environment. We have to recall how our conversation is shot through with colour language', *Theology After Wittgenstein* (Oxford: Basil Blackwell, 1986), p. 154.

17. D. Z. Phillips, *Wittgenstein and Religion* (New York: St Martin's Press, 1993), p. 124.

18. William Brenner, 'Creation, Causality, and Freedom of the Will', in Robert L. Arrington and Mark Addis (eds), *Wittgenstein and Philosophy of Religion* (London: Routledge, 2001), pp. 52–3.

19. 'Lecture on Ethics', p. 7.

20. *Remarks on Colour*, ed. G. E. M. Anscombe, trans. Linda McAlister and Margarete Schättle (Oxford and Berkeley: Blackwell and University of California Press, 1977–9), III, para. 317. See also 'Lecture on Ethics', p. 9, and *Tractatus* 6.44–5.

21. Brenner, 'Creation, Causality, and Freedom of the Will', p. 51.

22. On analogy, see David Burrell, *Analogy and Philosophical Language* (New Haven: Yale University Press, 1973), and Victor Preller, *Divine Science and the Science of God* (Princeton: Princeton University Press, 1967).

23. See Victor S. Preller, OGS, Third Mascall Memorial Lecture, delivered 31 October 1998, published in this volume, pp. 253–69.

24. James C. Edwards, *Ethics Without Philosophy: Wittgenstein and the Moral Life* (Tampa: University Press of Florida, 1982), p. 236. See also Kerr, *Theology After Wittgenstein*, p. 151.

25. Edwards, *Ethics Without Philosophy*, p. 240.

26. See Kathryn Tanner, *God and Creation in Christian Theology* (Oxford: Basil Blackwell, 1988), p. 89.

27. A Christian understanding of these will differ, though, from a Platonic understanding, insofar as the transcendentals are seen not solely as formal causes, but are taken as referring to a God who is also final and efficient cause of all goodness and being. See Rudi A. Te Velde, *Participation and Substantiality in Thomas Aquinas* (Leiden: Brill, 1995), pp. 33–4, 60–2.

28. I am grateful to Jeffrey Stout and Rob MacSwain for their thoughtful comments on an earlier draft of this essay.

12. Water into Wine

VICTOR PRELLER, OGS

In the 1997 Mascall Memorial Lecture, John Macquarrie told a familiar story about the canonization of Thomas Aquinas. When asked by the devil's advocate, 'Where in the case of Thomas are the two miracles required for canonization?', the Pope replied, 'There are as many miracles as there are articles in the *Summa*.' If not in the strictest sense of the word, we may speak, I believe, about miracles of grace – when human nature is transformed by the grace of God. Grace, we are told, does not destroy nature, but perfects it. Grace completes and complements human nature, restoring it to its intended integrity and ordering it to a supernatural end that transcends its inherent potentiality. In that sense, baptism itself is a miracle. I should argue that in the *Summa Theologiae*, Thomas Aquinas accomplishes something like a miracle of grace – we may call it a hermeneutical miracle – a miracle of interpretation through which Aristotle receives Christian baptism. Aristotle, regarded by both Church and State in the twelfth and early thirteenth centuries as the scourge of Christendom and a source of heresy, rises up from the waters of Aquinas's hermeneutical baptism looking very much like a disciple of Christ, articulating in what sounds like his own voice the truths of the Catholic faith. A miracle indeed.

The extent of that miracle can be appreciated if we recall the vehemence of the reaction of both the Empire and the Church to the reading and teaching of the newly discovered works of Aristotle, deprived of their Islamic clothing, standing out in bold defiance of the traditional wisdom of western Christendom. It is not surprising that the rulers of the Empire should find the *Politics* of Aristotle somewhat subversive. It is no more surprising that the magisterium of the Church should find (above all) the *Physics* but even the *Metaphysics* and *Ethics* of Aristotle bristling with heresy, and incompatible with the central teachings of the Catholic Church. As Gilson points out, the founding of the University of Paris was a cooperative attempt of the Empire and the Church to create a third arm of defence to protect Christendom against the corrosive influence of Aristotelianism. We shall look in a moment at some of the central aspects of Aristotle's philosophy that do in fact seem to be antithetical to the Christian faith – teachings of Aristotle that cannot be true if the Catholic creeds are not false. But first, we may briefly remark on the failure of both Empire and Church to eliminate the Aristotelian threat.

The Church attempted to halt the reading and teaching of Aristotle by means of the power of excommunication, which would submit its victims to the punishment of the Empire. From the time of the outbreak of Aristotelian teaching in the twelfth century through the height of Aquinas's career in the middle of the thirteenth century, pope after pope issued and reissued ban after ban, threat after threat. Originally, it was forbidden under pain of excommunication to read or teach any of the writings of Aristotle (apart, of course, from the *Logical Organon*, which was always a part of western tradition). Occasionally, a more limited ban was issued, allowing the teaching of Aristotle's *Physics*, but only if the purpose was to prove Aristotle wrong. None of those repeated threats of excommunication worked. Aristotle continued to be taught as a kind of natural philosophy, and Paris became more and more a centre of Aristotelianism and a source of threatening heresy. The last papal ban against the reading and teaching of Aristotle – the strongest form of the ban – was published in the middle of the thirteenth century, during the time that Aquinas was close to finishing work on the texts of Aristotle. Fr D'Arcy points out that earlier on the very day that the Pope issued that final ban on the works of Aristotle he had shared a quiet lunch at Castel Gandolfo with Thomas Aquinas. I am not normally given to conspiracy theories, but in this case I am sorely tempted. Perhaps Aquinas convinced the Pope that if baptized Christians could not be lured away from the pagan Aristotle, then Aristotle must become a disciple of Christ. Aristotle must undergo a baptismal transformation. Perhaps that final ban was an attempt to silence pagan readings of a pagan philosopher until that transformation was carried out. At any rate, by the end of the thirteenth century, after the work of Aquinas was over, the writings of Aristotle were required reading at many Catholic seminaries. They were read, of course, in the context of Aquinas's commentaries and the *Summa Theologiae*.

Now let's look briefly at what I take to be the basic source of the threat posed by Aristotle to the very foundations of Catholic theology. As stated above, there were many claims made by Aristotle that could not be true unless the Catholic creeds were false. Many of these, however, were relatively easy to counter. Denying them would in no way affect the principles of Aristotle's philosophy. They were incidental claims that could easily be discarded – such, for example, as Aristotle's references to the gods of Greek theology.

But it was not those incidental and historically contingent claims that threatened the very foundations of the Catholic faith. Within the writings of Aristotle, I should claim, every serious threat to Catholic truth derives from a basic principle of Aristotle's whole enterprise – an *arche*, a first principle, an assumed starting-point for all of his philosophical speculations on this world and on all of reality. I would call it the principle of the finitude of being. Aristotle argues that the first principles, the starting-points of every science, philosophy, or intellectual investigation, must be established by what he calls 'dialectic'. In the *Ethics* he gives a simple one-line definition of dialectical reasoning: 'Let all opposing positions cancel one another out, and see what is left standing.' In order to disagree on whether or not tea is a pleasant drink, we must agree on what tea is. In order to disagree intelligibly about anything, we must be able to define what it is that we disagree about. Behind every *dis*agreement, there must lie some more general *agreement* – something that we are both assuming – that we could in theory articulate and define.

In what he calls 'metaphysics' (and what Aquinas calls 'first philosophy'), Aristotle attempts to find the most universal agreements about reality that must be assumed if any rational argument or reasoning about reality is to be at all possible. Is there something that we must all implicitly assume in order to argue or reason about reality at all? What must we assume in order to argue or reason about what is? To start with, we must have the concept of 'being' (reality). And we can't, as it were, get *behind* that concept. 'Being is the first concept that falls under the intellect.' Is there anything absolutely universal that we must assume about *being* (about what *is*) in order to argue or reason intelligibly about anything in particular? It is here that Aristotle introduces the principle that was the ultimate source of his threat to the very foundations of the Catholic faith. It is a very seductive, a very plausible principle, and it has appeared again and again in one form or another throughout the history of western thought and philosophy. (It is plausible and seductive because it is so *nearly* true.) Here it is: in order to reason or argue intelligibly about what *is*, we must assume that whatever *is* is intelligible. Being is intelligible. To say that being is intelligible, however, is to say that any thing that *has* being must have some intelligible *form*. It must be capable of being conceived and defined. For Aristotle, that means that it must *be* something determinate – with limits or definable boundaries that would enable us to distinguish it from *other* beings. That is to say, it must be finite. Everything that has being must be finite. The notion of an infinite being (an *entity* that is infinite) is simply meaningless, totally unintelligible. Something that is nothing in particular, indeterminate. All that 'infinitude' could mean would be sheer chaos.

For Aristotle there is simply nothing more intelligible than finite being. We must simply assume, as our starting-point in all intelligible reasoning or arguing, the non-problematic status of finite entities. It would never occur to Aristotle to question the *existence* as such of finite entities. It would be irrational to ask: 'Why is there something rather than nothing?' The existence of finite entities is not a problem – it is what we must *assume* if we are to argue or reason intelligibly about anything. The *being* of determinate finite intelligible beings is an *arche*, a *given* starting-point of all understanding and rational argument about reality. There is nothing more intelligible than that determinate, delimited, finite entities *exist*. When Aristotle asks in the *Physics*, 'Could being come from non-being?', he is not asking if existence could come from non-existence. He is rather asking: 'Could finite entities with intelligible form come from some infinite chaos of nothing in particular?' The question answers itself. We cannot conceive of that possibility. The positing of something unintelligible can never be an answer to an *intelligible* question.

To give an explanatory role to anything that *we* cannot conceivably understand would be irrational in the extreme – utter nonsense. We must begin and end with that which is most intelligible to us, that which we tacitly assume in all our reasoning about reality, the unquestionable existence of *finite* beings. When Aristotle posits a prime mover outside the material universe, it is not to explain the existence of the world. It is to explain the eternal movement within the world – the endless movement of the generation and corruption of finite entities. Aristotle insists that the prime mover itself must be *finite*. *Any* entity of which we can intelligibly conceive is a delimited finite entity alongside other delimited finite entities. I claim that everything in Aristotle's writings that constitutes a real threat to the very foundation of the Catholic faith derives from that foundational principle of Aristotelian philosophy.

We cannot go into detail, but just think what it means to such notions as intelligent design and divine providence, the claim that things and events have a meaning and purpose that transcend every description or explanation that may be given in terms of the intrinsic nature – the form – of finite entities. Such a claim is excluded *ab initio* as irrational nonsense. Think of what it means for our understanding of the meaning and end of human life. Human life has (and can have) no *meaning* apart from our success or failure to acquire those goods that make it possible to live well and fare well in this world. Aristotle's world is a world in which tragic accidents and twists of fate have and can have no meaning apart from that supplied by a causal account of the finite factors that create them. The most virtuous and noble of human beings may through no fault of his own end his life in misery and agony, without friends or honour. And there *can be* no further reason or purpose for such innocent suffering, than that it just happens in our world of finite beings and intrinsic causes. Chance and fate have no further meaning than that of what *happens* in this world.

Think of what a transcendental proof for the impossibility of transcendence implies: a transcendental proof for the impossibility of there being anything that transcends the finitude of anything of which we can conceive. We cannot intelligibly entertain even the *possibility* that there might be a source of meaning that transcends the natural laws of finite beings – that might in some way redeem the tragic accidents and evils of human life. This is the way it is, and there is nothing more intelligible than that! There *is* nothing more to understand. I could go on, because this transcendental principle of the finitude of being colours everything that Aristotle writes. I have given so much weight to it in this lecture both because it is the central point on which Aquinas's hermeneutical miracle must turn, but also because we encounter it so often – in one form or another – in our own culture. Aristotle, in his dialectical argument for the principle of the finitude of being, is saying to us: 'That is as intelligible as it gets, and if we try to move beyond finite being, we will find ourselves positing something unintelligible and inconceivable.' To which Aquinas replies: '*Quo ad nos*, Aristotle, *quo ad nos*.' Unintelligible and inconceivable for *us*, Aristotle, for *us*.

Let us turn now directly to Aquinas and his hermeneutical miracle. There is one highly significant fact about Aquinas's discussion of Aristotle (and of all of his favourite authorities) in the *Summa*. He very rarely criticizes them directly, or overtly says that they were mistaken. Often, however, he quotes them with approval and then reinterprets what they said in such a way that it means something very different. In the *Secunda Secundae*, however, Aquinas directly criticizes Aristotle by name, calling him not the 'Philosopher' but Aristotle. And the point on which he criticizes Aristotle is just the point we have been discussing. Like all the ancient philosophers, Aristotle failed to raise the question of 'being' as such. Aristotle was not concerned about the being (the existence) of things *as such*, but with *this* entity, or that *kind* of entity. He was concerned with finite entities and their movement – the ways that they changed, the ways that they were generated and corrupted within this finite world. Aristotle failed to raise the question of their being or their existence as such. *Simpliciter*! Aristotle didn't see any problem. Aquinas then goes on to say that only *later* philosophers were able to see the question, the problem of the *existence* of finite beings *as* such. The commentators point out that Aquinas is referring more to the early Fathers, including, of course, Augustine, and to Maimonides. He was not referring to Plotinus, to the non-Christian Neoplatonists. They also did not provide us with the needed approach to finite beings. Why did it take Christian (and Jewish) philosophers to rise to the question of 'being' as such and to do what Aristotle could not do, to place into question, to make a problem of the very *existence* of finite beings? The answer to that question may help us better to understand Aquinas's views on the relation between grace and human nature, and the theological project of the *Summa* itself.

To start with, Aquinas is not surprised to find errors in the higher speculation of pagan philosophers on questions concerning being or existence. He often implies that such errors are inevitable. Aquinas also knows that if a philosopher says something that contradicts revelation, the philosopher must be wrong! Truth is one, and the truth of revelation is more certain than the conclusions of any human philosopher. The charitable, the *honest*, thing to do is to find the source of the error and correct it. Aquinas uses revelation, as it were, to help the philosopher see the truth – not the truth of revelation as such, but the truth within his own field and practice that he *missed* because he lacked the guidance of revealed truth. There was something that he failed to *see*. This is not the old view of theology as the Queen of the Sciences, the view that philosophy must serve theology, that it is merely a subsidiary of theology. In theory, philosophy could arrive at all the truth available to it without the help of revelation. In practice, however, it cannot and does not. Aquinas must, as it were, get Aristotle to see finite being as such as somehow problematic. But how is that to be done? And what is *really* its purpose? To put it another way, how do we get someone to experience *wonder* at the very being there of finite entities when these finite entities are intelligible as entities? And, again, to what purpose? Wonder is for Aristotle himself that which initiates our attempts to explain things, to get behind them and account for them in an intelligible manner. All truly creative thought begins in wonder.

But there *is* a rub. We can only resolve our wonder at something if we can turn that wonder into an intelligible question. But in order to do that, we must refer to something that we understand better, that we find more intelligible than that which produces *wonder*. And Aquinas agrees with Aristotle, and I agree with Aristotle, that there is nothing of which we can conceive that is more intelligible to us than finite beings and their existence. Indeed, Aquinas agrees with Aristotle, and I agree with Aristotle, that anything of which we can intelligibly conceive will be a finite being alongside of other finite beings. (No positing of infinity.) So, it would seem, if someone, for whatever reason, were to find himself wondering about the very existence of finite entities, he would have only two choices. The first is to say: 'Well that's the way it is! The very context in terms of which we define and resolve questions about the world (those finite entities that we understand most clearly of all – everything intelligible to me *as* a finite entity, anything of which I can intelligibly conceive) *none the less* has something about it, something at its very heart, something problematic, something that causes wonder. Not something peculiar to it, but something transcendental. Something that all conceivable entities have in common. We shall call it existence or being *as such*. It is not what a thing is that is unintelligible. It is rather that a thing is, that anything of which I can conceive exists at all. That is what is unintelligible. A *mere* given, not an *intelligible* truth. But I cannot conceive of anything that would resolve that wonder, that would render the existence of intelligible entities itself intelligible. So ultimately the world is without meaning and absurd, and my desire to find meaning and intelligibility in all that experience is a *useless passion*.' That is ultimately the response of Jean-Paul Sartre after he throws up next to a tree he regarded for too long.

The other possible reaction to experiencing wonder at the very being there of things (the very existence of finite entities) would follow the first one right up to the final move – the option for absurdity. One choosing the second option would say: 'There is something puzzling about everything that is most intelligible to me, everything of which I can intelligibly conceive, not *what* it is, but *that* it is. But I cannot conceive of *anything* that would remove that puzzlement, that would make intelligible the existence as such of the most intelligible, finite entities of which I can conceive. But it is unthinkable that the final context in which I *define* what is intelligible should itself be unintelligible. It is unthinkable that the *existence* of the universe of finite entities in which I find so much meaning and intelligibility should itself be absurd – an unintelligible brute fact! Therefore, I surrender. I give up my claim that the *human* intellect is the final judge or percipient of intelligibility, of all that is intelligible. There must therefore be something of which I cannot conceive such that, if I *were* able to *know* it, it would render fully intelligible to me the existence as such of all finite entities. So I shall posit such a being, and I shall call it an *infinite being*.

I shall call it God. Of *course* the term "infinite being" is an oxymoron, a paradox. An intelligible being must have *determinate* form of *some* sort. And yet that is exactly what the term "infinite" is meant to negate: determinate, delimited being. Nonetheless, there must *be* an entity with determinate, intelligible form that is *not* finite (or determinate) in the *way* that the finite beings that I *know* are finite or determinate. God must not be finite in the way that anything of which I can conceive would be finite. And yet God must have determinate, intelligible being in some way that I do not know and of which I cannot conceive. I shall therefore name God "infinite being"; but I do not know what those terms *signify in God*. I do not know the *res significata* of either of these terms in God. God remains for me *ut ignotum*, unknown. But such a being must exist. I admit the limits of my powers of intellect.'

Now that is the point to which Aquinas wants to bring Aristotle. Because Aquinas the *theologian* knows that such a surrender of a claim to transcendental intellectual power and judgement would restore the thinking of Aristotle (his *use* of his intellectual powers) to that openness to *transcendent* truth for which man *with* his intellect was created by God. To be *passively open* to the revelation of *truth*, of *being*, that the intellect cannot of its own power comprehend, understand, or conceive. But the question re-emerges: 'How is Aquinas to bring Aristotle to the point of wonder at the very being, the existence as such, of intelligible finite entities, and how is he to guarantee that Aristotle opts not for absurdity, but for a source and locus of intelligibility that transcends his own powers of intellectual conception?'

Well, I want to claim that it cannot be done through philosophical argumentation. And yet generations of Neo-Thomists have tried just *that*. Gilson, who correctly sees the question of existence at the heart of Aquinas's interpretation of Aristotle, tries to argue that Aristotle has a static view of being, or entity. Only if we see existing as a kind of *doing* (an activity) will we see that the existing (the existential doing) of finite entities requires some transcendent explanation. But surely Gilson is simply wrong about Aristotle. Aristotle, after all, uses the term *energeia* for the actualization of finite being: actual being is *energeia*. He does not have a static view of being. He simply sees no problem with the *energeia* (the existential doing) of finite beings. Eric

Mascall is closer to the mark. He also does not seek wonder at existence from argument, but rather from a kind of contemplation. There is no time now to discuss my reservations about Mascall's discussion of contemplation, but I call him to my side in saying that philosophical argument cannot of itself produce the result that Aquinas wishes to bring about in Aristotle. But the obvious objection to my position, it might be said, is that Aquinas attempted to do just that in his *de Ente et Essentia*, where he seems to argue for a real distinction between essence and existence, a distinction that *shows* the problematic nature of finite existence. I can only claim at this point that *de Ente et Essentia* ought not to be read as a philosophical work as such, and that if it were read by Aristotle, say, as a philosophical treatise, Aristotle would be unable to understand the distinction that Aquinas makes. There is no room in his vocabulary or philosophy for making that distinction as Aquinas *makes* it.

I shall now simply put all my cards on the table and say that whenever Aquinas writes he writes as a theologian, for a theological purpose, making use of theological assumptions. He talks about philosophy as a theologian. He does not *do* philosophy. That is true, I think, of his commentaries on Aristotle, it is true of *de Ente et Essentia*, and it is true of the *Summa Theologiae*. Aquinas is always writing as *catholicae doctor veritatis*, a teacher of Catholic truth. And in his interpretation of Aristotle, and his use of Aristotle, he tells us what Aristotle would say *after* his errors were corrected in the light of the *truth* of the Catholic faith.

Perhaps that claim will become more plausible if we look at the *Summa Theologiae*, and see how and where Aristotle appears in it as the Philosopher, the lover of wisdom. If someone were to ask me whether or not, based only on my reading of the *Summa*, I would say that Aquinas was an *Aristotelian*, I would hardly know how to reply. The *Summa* is certainly *not* an Aristotelian work. It is true that a version, an interpretation of Aristotle appears in it, and is given great authority. But it is also true that even more of Augustine appears in it, and is given even more authority. And Scripture appears in every question, and is given the greatest authority of all. Any reader should be struck at once by the fact that the entire framework of the *Summa*, that which gives it its basic structure and order, is radically theological and non-Aristotelian. The basic structure is that of the emergence of all things from God, and of the return of all things to God. The Neoplatonic model of emanation from God, and return to God (the *exitus* and *reditus*) controls the structure and the overarching message of the *Summa*. The *Summa* is patently an attempt to articulate the Catholic faith within an architectonic that lies closer to the Neoplatonists than to Aristotle. It is crucial to note, however, that the Neoplatonist model of emanation *from* and return *to* God (or the One) is not used in its original form; that model has to be corrected, just as Aristotle needs to be corrected, and on basically the same point – how we should think about the existence, the being, of finite entities.

The Catholic tradition replaces the pagan model of a necessary emanation of finite beings *out of* the very being of God with the model of creation *ex nihilo*. Finite entities derive from God, not as necessary finite specifications of his own universal, unified Being but as the result of a true act of creation *ex nihilo*. Created, contingent, dependent finite entities, in their intended order to one another constitute the external activity of God. It is the doctrine of creation that makes the distinction between what things are and the derived, dependent existence that they receive immediately thinkable. Aquinas knows full well that the shortcomings of the ancient philosophers (including Aristotle) on the question of the existence as such of finite entities were not corrected until Christian philosophers, informed by the doctrine of creation, turned their attention to what Aquinas calls being itself, the existence as such of finite entities. The *ex nihilo* doctrine of creation *revealed* to Christian philosophers the contingent status of finite entities, and thus enabled them to see their very *being* as contingent, and as *unintelligible* apart from reference to their infinite and inconceivable source. It is that picture of the existence of finite entities as the *result* of a freely chosen act of creation by the *same* incomprehensible being who revealed himself in Christ that opens up the space needed for purposeful design and providence – the intelligible space within which to ascribe to the events in this world a meaning and purpose that transcends the immanent forms of the finite *beings* in this world.

The entire framework of the *Summa* is radically theological, and even if it is dripping with Platonic and Neoplatonic language and images, they are largely derived from the Christianized, the corrected, interpretations of the early Fathers, especially Augustine and Pseudo-Dionysius. It is within this framework that Scripture is cited as the source for us of revealed truth. And it is within this framework that the language of Augustine and other Christian theologians is used to articulate the incomprehensible 'propositions' of the faith – what is proposed to us in the words of sacred Scripture for our belief. But it is also within this framework that the language of Aristotle is used *both* to *further* articulate the truths of revelation *and* to describe how the world and its entities are naturally understood by *us*, how the world appears *quo ad nos*. There is therefore a kind of stereoscopic vision of reality in the *Summa*: (1) the way things are to be understood from *God's* point of view, reality *quo ad Deum*; and (2) the way things are understood from our natural human point of view, *quo ad nos*.

The language of Aristotle dominates the *quo ad nos* part of this stereoscopic picture, but it is *also* used in the articulation of the *quo ad Deum* part of the same stereoscopic picture. Remember what I said when describing Aristotle's historical rejection of the notion of infinite being: it is very seductive and plausible, because it is so near to the truth. Everything that Aristotle said about the *limits for the human intellect* of what is intelligible is true! Aquinas agrees with Aristotle that only finite being is intelligible to us, and he agrees *as a theologian*. Aquinas *agrees* with Aristotle that infinite being is radically unintelligible to us. And he agrees *as a theologian*. We do not know God, we do not comprehend God, we do not see how the names and properties that we ascribe to God could *be* in God. We do not know, comprehend, or understand the *res significata*, the things signified in God by our language *about* God. On that Aquinas insists for theological reasons, on the ground of revealed truth! So when Aristotle's language is used in the *Summa* to portray the limits of what is intelligible from our natural human point of view, it serves a theological purpose. It becomes part of *theology*. All that Aquinas need do is to hold Aristotle back from denying on those grounds the very *possibility* of an infinite being that transcends those limits, and to do that he must somehow confront Aristotle with the question of 'being' itself and force him to acknowledge the unintelligibility, the problematic nature, of the *existence* as such of intelligible finite entities. He cannot do that by means of rational argument, but he can do it by forcing Aristotle to accept and articulate the revealed propositions of faith, including the doctrine of creation (the movement, as it were, of finite entities from non-existence, from nothing, to existence). That Aquinas has done just that shows itself in his use of the first three of the five ways in support and articulation of the revealed scriptural assertion that God's existence *can* be shown by seeing correctly the finite things of this world.

When Aristotle was forced to accept and articulate the revealed truths of the Catholic faith, his philosophy was corrected of that shortcoming that Aquinas finds in Aristotle's historical teaching. Aristotle the philosopher *sees* the very existence of finite entities as a source of wonder, as a question needing an answer. Thus, it would seem, revealed truth can perfect philosophy, as grace can perfect nature. Many Christians objected to Aquinas's *use* of philosophy in the service of theology. They objected to the use of philosophical language to articulate theological truth. In typical fashion Aquinas himself raises the issue. Is it proper, he asks, to use philosophy within theology? Objection: No, it is improper. The language of philosophy *waters down* the truth of theology. Reply: In the context of theology water becomes wine. Aquinas himself uses the image of Christ's first miracle to characterize what happens to the philosophy of Aristotle when it is used within theology in the service of theology. That miracle of Cana was a miracle of transformation. So, by baptizing Aristotle, Aquinas makes him accept and articulate the revealed truth of the Catholic faith. And when Aristotle does that, the shortcomings of his philosophy are corrected (given full integrity) and his philosophy is ordered to a supernatural end that transcends its own intrinsic power to comprehend or render intelligible – the Being and Truth of the *infinite* God.

Now on to another serious objection. While in theory philosophers could avoid errors about existence and human life in the world by the careful use of their intellectual powers (in practice they will never do so), can only something like Christian faith – the acceptance of revealed truth – *enable* them to do so? To that objection I would reply with a partial 'Yes!' What I am saying is that philosophers who rely entirely on their own ability to use their intellectual powers to understand the nature of the world, and the *meaning* and *purpose* of human

life, will in fact make mistakes of crucial importance to our understanding of reality and our place in it. And I am saying that something
like grace, the grace that opens us to the truth of revelation, is a *necessary* if not always *sufficient* condition of our avoiding those errors.
Philosophers who test their conclusions against revealed truth, and
look for the source of their error when there is patent contradiction,
are moving in the direction of perfecting their *use* (application) of their
intellectual powers.

It is parallel to what Aquinas says about virtue. In theory it is possible for a human being to acquire perfect virtue of the kind Aristotle
described, and that Aristotle calls natural, or political virtue, without
grace. In fact, however, without grace and the infused love of charity
no-one ever will. Our intellectual powers may not have been affected
by the Fall and by our sin, but our actualization of these powers – our
use of them – follows the *will*. Distorted love can affect our reasoning.
It can even affect what we find intelligible and what we do not.
Matters such as revelation and grace are not irrelevant to our pursuit
of the truth! As Aquinas remarks, God did not create Adam originally
in a pure state of nature, but in a state of nature and grace. Adam in
his original state possessed not only grace but even possessed, said
Aquinas, divinely infused charity which perfected in him the natural
love of friendship that is *agape*, the uniting principle of all *koinonia*.
When Adam fell, when he lost grace and the infused virtue of divine
love, his *nature – human* nature – broke. It was not destroyed, but it
became less than complete, less than perfect.

To demythologize, human nature cannot be complete or perfect in
its *own terms* without grace and the infused virtue of divine charity.
Without them human love and human longing will be distorted, and
that will in fact affect our search for truth, where we look for it and
whether we recognize it. If you want to find the true sources of the
view that science and philosophy are and ought to be *completely* 'free'
and independent of revealed truth, do not look to Aquinas. Look
rather to such opponents of Aristotle as Robert Grosseteste, who in
order to argue that Augustine had the truth and Aristotle did not,
relied on what he called a scientific method independent of both
philosophy and theology to prove the superiority of theology to
philosophy, and the superiority of Augustine to Aristotle. Ironically,

that introduction of a universally valid method to test for truth and falsity, a method independent of philosophy and theology, led I should argue to the actual historical separation of science – philosophy – from theology, and the concomitant transformation of theology into fideism: undoubtedly not by Grosseteste's intention. His two most important students were Wycliff and Roger Bacon.

Aquinas did not simply reject Aristotle because his teachings contradicted Catholic truth. He reinterpreted him in the light of revelation, made him capable of accepting and articulating the Catholic faith, and by doing so brought his philosophy nearer to full integrity and perfection. So great was Aquinas's hermeneutical miracle that Aristotle became a servant of Catholic truth. In the context of Aquinas's *Summa*, Aristotle's philosophy became theology. Water became Wine.

Editors' postscript

This lecture was delivered on 31 October 1998 at St Mary's Bourne Street in London as part of a lecture series in honour of the late Eric Mascall, OGS. Five lectures were planned and delivered in this series, and the other four contributors were Brian Horne, John Macquarrie, Rowan Williams, and Fergus Kerr, OP. Although Victor Preller's lecture was delivered in 1998, it was not published by St Mary's – in pamphlet form – until 2002, almost two years after his death. The lecture was prefaced with the following explanatory paragraphs:

> The Revd Dr Victor Preller, Professor Emeritus in the Religion Department of Princeton University, and Priest in the Oratory of the Good Shepherd, gave the Third Mascall Memorial Lecture at St Mary's Bourne Street, London, on 31 October 1998.
>
> Fr Preller delivered his address from a hand-written manuscript which he intended to revise for publication in the Mascall Lecture Series. Unfortunately, computer difficulties and ill health prevented his doing so, and when he died in January 2001 this lecture was found among his papers in its original hand-written form.
>
> Dr Mark Larrimore, Fr Preller's successor at Princeton

University, read the as-delivered, hand-written notes of the lecture and produced the typescript on which this text is based. A few words in the original manuscript were illegible and a few sentences fragmentary; in those rare cases Dr Larrimore followed his best judgement in reconstructing the sense. However, such textual problems were infrequent and minor, and they compromised neither the basic content nor clarity of the lecture. Dr Larrimore's typescript was then read by the Revd Dr Fergus Kerr, OP, of Blackfriars Hall, University of Oxford (who attended the actual lecture); Dr Eugene F. Rogers, Jr, of the University of Virginia; and the Revd Robert MacSwain of St Mary's Episcopal Church in Kinston, North Carolina. In only a few cases were any further editorial changes made, and then only to eliminate obscurity. The text was then prepared for publication by Mr John Greenhalgh of St Mary's Bourne Street.

Fr Preller was unable to polish this lecture to his satisfaction. Had he done so, he would have doubtless altered one or two points (e.g., D'Arcy's account of Aquinas's meeting with the Pope at Castel Gandolfo has been questioned by the most recent scholarship), and added explicit citations. However, we have persevered in bringing it to print because we believe not only in the inherent value of Fr Preller's lecture and its need for a broader hearing, but that Fr Preller would be very happy about its publication. This particular lecture mattered so much to him precisely because it was written and delivered in honour of Eric Mascall, a fellow priest in the Oratory of the Good Shepherd.

Aside from his significant study, *Divine Science and the Science of God: A Reformulation of Thomas Aquinas* (Princeton University Press, 1967), Fr Preller published very little in his lifetime and his influence spread primarily through his teaching. This lecture is thus an important statement of his reading of Aquinas. Furthermore, as the only member of the Mascall Memorial Lecture Series who was – like Eric Mascall – a priest in the Oratory of the Good Shepherd, it would have been most unfortunate if only Fr Preller's lecture remained unpublished. It would have also been regrettable if the series remained incomplete. But with the publication of this, the Third Mascall Memorial Lecture, all five have now been put into print and our tribute to Eric Mascall's life and ministry among us has reached its intended shape.

The St Mary's Bourne Street pamphlet also noted, 'This edition is for private circulation among members of the congregation of St Mary's, friends and pupils of Victor S. Preller, and the brethren of the Oratory of the Good Shepherd.' The editors of this volume are grateful to both St Mary's and the Oratory for allowing us to include Victor's final lecture in our Festschrift.

13. Memoir: Living *in medias res*

(Victor S. Preller 1931–2001)

MARK LARRIMORE

Die Lösung des Problems, das Du im Leben siehst, ist eine Art zu leben, die das Problematische zum Verschwinden bringt.

Daß das Leben problematisch ist, heißt, daß Dein Leben nicht in die Form des Lebens paßt. Du mußt dann Dein Leben verändern, und paßt es in die Form, dann verschwindet das Problematische.

Aber haben wir nicht das Gefühl, daß der, welcher nicht darin ein Problem sieht, für etwas Wichtiges, ja das Wichtigste, blind ist? Möchte ich nicht sagen, der lebe so dahin – eben blind, gleichsam wie ein Maulwurf, und wenn er bloß sehen könnte, so sähe er das Problem?

Oder soll ich nicht sagen: daß, wer richtig lebt, das Problem nicht als *Traurigkeit,* also doch nicht problematisch, empfindet, sondern vielmehr als eine Freude; also gleichsam als einen lichten Äther um sein Leben, nicht als einen fraglichen Hintergrund?

Ludwig Wittgenstein, Vermischte Bemerkungen[1]

To write about Victor Preller is not easy: more than most people, he was multiple. One of the Princeton colleagues who knew him longest sees Preller as Robert Lifton's 'protean man', the quintessential post-war person whose life is a series of radical reinventions. For another, Preller was the Augustine of his time, someone who really lived the changing moods of the second half of the twentieth century, not just as an observer from the sidelines. Preller drank deep of what each period offered, and then moved on, impatient with the compromises by which most of us live. I knew him during the years of his life when things finally came together – the years as Master of the Princeton University Graduate College and, after his retirement, as a *de facto* full-time priest at last.

One could essay a reconstruction of the life of this son of a Camden, New Jersey sheet-metal worker, called already as a young teenager to the priesthood in the Episcopal Church. One could try to recreate Preller's experiences as an undergraduate at Princeton in the early 1950s, sharing cocktails with full professors rather than with his snobby fellow students. One could retrace his theological training at Keble College, Oxford, and at General Theological Seminary in New York, his ordination, and the stint as hospital chaplain in Chicago. One could speculate about the reasons for his return to Princeton's Department of Religion for his doctorate (he'd been a philosophy major as an undergraduate), where he was to stay. But account would also have to be taken of Preller's oft-repeated claim that he had spent his life 'trying to leave Princeton'. And even after his return to the Episcopal Church and to the Oratory of the Good Shepherd, he was persuaded that 'the Church is the cross on which Christ is daily crucified'.

Perhaps one could retrace an intellectual trajectory spanning Aquinas, Sellars, Heidegger, Freud and Jung, Vedic and Buddhist philosophies, Wittgenstein, Dilthey, Gadamer, and Aristotle, but it would be difficult, since he left little written trace. Preller published about as little as was legally possible for a professor of his generation. ('I write through my students,' he said semi-seriously.) Most of his heavily marked books were destroyed in a flood in the late 1980s, so one's main source would have to be the courses Preller taught at Princeton for nearly three decades. These courses covered a remarkable range of topics from Aristotle, medieval philosophy, ancient Buddhism, fairy tales, and the theory of religion to contemporary philosophy of language and hermeneutics.

Or maybe the arc of Preller's life would be best captured by favourite poets: Eliot, Heine, Herbert . . .

But any of these narratives would make Preller's life make too much sense. What should one do with the two post-doctoral years spent in pre-Olympic Munich, years decidedly *not* spent working with Karl Rahner but – among other things – helping subtitle Marx Brothers movies in German? During those years Preller claimed he lost the use of English! What about the visible and risible role Preller played in the counterculture at Princeton during the Vietnam War, when he accepted even hand-made pottery as a final project? These years were among those Preller later described as his 'years in the wilderness', years of religious exploration and atheism.

It would be untrue to Victor Preller in a very deep way to essay an official version of his life, however. Were the 'years in the wilderness' necessary to fill out an *exitus–reditus* cycle? He did not say so, and the grammar of grace prohibits it. Grace, Preller believed, completes nature in a manner at once thoroughly unpredictable and, when it has happened, entirely fitting. Victor Preller's life – like anyone's – added up to more and less than a whole. Yet generating an official 'life' would be untrue for another, related reason. Several people over the course of his life, Victor Preller was also several at every point in his life, and this not through a lack of character but through a kind of surfeit of it. At least for the dozen years I knew him, Preller was different things to different people. Most of his students were unaware that he was a priest, or even a believer, and it took years for me to find out that he liked baseball.

The penny drops

Victor Preller was among the most impressive teachers I have ever encountered. I doubt I am the only one for whom he was a kind of incarnation of the teaching vocation. His manner of teaching is tricky to describe, however, because Victor purveyed mind-altering intellectual substances, ideas which radically changed one's view of the world and one's place in it. The order of discovery, he often said, is almost always different from the order of exposition. Here it will have to be, as the moment of comprehension makes it hard to go back to a state of unknowing, as hard as remembering what it was like not to 'get' imaginary numbers, or the subjunctive, or the way the impossible liberty of indifference of which the modern age dreams would not confirm but destroy human dignity.

Preller had a phrase for the moment when a student 'got' what it was one of his courses was about: 'the penny dropped'. But the penny almost never dropped *during* the course in question. It was usually well after the course had ended – perhaps deep into a new Preller course, quite possibly a course ostensibly on something completely unrelated. The moment when the penny dropped was something like when you suddenly stop in the street and burst out laughing (or perhaps just smiled), having just 'got' the point of a funny story you'd been told minutes – or hours – before. The 'getting' in question was like getting a joke, because what was at issue was a change of aspect. Finding everything as it was and yet nothing quite the same, you recognize the familiar as familiar in a thoroughly *unfamiliar* way. It makes for a kind of inside-out experience of the uncanny. There was also an element of delight based in the experience of language's *working*. It can obscure, but also disclose the nature of our engagement with each other and with the world.

The Aquinas penny dropped for me when a real-life case (I can't even recall which – it doesn't matter) made one of the thought experiments Preller had used in class suddenly lose its air of arbitrariness. All at once the Thomistic locutions seemed not cumbersome if gothically elegant redescriptions of things already known but, rather, illuminations of things heretofore unremarked. So *that's* what all that was about, I thought, and suddenly the view of the larger argument Preller was presenting opened up, like the vista when you reach the summit of a mountain. Virtually at once the point of *all* the examples became clear. For less figurative-minded people, the penny doubtless dropped at different times, but I doubt it was ever just the words and concepts rearranging themselves in one's mind. The wisdom involved was *practical*, so the trigger must have been something one cared about.

Since the penny generally didn't drop until after the seminar was over, the experience of attending a course with Victor Preller was one of something other than a full understanding of what was up. Going back is like trying to remember what it was like to hear a funny story uncomprehending. Even without getting it, one can admire and even enjoy the skill and love with which the storyteller chooses his words, pauses meaningfully, raises an eyebrow – all pleasures afforded by Preller. Awe at Preller's comprehension of important truths was preceded by awe at his astonishingly deep and resonant voice, his intensity, his manifest intelligence. One could enjoy his innuendos even without knowing what they were about.

Prelline pedagogy

Preller's counsel to me as I began to teach was: 'never pander'. It is a disservice to students to let them think they get it when they don't. If what you are endeavouring to teach is really structurally different from what students are likely to know, a rapprochement with their terms before they realize the *possibility* of such a difference would be fatal. It would foreclose for them the possibility of really understanding. They need to realize there are things they are *not* getting. Besides: there is no single universally accessible approach. What might make things easier of access for some would make it needlessly harder for others.

At least some subject matters are best taught as languages, through a kind of total immersion. 'Understanding', Preller liked to say, 'begins *in medias res*'. Right from the start, the teacher speaks only the target language. To do this without alienating or discouraging the students is an art indeed. On this analogy the penny dropping can be likened to the point at which you catch yourself thinking in the new language, or, even better, dreaming in it. Of course, this is just the first time you've caught yourself doing this, not necessarily the first time you've done it. A new language permits the articulation of new sentiments – which nevertheless may feel like they've always been there, waiting to be recognized.

It is only after learning another language well enough to see the danger in translations that one is in a position really to see one's own language as language. (How curious that so little is made of the bilingualism of Wittgenstein's existence.) Only now does one realize that the problem of translation cannot be evaded even by confining oneself to a single linguistic tradition, as interpretation between different but always shared human subjectivities, at once necessary and impossible, is at the heart of the transmission of tradition, too.

Recalling the experience of Preller's teaching is difficult for another reason. The seminar was only part of Prelline pedagogy, and not perhaps the more important. (The end of a syllabus was as good as never reached, occasionally generating interesting torsos, like the course 'The idea of freedom from Augustine to Luther', which ended up as 'Freedom from Augustine'.) Already as a graduate student,

Preller was known for taking the time for long conversations with students over tea – closer generally to three hours than to one. At the end of his life, Preller would often be exhausted for the rest of the day by a telephone conversation of two or three hours with a parishioner or ex-student.

This most important part of Preller's teaching cannot be described in general terms. If in seminars Preller presented the object language alive and dauntingly complex, in the intimacy created by the steeping of a shared pot of tea he spoke *your* language. These conversations were moments of near-perfect communication, tailored so well to the terms and concerns of the parties as to be genuinely open.

I suppose this is what tutorials ideally are, discussions which flow freely back and forth between texts or issues of immediate concern and something close to spiritual direction. But the communication wasn't just one-way. The time Preller took for conversation, and the way he took it, evinced a commitment not only to his interlocutor and to the material taught, but to the value of *shared* enquiry toward understanding. The hermeneutics of charity is imperialist only when one thinks one has already understood everything worth knowing. Quite different is an approach which supposes that something vital is to be learned from every attempt at truthfulness and comprehension, that more of the mountain's grandeur is illuminated by each path to its summit. I can't help thinking that what enabled Preller so to inhabit this form of communication also explains his distaste for the impersonality of publishing.

It is a sign of a good listener to hear things you aren't even aware you are saying. One of Preller's favourite tricks – if a trick it was – was to find in what you had just said the very thing you were looking for. 'That's exactly right,' he would say, and rephrase what you said in just the terms you were grappling to understand. You might protest: that's not what I meant, that's not what I said, that's not what I meant to say – but in protesting you often found that it *was* indeed what you *wish* you had said, and quite possibly what you were meaning to say after all.

Adversus Stoicorum

In one respect likening understanding to getting a joke doesn't entirely capture the moment of the moment when the penny dropped. For the aspect change involved wasn't a mere matter of a duck–rabbit but something more like figure and ground. The penny's drop discloses a world alive with unsuspected significance – the world we already inhabit. We live in the midst of things, of practices and friendships which already ground our existence, which already move us to live as we do. The penny dropping was like learning how a magician does his tricks, only to find out that the objects in fact move on their own!

What happened when the Aquinas penny dropped was that I saw, as if for the first time, what it means that human beings act under a description of the good, and thus what distinguishes human action from the mere acts of a human. I saw why Preller always insisted that the first principle of the natural law for Aquinas – that good is to be pursued and evil avoided – doesn't so much define a set of licit acts as render human action intelligible in the first place. All our actions are oriented to goods, and (so) fall under justice. We can be mistaken about goods, but never more than when we think they're only in our minds.

That we don't see these things is a result, Preller thought, of what he called the 'Stoicism' of so much of modern thought and culture. In the futile quest for perduring goods, ahistorical certainties, and complete autonomy, moderns lose the world and themselves in loveless indifference. And yet the goods of this world are not less but more precious for their fragility! Ethical deliberation is not less but more important for the fundamental uncertainty of the particular case. And human beings are not less but more lovable for their fallibility and interdependence.

If you brought up theology, Preller might add that this modern 'Stoicism' is symbiotic with too pronounced a theology of the Fall and too feeble a theology of creation. We moderns do not trust the world nearly enough, nor even our most considered responses to it. We are not moved enough by love of the true goods of this world, and we are not angry enough when they are destroyed, or at their unjust distribution.

276

If you didn't mention theology, Preller might have encouraged in you a response to the serendipity, the genuine delightfulness of goods like friendship, understanding, music. He was much moved by the efforts of the late Philip Hallie to articulate the sense in which human goodness is at once startling and yet in its own way matter-of-course, an 'utterly clear mystery'. It may be exceptional in our world, but goodness doesn't understand itself as exceptional. It is habitual, and anchored in the real. Though a thoroughly secular thinker, Hallie found the good to have 'something supernatural in it'.

One should not wonder that Preller did not insist on introducing theological considerations in every case. This went beyond a fierce opposition to preaching in the classroom. The 'openness to gratuity' Victor Preller thought so rare and precious a trait of some people – if only we could all learn it! – doesn't derive from theological as opposed to philosophical reflection, though it can lead to it. At the point at which we reach bedrock, our spade naturally turns *up*.

Music

It would not be right to speak about Victor Preller without mentioning music, and not just because music was so often part of the experience of a conversation with him. Preller approved of Arvo Pärt's enigmatic claim that he couldn't say whether he understood God through his music or vice versa. With time, Preller said, he found music ever more indispensable to understanding meaning of all kinds.

The flood which destroyed Preller's books also wiped out a vast collection of classical and jazz LPs. He decided to reconstruct only the classical collection, though he remained an avid lover of jazz, and the great ladies of the blues found their way back, too. How the new collection grew was revealing: Preller bought with a kind of knowing abandon. A recording of a work he knew by a performer he did not know would arrive, recommended by a friend or by *Grammophone*. If this performance delighted, Preller would acquire as many other recordings by this artist as he could. This would inevitably introduce pieces by composers he did not know, old or new. Preller would then acquire as many other recordings of work by this composer as he could. Of a newly discovered piece he sought multiple interpretations. And so it continued, crossword-puzzle style.

The three thousand compact discs left at Preller's death were the winnowed results of tens of thousands of hours of always concentrated, often enraptured listening. Each disc is there for a reason. (Recordings which did not pass muster were sold in great stacks to the Princeton Record Exchange.) Of favourite pieces – Bach's sonatas and partitas for solo violin, for instance – Preller might have as many as a dozen different interpretations, and he was always open to a new one. There were two or more recordings of each of the Shostakovich symphonies, but no complete set by any one conductor. A good rendition is one which discloses aspects of a work we had not heretofore noticed, which brings out contrasts or cadences, subtexts or underlying structures, kinships with other works by the same composer or in the same genre – or beyond. When Preller lent you CDs to introduce you to a new work or composer, he rarely lent you just one interpretation.

I mention these details of Preller's collecting because they reveal, I think, an ongoing course of instruction in *listening* which parallels his approach to texts and to conversation. Music is available to us only through the gifts of performers (Preller played no instrument, although he had taught himself to read music to follow complicated orchestral works), and more of it is revealed to us by each good new performance. The lover of Mozart's or Bartók's string quartets or of the operas of Handel or Rossini or Janaček is always on the lookout for a new rendition – and for new works. This is faithlessness neither toward the works one loves nor toward the performers one trusts. Preller thought that each new interpretation revealed things we could not see or hear before, in the process casting its predecessors in a new light. Strauss's operas deepen our appreciation of Mozart's, as Adès's open up new ways of hearing Strauss. As jazz lovers know, true goods are not competitive. They complement and indeed compound each other. The future of music but also its past are changed by a new voice.

It is at once the most remarkable and the most natural thing in the world when a new interpretation or work clarifies something we thought we knew. When Mabel Mercer (one of Victor Preller's lifelong loves) sang their songs, songwriters often said that they felt they were hearing their own songs for the first time. Hearing and rehearing new and old interpretations, one learns to enjoy the particularity of the piece, of the composer, of the performers, of the instruments, and the serendipity of their ever-changing ways of coming together. Victor Preller loved music as an interpretive and participatory good which binds us to our fellows present, future, and past. It is a natural tributary to the love of friendship. But so are all the goods in whose midst we live.

Note

1. 'The way to solve the problem you see in life is to live in a way that will make what is problematic disappear.

The fact that life is problematic shows that the shape of your life does not fit into life's mould. So you must change the way you live and, once your life does fit into the mould, what is problematic will disappear.

But don't we have the feeling that someone who sees no problem in life is blind to something important, even to the most important thing of all? Don't I feel like saying that a man like that is just living aimlessly – blindly, like a mole, and that if he could only see, he would see the problem?

Or shouldn't I say rather: a man who lives rightly won't experience the problem as *sorrow*, so for him it will not be a problem, but a joy rather; in other words for him it will be a bright halo round his life, not a dubious background.'

(ET: *Culture and Value*, ed. G. H. von Wright in collaboration with Heikki Nyman, trans. Peter Winch (Chicago, 1980), p. 27; passages marked and underlined by Victor Preller.)

Subject and Name Index